Management Accc
Business Students

GW00370894

David Crowther

Stanley Thornes (Publishers) Ltd

First published in 1996 by:
Stanley Thornes Publishers Ltd
Ellenborough House
Wellington Street
Cheltenham
Glos. GL50 1YW
UK

96 97 98 99 00 / 10 9 8 7 6 5 4 3 2 1

ISBN 0 7487 2246 7

Typeset by Northern Phototypesetting Co Ltd, Bolton
Printed and bound in Great Britain by
Redwood Books, Trowbridge, Wiltshire

Contents

How to use this book

This text is designed as an introduction to management accounting, particularly for business students. Throughout there is an emphasis on the ways management accounting supports decision making throughout a business. Chapters are organised around case studies illustrating particular business problems. We believe students will understand management accounting skills best if they can relate them to particular situations and to the wider needs of business.

The sequence of chapters is designed to build knowledge and skills progressively, but can be read either in sequence or independently. To provide maximum flexibility for both lecturers and students, chapters are designed to be as self-sufficient as possible so that they can be fitted around the structure of a particular course, or read more selectively by students. Where possible, chapters make clear what background knowledge is needed to get the most out of them.

The book recognises the fact that, as teaching loads get heavier and student/lecturer ratios worsen, there is both more pressure on students to learn more independently, and to provide time-saving support for lecturers. To meet the first need, chapters include learning objectives, summaries, suggestions for further reading, self-review and additional questions. Self-review questions are designed to help students check their own understanding of the chapter quickly. We suggest that, when a student has read the chapter once, she or he jots down answers to the self-review questions and then checks them against the suggested page references. These refer the student back to key parts of the chapter to consolidate knowledge and understanding. Alternatively, they can be used by the lecturer as discussion points in tutorials. Guideline answers are also provided in the lecturer's pack, available to adopting lecturers.

Additional questions provide exercises for students to complete to test their knowledge. Answers to those questions where the question number is shown in a box are included at the back of the book. Answers to the remaining additional questions are provided in the lecturer's pack. This also contains the following material:

- summaries of the main teaching points from each chapter (for use as overheads or handouts in lectures, or as a basis for individualised learning packs)
- masters of key definitions, formulae and diagrams (for use as above)
- further questions and answers (for use in tutorials or learning packs).

Copies of the lecturer's pack are available free to adopting lecturers from:

Francis Dodds
Higher Education Publisher
Stanley Thornes (Publishers) Ltd, Ellenborough House, Wellington Street, Cheltenham, Glos. GL50 1YW. Tel: 01242 228888; Fax: 01242 221914.

We hope that the text will prove useful for both students and lecturers.

1 Accounting for business decisions

Objectives

After studying this chapter you should be able to:

- describe the main features of a manager's job
- outline the key elements of information provision
- describe the nature and functions of management accounting
- discuss the relationship between performance measurement and accounting in a modern business environment
- outline the relationship between ethical behaviour and business performance.

The role of a business manager

Managers of any modern business have a difficult job to perform. A crucial part of their job is to meet the objectives of their organisation and in order to do so they must pay attention to a number of important issues. In this book, we will look at these issues and the ways in which accounting information can be used to help managers.

Although the exact nature of a manager's job may vary quite significantly from one organisation or department to another – so that the role of a marketing manager, a production manager or a manager of a supermarket may appear to be quite different – there is considerable similarity in terms of the fundamental tasks to be performed. These tasks can be categorised as shown in Figure 1.1.

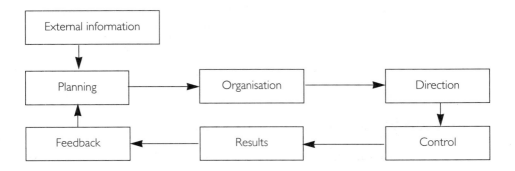

Figure 1.1 The tasks of management

Every manager plans his or her work and the work of others as well as organising him or herself and others, directing others as to what to do, motivating them and exercising control over situations and other people. The results are fed back into the planning process in order to modify future plans for the business.

All managers are concerned with working with people: those that are contemporaries, those they supervise, those they report to, and those who are the customers for the product or service which is provided by the organisation's area for which the manager is responsible. All managers are therefore naturally concerned with the output for their particular area of responsibility and so are also concerned with the inputs, whether these be raw materials, information or goods to be displayed and sold.

Using the information available, a manager must plan for the future of the business. In this context, he or she must:

- decide upon the courses of action which need to be taken in order to achieve the best results
- consider what alternative courses of action are available
- assess the consequences of any particular decision taken.

The manager of a restaurant, for example, will need to decide what its opening hours need to be and how these might affect possible customers who might want to dine when the restaurant is closed. The manager however also needs to decide upon the ingredients of the menu and how much of each one to order. In doing so, he or she needs to consider what the effect of not ordering enough of a particular ingredient might be in terms of dissatisfied customers and the possible effect this might have upon the future of the business. Balanced against this, he or she has to consider the effects of over-ordering and how the consequent waste might affect the profitability of the business. The manager therefore needs to consider alternatives and their consequences, and decide what course of action to take after considering all the facts.

Decision making is a crucial part of the job of any manager, and decisions need to be made between conflicting alternatives. These decisions are often conflicting in their possible outcomes and there is a degree of uncertainty surrounding the consequences. Selecting the best possible decision to make is therefore often a difficult and skilful process but it is important that the decisions made are the right ones. Because of this a manager needs tools to help him or her to evaluate the consequences of the alternative decisions which have to be made. These tools will assist in better decision making.

Within most organisations a key dimension in decision making is financial. In the case of a restaurant manager, for example, he or she will need to balance the cost of the ingredients bought against the income from providing meals. Management accounting has been developed as one tool which can help managers in decision making through helping them to assess the financial implications of any courses of available action.

The need for accounting information

It is impossible for a manager to ignore the financial implications of any decision which he or she might make and so the evaluation of any decision in financial terms is a crucial part of the decision-making process. As accounting is the method by which a business records its operations it is an important part of the business and cannot be ignored by any manager. Accounting information however takes time and effort to collect and process, and so is costly to produce. Such information therefore is valuable to a business and so needs to be used to maximum benefit.

In order for accounting information to benefit the business it needs to enable the users of that information (the managers) to alter their behaviour as a result of considering the information which has been provided. The information therefore needs to be *meaningful* to the recipient and also *relevant* to the purpose for which it is provided. It also needs to be provided at a *specific time*. Finally, the information must be *accurate* and provided in an *understandable format*. Therefore, the key elements of information are:

- meaningfulness
- relevance
- timeliness
- accuracy
- format.

Information can be distinguished from data; *data* are a set of facts which are not capable of influencing behaviour. In order to be useful, information must be communicated in a form which is understandable to the recipient and the quantitative nature of accounting information enables it to be more precisely understood.

Accounting information can be divided into two types according to its use:

- *external information* is provided for people who need to know about the business but are not involved in the running of the business, such as shareholders, investors in the business and government departments (e.g. Customs & Excise or the Inland Revenue)
- *internal information* is provided for use within the business and is the kind of information which managers need to help them make decisions on how to run the business.

Each type of information is provided by a different type of accounting.

Different types of accounting

Accounting can be categorised into three distinct types, depending upon its function.

Financial accounting

This is concerned with the provision of external information about the business, with the determination of profit, and with the production of the final accounts which a business needs to produce on an annual basis. It is therefore concerned with meeting statutory requirements in this respect. Financial accounting is also concerned with the raising of finance for a business and with the acquisition of assets. It is largely historical in perspective and concerned with recording what has happened in the business and the effect which this has had.

The key functions of financial accounting are:

- meeting statutory requirements
- record keeping
- the production of final accounts
- the raising of finance.

Management accounting

This is concerned with the internal information needs of the business. Its focus is upon the future rather than the past and with the evaluation of alternative possible courses of action. It is therefore essentially part of the management decision support system but also part of the planning and control aspects of the business. Management accounting enables performance to be measured and evaluated.

The key functions of management accounting are:

- controlling business operations
- decision support
- business planning
- performance measurement.

Cost accounting

This is often considered to be a part of management accounting and is the base from which management accounting was developed. In reality however cost accounting needs to be viewed as a separate branch of accounting which provides the basic information for both financial and management accounting. It is concerned with the identification and allocation of the various costs of production and with determining the value of the goods produced.

The key functions of cost accounting are:

- identifying and attributing costs
- cost accumulation for product costing
- stock valuation
- the provision of source data for financial and management accounting.

This book is concerned with accounting as a tool for business decision making and is therefore concerned with *management accounting*. It is impossible however to consider this without a basic understanding of cost accounting and so this type of accounting is also considered.

The nature of management accounting

Management accounting is concerned with the analysis and reporting of financial information for managers within a business in order to assist them in the performance of their jobs. The collection of this financial information is crucial to management accounting and cost accounting has a large part to play in this. However, other sources of information are also needed and not all information will be expressed in financial terms. Information regarding quantities of resources (in terms of physical units) may be important, as may qualitative information, and so these also fall within the scope of management accounting.

Management accounting is essentially a part of management decision making which is of use to all managers. It is used throughout the business rather than being focused within the finance department and can help managers with decision making in the following areas:

- *planning*: to decide what to produce and how best to meet the objectives of the organisation
- *control*: to ensure that the outcomes correspond to those planned
- *decision making*: to choose between alternative courses of action by evaluating the consequences
- *measuring performance*: to evaluate whether performance matches the expectations set out in the plan and to take corrective action if not.

This book investigates the types of problems which managers face in these four main areas and the ways in which management accounting can be used to help solve them.

Accounting information systems

Management accounting information will be generated, to a large extent, by the accounting information system which the business possesses. As far as managers are concerned, this system is a means of collecting and communicating information to aid in decision making. The system therefore needs to have been developed to meet the requirements of the managers of the business, along with its other function of satisfying the financial accounting and reporting requirements of the business. These requirements will vary greatly according to the nature of the business and the role which each individual manager plays in that business. The information needs of a warehouse manager will obviously be very different to those of a sales force manager, while a manager in a hospital will have quite different information reporting needs to those of a textile company's manager.

These information needs will, to some extent, be dependent upon the structure of the organisation, the manager's place in that structure, and the culture of the organisation. Organisational structure and culture will tend to vary from one organisation to another, thus placing different demands upon the accounting information system.

The technology upon which an accounting information system is based will also vary greatly and will depend partly upon the size of the organisation. Nevertheless, there are certain functions common to all such systems, namely:

- *Information collection and recording*. This function ensures that the relevant information is identified and stored in a systematic way so that it can be used for the future.
- *Information analysis*. This function involves the interpretation of information and the sorting of it into such a form that it can be used to help the manager in the business.

● *Information reporting.* The relevant information needs to be communicated to managers in such a way that it enables them to use it to help make decisions. It is vital that information is reported in time to enable decisions to be made.

The tasks of a manager

We have seen how the role of a manager of a business will vary greatly according to area of responsibility. We have also seen how the manager needs to help the organisation meet its objectives and that these can vary significantly from one organisation to another. The roles of different managers are very different and therefore the tasks which they undertake to perform their roles also differ. Nevertheless, we can classify these different tasks into one of several types, according to their nature, as follows.

Planning

A manager needs to plan for the future in order to decide how best to meet the objectives of the organisation. He or she needs to decide what can be achieved and what inputs are needed to help meet plans. Planning therefore needs to be not just qualitative but also quantitative, in order to evaluate the plan and determine its inputs and outputs.

All business processes can be considered as taking a set of inputs and performing operations in order to add value and transform them into outputs. The function of any business can therefore be viewed as one of adding value through the transformations made during its processing (see Figure 1.2).

Figure 1.2 The transformation process

Planning needs to consider alternatives, not just in terms of alternative targets to set but also in terms of alternative methods of achieving these targets. Planning cannot be done in isolation but needs to take into account what effect a particular course of action has upon the plans of other managers within the organisation. This is especially true when the inputs of this plan come from the outputs of another manager's plan, or when these outputs affect the planning of another manager. Thus a sales manager cannot plan how much to sell without taking into account the production manager's plans concerning how much will be produced; the production manager cannot make plans for production without taking into account the planning of the sales manager regarding how much can be sold. The planning tasks of the manager therefore cannot be made in isolation.

Control

Control is concerned with making sure that things happen in accordance with the plan. It therefore involves monitoring the plan and the progress being made in accordance with the plan, and taking action when things are not going in accordance with the plan to change things so that the plan can be achieved. Control is an ongoing activity for a manager and involves comparing actual performance with targets, providing feedback on actual performance and taking action to change performance when it diverges from the plan. Although the manager may be able to achieve this by physical observation and communication with people, it is likely that this will not be sufficient. He or she will probably be reliant on reports in order to exercise control. The reports which management accounting provide are therefore crucial in assisting a manager to exercise control.

Decision making

One of the key aspects of a manager's job is concerned with making decisions. There is always more than one course of action which a manager can take in any particular situation (even if one of the courses is to do nothing!) and so he or she needs to decide between the alternatives in order to make the decision which is most beneficial.

In order to make a decision the manager needs to identify the possible alternative courses of action, to gather data about those course of action and to evaluate the consequences of each particular alternative. The stages in the decision-making process are shown in Figure 1.3. This illustrates that the decision-making process is not complete when an alternative has been selected and implemented but that the outcomes of the decision need to be followed through into the control process.

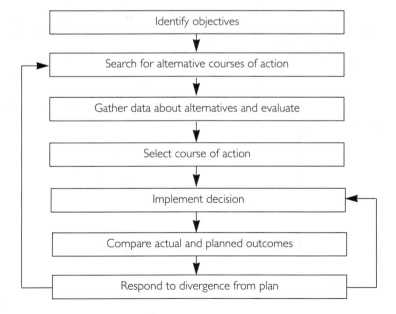

Figure 1.3 The decision-making process

In order to make a decision a manager needs information. Management accounting is one tool which exists to help the manager by providing information about the consequences of the alternatives open to him.

Performance evaluation

While the performance of organisations is evaluated by such measures as return on capital employed, the organisation in turn needs to evaluate the performance of its units and the managers running these units. The managers likewise need to evaluate the actual performance of their tasks against that which has been planned. In order to evaluate performance there needs to be acceptable measures of performance. Measurement must be relative to be meaningful – to compare performance with plans and with past performance. Performance measures also need to be quantitative in order to enable comparisons to be made and financial information provides important data for the measurement of performance.

Unless performance can be evaluated managers have no basis upon which to exercise control, to make decisions and to plan for the future. The role of management accounting in this context is therefore of crucial importance in enabling managers to carry out their tasks.

Communication

Information available to help managers in their tasks needs to be communicated to them, and managers in turn need to communicate their plans and decisions to others. Communication involves both the sender of information and its recipient, and for the information to be of value it needs to be understood by the recipient *as intended by the sender.* Any interference which prevents the message being received by the recipient is known as *noise.* Figure 1.4 shows that two types of noise prevent a message being received as transmitted.

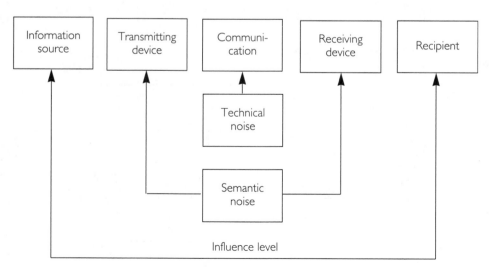

Figure 1.4 The communication of information

Technical noise is that such as occurs on a telephone or radio and concerns the technical means of communication. A more crucial type of noise however is *semantic noise* which occurs because a message is not transmitted in a clear and unambiguous manner and so is not correctly understood by the recipient. Quantitative information is less likely to be misunderstood than qualitative information and this is one of the importance features of accounting information. Management accounting therefore has an important part to play not just in enabling decisions to be made but also in the communication of information.

The importance of performance measurement

In order for a business to be able to control its operations it is necessary that the managers of that business are able to measure the performance of the business as a whole and its constituent parts. We will look at examples of how management accounting can help a manager to do this. It is important however to remember that businesses, and the environment in which they operate, are continually changing. As the business environment changes so too must accounting in order to respond to the changes and to provide business managers with the tools needed to manage in such an environment. In an ever-changing environment there is a constant need for managers to keep abreast of developments in order to be able to perform to optimum effect.

As well as having to measure and evaluate the performance of the business as a whole and of its individual parts the ability to evaluate the performance of individual managers is just as important. This is not only of importance to the business but concerns the managers themselves, as their rewards are increasingly based, at least in part, upon an assessment of their performance. Thus management accounting needs to be able to perform this function although it has been criticised for its failure in this respect.

Johnson and Kaplan (1987) have argued that the role of management accounting has changed so that it is no longer relevant to managerial needs. In considering management accounting systems they state:

> Their original purpose of providing information to facilitate cost control and performance measurement in hierarchical organisations has been transformed to one of compiling costs for periodic financial statements.

While we will see, in our consideration of the various techniques of management accounting, that this is not entirely the case and that management accounting does in fact facilitate the measurement of performance, it is important to recognise that a business manager, when using management accounting, operates within the broader environment of the organisation, and that accounting is used to satisfy other needs within the business. These other needs necessarily relate to financial accounting and the relationship between costing, management accounting and financial accounting needs to be recognised, as does the role of accounting information and control systems within the organisation. It is also important to recognise that management accounting is subject to criticism and has limitations in its use. Thus each technique which a business manager might employ to help solve a problem gives both benefits and limitations, and we will explore both aspects of each of the techniques considered. It is important for a manager to recognise these limitations.

We will see that accounting is presented as a quantitative subject which enables the analysis of facts relating to business decisions in order for rational decisions to be made. Equally, the use of accounting information can affect individual behaviour within the company and lead to either increasing or reducing the motivation of individual managers. The way in which control systems are designed and the way in which accounting information is used can therefore have a significant effect upon the performance of a business. It is important for business managers to recognise this and be aware of the effects of accounting upon themselves and others within the organisation. This awareness will help lead to better decision making and subsequently to better performance by the manager.

Managers and business ethics

Business ethics is a subject of considerable importance to any organisation and accounting information has often been accused of providing an excuse for unethical behaviour. Indeed this accusation has been extended to accountants and business managers generally who have been accused of behaving unethically in their search for profits to the exclusion of all else. The unethical ways in which accounting information has been used have been described in detail by Smith (1992) who describes the way in which new accounting techniques have been created with the sole purpose of boosting reported profits. These techniques have become known as *creative accounting* and have been the subject of much media attention. (Smith's book, *Accounting for Growth*, makes interesting reading for any prospective business manager.)

Other writers have however been concerned with highlighting the value of ethical behaviour and have claimed that this actually leads to better business performance. Thus McCoy (1985) considers that ethics need to be at the core of business behaviour and that effective business management is based upon ethical behaviour. He claims that this recognition, and acting accordingly, actually increases the performance of a business.

The UK accounting bodies are also concerned with business ethics and all have a stance on this matter, incorporating a requirement for ethical behaviour into their codes of conduct. The subject of ethical behaviour amongst businesses has also had an effect upon auditing practice and upon the financial reporting of businesses.

Any manager operating in a business environment needs to be aware of the importance of ethical behaviour. Equally, in attempting to behave ethically, he or she will experience conflicts between different alternative courses of action, and may find conflicts between the company's objectives and his or her own personal motivation and objectives. No ready solution to these conflicts is available but managers should be aware that research has shown that ethical behaviour leads to better performance in the longer term and so should be encouraged to act accordingly.

The organisation of this book

This book is concerned with the problems which managers have to face in the performance of their duties and with the decisions which they need to take in order to be effective. Management accounting is a tool which is available to managers to help them achieve better job performance and to make better decisions. Therefore, this book is organised around the problems which managers face and explains how the techniques of management accounting can be used to assist.

The book is divided into four parts, as follows:

- *Part 1* considers the way in which cost accounting classifies costs in an organisation and attributes them to the products or services which are responsible for the income of the organisation.
- *Part 2* takes the argument further by looking at different ways of attributing costs in assisting managers to make decisions about these products or services.
- *Part 3* explores the broader range of techniques which management accounting provides to assist managers in appraising and pricing projects.
- *Part 4* shows how, once a particular course of action has been decided upon, management accounting can help managers to monitor and control progress to meet agreed targets.

The structure of the book is shown in Figure 1.5.

Introduction

Accounting for business decisions	Accounting and business strategy

Part 1 Classifying and absorbing costs

The nature of cost behaviour	Establishing the cost of a product	Absorption costing	The different costing methods used in industry

Part 2 Attributing costs for decision making

Manufacturing technology and accounting systems	Activity based costing	Marginal costing

Part 3 Appraising projects

Planning of profit and volume	The pricing decision	The relevant costs for operational decisions	Making operational decisions
Making capital expenditure decisions	The effects of risk and uncertainty	Internal supply in divisionalised companies	

Part 4 Controlling business performance

The control of stock	Setting targets	Using budgets for planning and control
The use of standard costing	Analysing variances	Evaluating managerial and divisional performance

Figure 1.5 The structure of the book

Summary

- The role of the manager is complex and is concerned with:
  - planning
  - control
  - decision making
  - performance evaluation
  - communication.
- A manager operates within the context of the organisation and its objectives (which can be multiple).
- Management accounting is a branch of accounting which is concerned with assisting managers in performing their duties.
- Performance measurement is an important element of business management and the changing nature of business has caused accounting to change accordingly. These changes are continuing and affect the role of the business manager.
- Ethics form the basis of business behaviour and ethical behaviour has been shown to lead to improved performance in the long term.

Bibliography and further reading

Clutterbuck D and Snow D, *Working with the Community*, Weidenfeld & Nicolson 1990

Handy C, *Understanding Organisations*, 3rd edition, Penguin 1985

Johnson H T and Kaplan R S, *Relevance Lost: The Rise and Fall of Management Accounting*, Harvard Business School Press 1987

McCoy C S, *Management of Values: the Ethical Difference in Corporate Policy and Performance*, Pitman 1985

Mintzberg H, *The Nature of Managerial Work*, Harper & Row 1973

Sizer J, *An Insight Into Management Accounting*, 3rd edition, Penguin 1989

Smith T, *Accounting for Growth*, Century Business 1992

Self-review questions

1 Why is quantitative information important for a manager?
(See page 9.)

2 What are the key components of an accounting information system?
(See page 5.)

3 Distinguish between external information and internal information. What kind of information is of particular concern to the manager of a business?
(See page 3.)

4 What is the main way in which management accounting can help in each of the five main tasks of a manager?
(See page 6.)

5 Outline the changing nature of performance measurement in a company and the implications for management accounting information.
(See page 9.)

6 Explain the significance of business ethics to a business manager and how they affect the use of accounting information.
(See page 10.)

Additional questions

1.1 List the main inputs for a company and then list the main outputs from the transformation process.

1.2 Information is one of the key resources of any business manager. Distinguish between information and data, and describe the key elements of information.

2 Accounting and business strategy

Objectives

After studying this chapter you should be able to:

- describe the purpose of strategic planning and the steps in the planning process
- explain the nature of emergent strategy
- discuss the relationship between strategy and organisation structure
- describe the effect of information technology (IT) upon the role of a business manager
- outline the possible objectives of an organisation.

Introduction

In this book we will be investigating the way in which management accounting can help the business manager to perform better his or her job through:

- planning the operations of the business
- controlling the plan in operation
- making decisions which will help in the operation of the business.

All of these functions are vital to a business but are essentially inward looking and concerned with the internal operations of the business. A business manager however must also be concerned with the external environment in which the business operates – that is with his or her customers and suppliers, with competitors, and with the market for the products or services supplied by the business.

Such concerns of a business manager comprise the *strategic* element of the manager's job and a manager must be familiar with this aspect of management, and with the way in which accounting can help in this area. This chapter therefore is concerned with the external environment of a business and with the strategic part of a manager's job. First however we need to consider the various objectives which an organisation might have.

The objectives of an organisation

We have seen that management accounting exists as a tool to help the managers of a business in meeting their objectives, but the objectives of managers need to be considered in terms of how they help to meet the objectives of the organisation. While most business organisations aim to make a profit this is not true of all and the not-for-profit sector of the economy is one which is increasing in importance. Profit making is not the only objective of most organisations.

The following possible objectives of an organisation can be identified.

Profit maximisation

For organisations which exist to make a profit it seems reasonable that they should seek to make as large a profit as possible. It is not however always clear what course of action will lead to the greatest profit and it is by no means clear whether profit maximisation in the short term will be in the best interests of the business and will lead to the greatest profit in the longer term. Thus profit maximisation may not be in the best interests of a business and it certainly may conflict with other objectives which a business may have.

Maximising cash flow

Cash flow is not the same as profit and an organisation needs cash to survive. In some circumstances, this cash flow may be more important than profit because a lack of cash can threaten the survival of an organisation.

Maximising return on capital employed

Return on capital employed is a measure of performance of a business in terms of its operating efficiency and therefore provides a measure of how a business is performing over time. Comparative measures are useful in helping the owners and managers of a business to decide what course of action may be beneficial to the business.

Maximising service provision

This is the not-for-profit sector equivalent of maximising the return on capital employed and thus provides a similar means of evaluating decisions.

Maximising shareholder value

The value of a business depends partly upon the profits it generates and partly upon the value of the assets it possesses. These assets can be made up partly of *tangible assets*, such as plant and machinery or land and buildings, and partly of *intangible assets*, such as brand names. Thus the value of Coca Cola as a business far outweighs the value of its fixed assets because of the value of its brand name which is recognised world-wide. Maximising the value of the business to shareholders therefore involves much more than maximising the profit generated.

Growth

Growth through expansion of the business, in terms of both assets and earnings, and the increase in market share which the business holds is one objective which appeals to both owners and managers. If this is an objective of the business then it will lead to different decisions to those of profit maximisation.

Long-term stability

The survival of a business is of great concern to both owners and managers and this can lead to different behaviour and a reluctance to accept risk. All decisions involve an element of risk and seeking to reduce risk for the purpose of long-term stability can lead to performance which is less than desirable.

Satisficing

All an organisation's objectives are dependent upon the people who set them and business behaviour cannot be considered without taking this into account. *Satisficing* is a way of reducing risk and taking multiple objectives into account by making decisions which are acceptable from several viewpoints without necessarily being the best to meet any particular objective.

Any business is likely to seek to pursue a number of objectives at any one time. The precise combination of them is likely to vary from one organisation to another, and from one time to another, depending upon the individual circumstances of the organisation at a particular time. The organisation will not however view all the objectives which it is pursuing at any particular time as equally important and will have more important ones to follow. These objectives will therefore tend to be viewed as a hierarchy, which may vary over time.

Strategic planning

Strategic planning is concerned with the future of the business and with how the company can best supply what the market desires. This requires an analysis of the market in which the business is operating in order to decide what the market (i.e. potential customers) wants and what price it is willing to pay for the satisfaction of its wants. This is then followed by an analysis of what the company is able to produce and supply (and at what price). This then determines how the company will organise its activities in order to provide these goods or services.

Strategic planning is not concerned with the present but rather with the future and is therefore especially concerned with changes to current patterns of demand, and with ensuring that the company's capabilities change to meet the changes in market demand. Thus strategic planning is concerned with ensuring the future of the business by ensuring that the company changes to reflect changing market conditions. This can be modelled as shown in Figure 2.1.

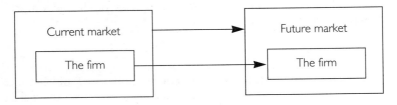

Figure 2.1 Strategic planning and market development

Without strategic planning there is a danger that the market would change without the company being aware of this change and reflecting it in its own pattern of operations. Thus the company would find itself outside the market (see Figure 2.2) and effectively go out of business.

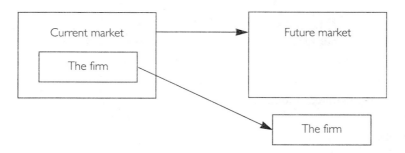

Figure 2.2 Market development without strategic planning

The implementation plan

Strategic planning is concerned with the future direction of the business. This planning must of course ensure that the business has the capability of achieving whatever direction and objectives are determined in the planning stage. Thus the strategic plan must define a set of objectives for the business and the steps necessary to ensure the achievement of these objectives – in other words an *implementation plan*. Most managers of organisations, at the start of their strategy development process, begin with a vision of where they see the organisation being in the future. This is known as a *strategic vision* and is often promulgated throughout the organisation in the form of a *mission statement*, which sets out, in broad terms, the reason for the organisation's existence.

The strategic planning process can be modelled as shown in Figure 2.3.

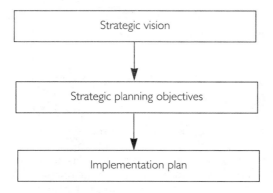

Figure 2.3 The strategic planning process

The implementation plan will involve the following elements.

An operations plan
This ensures that the company has the resources (i.e. manpower, capital investment, working capital) and capabilities to achieve the objectives of the plan. These capabilities include:

- technological capability (see Chapter 7)
- capacity planning (see Chapters 10 and 14)
- the ability to produce required costings (see Chapters 4, 7 and 8).

A marketing plan
This ensures that the company is able to:

- produce the required amount and maintain adequate stocks (see Chapter 17)
- price the product correctly (see Chapter 11).

A financial plan
This ensures that the company has the financial resources to:

- manage operations (see Chapters 19 and 22)
- undertake any necessary capital investment (see Chapter 14).

The strategic plan is as shown in Figure 2.4.

Figure 2.4 The components of the strategic plan

Corporate planning

The strategic plan sets out the objectives of the business for the future in outline terms. It also considers the options available to the business and how capable it is to meet this plan. Once the future direction of the business has been determined by this planning there is a need to develop the plan into a more definite one which can be expressed in quantitative terms. This is the function of the corporate plan, which we will look at in detail in Chapter 19.

The *corporate plan* provides a detailed plan for the organisation, and its components parts, in order to enable it to organise its future activities and to communicate this planning throughout the organisation. This in turn leads to the development of the organisation's short-term plan, or *budget.*

The planning stages of the organisation are as shown in Figure 2.5.

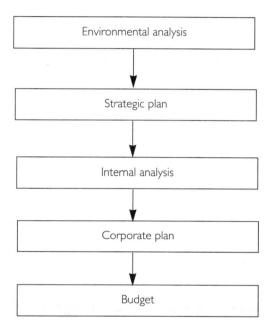

Figure 2.5 Stages in the corporate planning process

The environmental analysis will enable a company to develop its strategic plan through an examination of the external environment in which the company is operating. An examination of the internal environment will enable a company to translate this plan into a corporate plan for implementation. Part of this analysis will comprise a *gap analysis* which will inform the managers of the company of its ability to meet the plan and any gaps in resources which need to be addressed. Gap analysis will enable the managers of the business to determine what resources are needed in order to implement the plan and this will feed through into both the operating budget and the capital investment budget.

We can see that the business manager needs to be involved at all stages of this planning process and that the accounting techniques which we have discussed have an important part to play in helping at all levels and at all stages of the planning process. Thus management accounting is of importance to a business and its managers, not just operationally but also strategically.

Planned and emergent strategy

Although an organisation develops its strategy through a planning process, it is often the case that the effects of this strategy do not materialise in the manner intended. While following a strategy, the managers of the business will continue making decisions on a day-to-day basis. These decision will inevitably affect the strategic direction of the organisation and may cause changes to the way the strategy evolves. This is known as *emergent strategy* and can be modelled as shown in Figure 2.6.

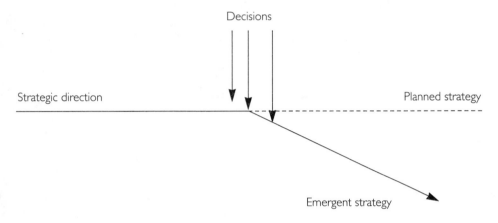

Figure 2.6 Planned and emergent strategies

Accounting and organisational design

An important part of strategic planning is to ensure that the organisation is structured in such a way that the plan can be achieved, and that the control systems of the organisation provide appropriate feedback to managers. This feedback is necessary in order to ensure that managers are able to measure performance against the plan and take corrective action as necessary (see Chapter 22). Thus the structure of an organisation needs to be determined by its planning while its control systems need to determined by its structure (see Figure 2.7).

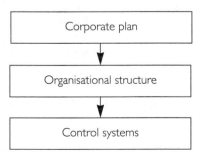

Figure 2.7 Planning and control systems

The control systems provide a feedback loop as shown in Figure 2.8.

Figure 2.8 The feedback loop

Organisational design is therefore dependent upon the planning of the business and accounting information is used to provide managers with feedback via the control systems in order to measure performance. Although each organisation tends to be unique in its structural design and control systems, various attempts have been made to classify organisations according to these elements. One such classification was undertaken by Miles and Snow (1978) who classified organisations according to the way in which they responded to their external environments. They identified four types of organisation, as follows.

Defenders

These organisations are strong on control systems, operate in stable markets where growth is slow and incremental, and tend to have hierarchical structures.

Prospectors

These organisations are concerned with exploiting market opportunities and therefore tend to have little formal structure, and control systems which are only concerned with overall results rather than detail.

Analyzers

These organisations tend to operate in a matrix structure rather than hierarchically, and tend to have extensive planning systems, and elaborate control systems to measure performance against budgets.

Reactors

These organisations react to market changes rather than planning their strategy. Their structure and control is therefore viewed as often inappropriate to their needs and their performance is consequently below that achieved by other types of organisation.

Trends in design

Organisation theory is also concerned with other issues such as whether an organisation is *centralised* or *decentralised* and whether this affects the performance of the organisation. We will consider the organisation of a business into divisions in Chapter 16 and see that this form of decentralisation can lead to increased performance. We will also consider decentralisation in Chapter 22 and see how this can lead to increased motivation for managers and consequently to increased business performance. Decentralisation tends to be a key feature of modern organisations and this has had the effect of giving more responsibility to individual managers. Such managers therefore have more decisions to make and so need to understand the techniques which we have considered in order to be able to use them to help in managing their individual areas of responsibility.

One further trend in organisational design which is of significance to modern business managers is the trend away from hierarchical organisations towards a flatter structure with fewer levels of management. This is known as *delayering* and has been a feature of organisational design in the 1990s. This trend too has had the effect of giving greater responsibility to individual managers. It has also had the effect that the accounting departments of some organisations have been delayered, thus providing the individual managers with less technical support from accountants. This means that all business managers need to have a sound grasp of the techniques of management accounting and to be able to apply these techniques to appropriate business problems without relying upon the support of others in the organisation.

The impact of information technology upon business management

One of the features of business in recent years which looks set to progress into the future is the increasing use of information technology (IT) by the company as a whole and also by individual business managers. One feature of the increasing use of IT is that the techniques of management accounting have become easier to use because of the processing capabilities of the software available to managers. This is particularly true of the more statistical and mathematical techniques. Thus analysis prior to decision making has become easier and this has given business managers the opportunity and ability to undertake more detailed analysis and to compare alternative decision outcomes in greater detail. This should have the effect of improving managerial decision making by providing better support for these decisions. It has had the effect of increasing the role of management accounting in managerial decision making.

Another feature of the increased use of IT however is that it has made much more information available to the manager and has meant that the information provided is not just more detailed but also more speedily produced and hence more up-to-date. This improved feedback is valuable from the point of view of measuring performance and enabling corrective action to be taken when necessary. Also, because the information is more up-to-date, corrective action can be taken earlier and therefore tends to be less dramatic.

One problem with this increased volume of data available to managers however is that of *information overload*. This means that it is more difficult to identify the significant information from within the increased volume of data available. It might be argued therefore that although the quantity and speed of feedback from control systems has improved the quality of that feedback has deteriorated. This means that a manager must be more skilled to identify and react to the relevant and significant information. As much of this information is financial in content this too means that the accounting expertise of each individual manager needs to be higher, as well as his or her IT competence.

This skill trend looks set to continue into the future and means that the required skill level of each manager, as far as management accounting is concerned, appears to be continuing to increase.

Conclusion

Managing a business, or a part of one, is a complex process and requires a manager to address a variety of problems. It also requires him or her to possess a range of skills in order to be able to do so. In this book we will consider a variety of problems which business managers face in the course of their work and look at how the techniques of management accounting can help the manager in finding solutions to these problems. We will consider both the strengths and weaknesses of these techniques and see that, on balance, their use allows managers to arrive at better solutions to their business problems, and so enables them to manage their businesses better. We will also consider the relevance of these techniques of management accounting to managers in all areas of a business and see that they are equally relevant to all areas of management.

Therefore, it is hoped that you, as a prospective business manager, will become a better manager through the use of these techniques in appropriate situations.

Summary

- Strategic planning is concerned with the future of the business in order to decide the future activities of the company.
- Strategic planning includes environmental analysis and implementation planning. It also includes:
  - operations plans
  - marketing plans
  - financial plans.
- Emergent strategy arises from the effects of day-to-day decisions upon the strategic direction of the organisation.
- Strategic planning leads to the development of a corporate plan and then to the development of the budget.
- Organisation structure needs to be determined by the corporate plan. Control systems need to be determined by the organisational structure. Control systems provide a feedback mechanism.
- Organisation theory is concerned with the way organisations are structured. This includes such issues as hierarchies and centralisation or decentralisation.
- The increasing use of IT in business is having a continuing effect on the role of a business manager.

Bibliography and further reading

Emmanuel C R, Otley D T, and Merchant K, *Accounting for Management Control*, 2nd edition, Chapman & Hall 1990, (Chapter 2)

Miles R E & Snow C, *Organisational Strategy Structure and Process*, McGraw-Hill 1978

Mintzberg H, *The Rise and Fall of Strategic Planning*, Prentice Hall 1994

Peters T J and Waterman R H, *In Search of Excellence*, Harper & Row 1986

Porter M E, *Competitive Advantage*, The Free Press 1985

Ryan B, *Strategic Accounting for Management*, Dryden Press 1995, (Chapters 2, 4 and 9)

Smith T, *Accounting for Growth*, Century Business 1992

Self-review questions

1 What is the main purpose of strategic planning?
(See page 16.)

2 Distinguish between planned and emergent strategies. Why does this difference arise?
(See page 20.)

3 Explain how organisational structure needs to be determined by the corporate plan, and how control systems are affected by an organisation's structure.
(See page 20.)

4 How has the increasing use of IT in business affected the role of accountants?
(See page 22.)

5 List five possible objectives of an organisation and suggest how they might conflict with each other.
(See page 15.)

Additional questions

2.1 The managing director of Cable Co Ltd is concerned that the strategy of the company as determined by the board never seems to materialise exactly as planned. He attributes this to a faulty planning process. Do you agree with him?

2.2 Decentralisation of control tends to be a feature of modern organisations. How does this affect the requirements for managers to use management accounting techniques in the decision-making process?

2.3 Accounting information provides detail which is essential to the planning of a business but only considers the internal operations of the business. A successful business manager must also be concerned with the external environment in which a business is operating. Discuss.

Part 1
CLASSIFYING AND ABSORBING COSTS

3 The nature of cost behaviour

Objectives

After studying this chapter you should be able to:

- describe the purposes for which costs are classified
- differentiate between fixed costs, variable costs and mixed costs
- explain the limitations of cost classification for cost prediction purposes
- classify costs appropriately for product costing purposes.

Stanley Brown – the transport manager

Stanley Brown is the transport manager of a food manufacturing company, based at its distribution centre, and he controls the operation of a fleet of vans. He needs to know the operating cost of the vehicles under his management in order to calculate delivery costs so the company's customers can be charged for the products delivered.

His assistant has provided him with the following information in terms of cost per vehicle:

Purchase cost	£25,000
Expected sale value after two years	£7,000
Vehicle licence per annum	£500
Insurance per annum	£500
Maintenance – each six-monthly service	£250
Replacement parts (per 1000 miles)	£75
Tyre replacement after 25,000 miles – 6 tyres	@ £80 each
Average mileage per annum	30,000
Diesel fuel per 5 litres	£2.50
Average miles per 5 litres	15

Stanley needs to classify this data in some way in order to be able to arrive at an estimated running cost per mile for his vehicles so that he can determine the cost of delivery to his customers.

The classification of costs

Although you may think that a cost to a business is simply that – a cost – in actual fact accountants spend a lot of time considering the nature of cost behaviour and attempting to arrive at a classification of costs which is appropriate to their purpose and to the needs of the business.

If we look at the problem facing Stanley Brown we can see that he has information concerning the costs of his vehicles which he needs to classify or organise, in some way, in order to be able to work out the cost of delivering goods to his customers. The information which he has been presented with will not enable him to do this until he has classified it in some way and we need to consider how he might do this.

As we work through this book we shall look at various methods of classifying costs, that is grouping costs according to their meaning in a particular context, and we will investigate how these cost classifications can be used to help business managers solve some of the problems they face in managing a business. As a starting point however it is necessary to recognise that costs can be classified in a variety of ways, depending upon the purpose of the classification. Costs can be classified in the following ways:

● according to their behaviour
● according to their relevance to the production of goods and services
● according to the nature of the decision to be made.

In this book we will look at these different classifications and see how they can help business decision making. In this chapter we will consider the first of these classification methods and we will look at the other methods in Chapters 4 and 12 respectively.

Cost classification according to behaviour

While business managers are concerned with what their costs have been in the past, they are naturally much more concerned with what their costs will be in the future. *Cost prediction*, the estimating of future costs, is therefore of crucial importance to business planning. In order to be able to predict costs it is necessary to be able to understand the behaviour of costs and how they will be affected by changes in methods of operation or levels of activity. The classification of costs according to their behaviour is therefore the basis of cost prediction and this is normally undertaken in relation to changes in the activity level, or output, of the company. In this context, costs can be classified into two types:

● fixed costs
● variable costs.

Fixed costs

A *fixed cost* is one which is not dependent upon the level of activity but which will be incurred on a recurring basis whatever the level of activity the company undertakes.

> Thus for Stanley Brown the purchase cost of a van is a fixed cost which must be incurred whether or not the van is actually used.

Fixed costs are relevant to time periods rather than activity levels and in terms of cost prediction the cost behaviour can be predicted into the future without regard to the expected activity level. Such costs are unchanged according to the level of activity and can be shown as in Figure 3.1.

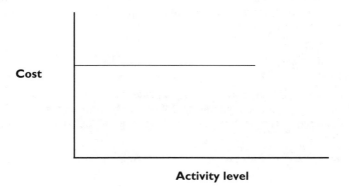

Figure 3.1 Fixed costs

Fixed costs are not however fixed indefinitely for all activity levels and at a certain point additional fixed costs will be incurred.

> Thus for Stanley Brown, when the number of deliveries increases above a certain level an additional van will be required. This is known as a *step change in fixed costs* and is shown in Figure 3.2.

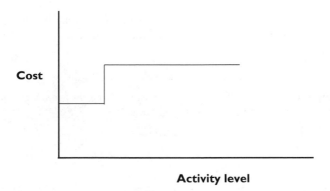

Figure 3.2 Stepped costs

Variable costs

A *variable cost* is one which is directly related to the level of activity of the company and can be predicted to increase or decrease in direct proportion to an increase or decrease in the level of production.

> Thus for Stanley Brown, diesel fuel can be considered to be a variable cost and a 10 per cent increase in the annual mileage of one of his vans can be expected to lead to a 10 per cent increase in the annual cost of diesel fuel. This can be shown as in Figure 3.3.

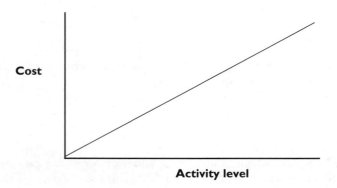

Figure 3.3 Variable costs

Variable costs therefore are related to the level of activity of the business and for cost prediction purposes cannot be estimated for the future without a consideration of the estimated level of activity, as any changes to this will lead to a change in cost.

Although costs are predicted in total for a time period, for variable costs it is useful to understand the cost behaviour in terms of unit cost – i.e. cost per unit produced, per 1000 units produced or per batch, or whatever unit is appropriate.

For Stanley Brown an appropriate unit measure is cost per mile so variable costs such as tyre replacement can be predicted in terms of cost per mile.

This classification of costs into fixed and variable according to their behavioural characteristics is an essential preliminary to being able to undertake any sort of cost prediction.

For Stanley Brown therefore it is possible to classify his costs in this manner, as follows:

Fixed costs
       purchase cost
       vehicle licence
       insurance
       maintenance

Variable costs
       replacement parts
       tyre replacement
       diesel fuel.

For cost prediction purposes it is necessary to convert these into costs per time period and in this case costs are considered on an annual basis as follows:

Fixed costs

	£	£
Purchase of vehicle:		
Purchase	25,000	
Less resale value	7,000	
	18,000	
Cost per annum (over 2 years)		9,000
Vehicle licence		500
Insurance		500
Maintenance (2 services @ £250 each)		500
Annual fixed cost		10,500

Variable costs

	£
Replacement parts:	
£75 per 1000 miles – annual mileage 30,000	2,250
Tyres:	
£80 x 6 tyres every 25,000 miles –	
annual mileage 30,000	
i.e. 80 x 6 x 30,000/25,000	576
Fuel:	
£2.50 per 5 litres @ 15 miles per 5 litres	
annual mileage 30,000	5,000
Annual variable cost	7,826

In order to be able to predict costs in the future for calculating delivery costs to customers Stanley Brown, having now classified costs appropriately, is able to calculate a cost per mile as follows:

	£
Fixed cost	10,500
Variable cost	7,826
Total cost	18,326
Cost per mile:	
Fixed cost (10,500/30,000)	0.35
Variable cost (7,826/30,000)	0.26
Total cost	0.61

Because Stanley has classified his costs into fixed and variable costs he is able to predict costs in the future at different levels of activity. The fixed costs will not change in total but if the average mileage changes they will change in terms of cost per mile. The variable costs on the other hand will change in total in direct proportion to the changed activity level but will remain the same in terms of unit cost per mile. Thus, for example, if each van is expected to travel 35,000 miles per annum in future instead of 30,000 miles per annum costs can be predicted as follows:

	£
Fixed cost	10,500
Variable cost (£0.26 per mile x 35,000 miles)	9,130
Total cost	18,326
Cost per mile:	
Fixed cost (10,500/35,000)	0.30
Variable cost	0.26
Total cost	0.56

Problems relating to the classification of costs

Although this classification of costs forms the basis of cost prediction it needs to be recognised that it is not necessarily simple to achieve, nor is the prediction of cost based upon this classification as absolute as might be understood from the example. We will consider some of these difficulties in future chapters but for the moment the following problems relating to the classification of costs need to be understood.

Mixed costs

Not all costs can be classified as purely fixed or purely variable and many have an element of both fixed and variable costs. Examples include telephone charges or photocopy machine charges which have a fixed element of rent and a variable element depending upon usage. These costs are known as *mixed costs*, or *semi-fixed* or *semi-variable costs*. Cost prediction must therefore recognise these types of cost and how they behave, and attempt to separate the two types of cost in order to predict future behaviour. This can be a difficult exercise and prediction is often made using statistical methods based upon an analysis of past cost behaviour. Such costs can be illustrated as in Figure 3.4.

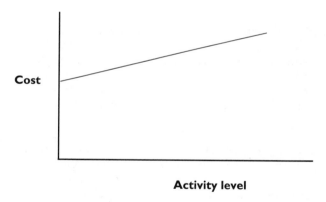

Figure 3.4 Mixed costs

Short-term and long-term effects

The classification of costs into fixed and variable costs for prediction is basically only valid for short-term prediction, i.e. for the next time period or the next year. In the longer term all fixed costs can be regarded as variable and even long-term costs, such as the factory costs themselves, can be varied as existing factories can be disposed of or new factories built given sufficient time. In the long term there are also likely to be technological changes which will affect production methods or economic changes which may affect demand for a product. Cost prediction cannot therefore be made indefinitely into the future but only for fixed, relatively short time periods.

Linearity

In predicting costs it is normally assumed that variable costs vary in direct proportion to changes in the level of activity, but in reality this may not be strictly true. Thus the assumption is made that a 10 per cent increase in output will result in a 10 per cent increase in variable costs and a 20 per cent increase in output will result in a 20 per cent increase in variable costs. The reality may however be a 12 per cent increase in costs for a 10 per cent increase in output and a 19 per cent increase in costs for a 20 per cent increase in output. Cost behaviour is somewhat irregular, and even when regular the relationship may not actually be a linear one but may be a *curvilinear relationship* with costs changing predictably with changing activity levels but not in a linear manner. Nevertheless, while recognising this, it is often reasonable in predicting costs to make an assumption of linearity and calculate costs on this basis. For small changes in activity levels this assumption is usually sufficient and it is often not worth the effort to determine the exact nature of the cost behaviour. The bigger the variation in activity level however the less precise such approximations are likely to be.

Relevant range

Both fixed and variable cost relationships only hold true within a specific range of activities, termed the *relevant* range, and outside this range the relationship no longer holds true. For example, with fixed costs an increase in the level of activity beyond a particular point may necessitate the introduction of a new production plant or an additional assembly line, hence causing an increase in the level of fixed costs. Fixed costs tend to increase in steps rather than gradually as the level of activity increases and these increases are known as *stepped costs* in the production process (see Figure 3.2). For variable costs the changes tend to be more gradual but, for example, an increase in activity may result in the need to recruit extra labour, overtime working at premium rates, or a new shift working pattern. The effect of this is to change the unit cost of production beyond a particular level of activity and to move the variable cost behaviour into a different cost behaviour relationship. In predicting costs therefore it is necessary to recognise the relevant range within which a particular cost behaviour applies.

Economics versus accounting

Economic theory suggests that costs behave in a predictable way, whatever the range of activity, and that one cost function applies to all levels of activity. Economic theory further suggests that a cost function is not linear, but rather curvilinear. The difference between costs in accounting and in economics is considered in detail in Chapter 11.

Multiple causes of behaviour

It is often assumed that a variable cost is related to the level of production and varies directly with changes in the level of production. In reality, variable costs may vary in relation to a number of different activities within the production process. Thus, for example, labour costs may vary according to the number of orders received, the number of batches processed, the number of times machines need to be reset for different production processes, or more likely for a combination of such reasons. It is an over-simplification to relate all variable costs to a sole activity measure, such as output, but one that is frequently assumed by manufacturing companies. Such an assumption however is often sufficient to classify costs for prediction purposes. At other times however the results from this may be misleading and it is for this reason that other methods of determining cost relationships have been developed. Activity based costing is one such method which we will consider in detail in Chapter 11.

The objectives of cost classification

In order to consider how we might wish to classify the cost information which is available to us in a useful way it is a good starting point to consider the objectives which we have in mind for such a classification. Broadly speaking there are three reasons or objectives for wishing to classify costs, namely:

- stock valuation
- decision making
- control,

and we will look at each of these in turn.

Stock valuation

In order to value stock we need to be able to calculate its cost of production. This is important because it is crucial for a business to know whether or not it is operating profitably and to know whether or not each product made is being sold at a profit. Most companies manufacture more than one product and so need to know the costs of production for each product separately. This also applies to service industries and a company such as Macdonalds will want to know the cost of production of a Big Mac separately from the cost of production of French Fries in order to know whether it is making a profit from producing and selling each of these products.

Not all of the costs which a company incurs are directly associated with the production of individual products. In the case of Macdonalds its television advertising is concerned with all of its products from a sales point of view and not with production. Similarly, the heating and lighting of its individual restaurants is not solely for the production of individual products. We shall look at production costs and at stock valuation separately in later chapters but at this point it is important to be able to classify costs into two separate types:

- product costs
- period costs.

Product costs
These are the costs associated with the actual production of the product itself. They include the cost of raw materials involved in the production, the labour time involved

in the production process, and a variety of other costs such as the cost of running machinery which is necessary to produce the finished goods. *Product costs* are similar to s*ervice costs* depending on the company's business activity.

Period costs

These are costs incurred by the business which are not related to actual production but which are incurred because the company is in business. They are known as *period costs* because they are generally associated with a time period. For example, business rates are payable annually, telephone bills are payable quarterly and the managing director's salary is payable monthly. None of these costs can be considered to be directly attributable to the costs of producing any particular product.

> If we look at the costs involved in running the vans which Stanley Brown is responsible for we can see that such items as insurance and vehicle licence can be classified as period costs whereas costs such as tyre replacement and fuel costs can be classified as product costs – or in this case as service costs.

Decision making

One of the prime functions of a business manager is the making of decisions and it is obvious that the best decisions are those that are based on the most accurate and meaningful information. Part 4 of this book is devoted to decision making and the way in which management accounting can assist the business manager to make decisions. As far as the classification of costs is concerned we can simply state at this point that some costs are affected by a decision and change depending upon that decision while others are not affected by the decision. We can therefore classify costs into the following two types:

- *relevant costs* – those costs which change depending upon the decisions made or that are incurred because a decision is made
- *irrelevant costs* – those costs which are not affected by the particular decision to be made.

We will examine the implications of this method of classification in greater detail in Chapter 12.

Control

Controlling the operations of a business, or a part of a business, to ensure that objectives are met, is also a major part of the work of a manager. Stanley Brown is responsible for the control of a fleet of vans to ensure that the objective of the delivery of the company's products to its customers is achieved. Part 4 of this book considers the control of a business and the way in which accounting information can help the manager to achieve this. As far as the classification of costs is concerned it is important to recognise that some costs are within the control of the business, or a particular manager, and some are outside that control. Costs can therefore be classified into:

- controllable costs
- uncontrollable costs.

> For Stanley Brown, costs such as the vehicle licence and the cost per gallon of fuel must be regarded as *uncontrollable costs* because he is unable to influence the cost of these items. Maintenance costs however can be considered a *controllable cost* because Stanley Brown can directly affect this cost and can even vary the time period over which the maintenance is undertaken.

Other methods of cost classification

Although the basic method of classifying costs for product costing and for the prediction of future costs is in relationship to the behaviour of those costs, there are other methods of classifying costs which are used and are of some importance to the business manager. These classification can be considered to be sub-divisions of the cost classification system which are used to indicate the way in which the costs arise rather than indicating their behaviour. Three different classifications will be considered here, namely:

- direct and indirect costs
- prime cost and overheads
- departmental costs.

Direct and indirect costs

Direct costs are those which can be directly identified with a particular product or service which the business provides. These can be categorised into three distinct types:

- *direct materials* – the raw materials which go into the product
- *direct labour* – the costs of labour which are directly involved in the production process
- *direct expenses* – expenses which are incurred specifically in the making of a particular product, such as royalties paid or hire of a particular piece of equipment.

Indirect costs are all those costs of materials, labour and expenses which are incurred in the production process but which cannot be identified with one particular product. Examples include the cost of foremen and maintenance staff in a business producing a range of different products, or consumable materials used by machinery involved in the production process.

Prime cost and overheads

The total of all direct costs is known as *prime cost* and therefore:

Direct materials + Direct labour + Direct expenses = Prime cost

Indirect costs are also known as *overheads* but overheads include not just production overheads as indirect costs but also other categories of overheads, such as administration overheads and selling overheads. The total cost of a product therefore is the sum of the prime cost and overheads, thus:

Prime cost + Overheads = Total cost

The manufacturing cost of a product however is defined as the sum of the prime cost and production overheads, rather than all overheads, thus:

Prime cost + Production overheads = Manufacturing cost

The classification of cost by this method and the treatment of overheads will be considered in greater detail in the next chapter.

Departmental costs

Most businesses, and certainly all large businesses, are organised into departments, with each department being the responsibility of an individual manager. Costs are classified as being attributed to a particular department both to facilitate their control and to allocate responsibility for them to a specific individual manager. The implications of this classification regarding control are considered in detail in Part 3 but at this point it should be understood that this classification of costs is for control purposes rather than for cost prediction purposes.

Departments can be categorised into:

- *direct departments* – those departments involved in the production process
- *service departments* – those departments which perform functions for the business generally rather than for the production process.

Stanley Brown therefore is the manager of a service department which fulfils a service function to the business which is concerned with the production of food products. Other departments will be directly concerned with the manufacture of food products and these will be the direct departments. As Stanley is in charge of the transport department he controls the costs of that department and is responsible for its operations, but has no control over other costs of the business which will be the responsibility of other managers.

Summary

- Costs are classified for three main purposes:
  - for stock valuation
  - for decision making
  - for control.

- Costs can be classified according to behaviour for prediction purposes into:
  - fixed costs
  - variable costs.
- Limitations to cost predictions based upon cost behaviour arise due to the following:
  - mixed costs
  - short- and long-term effects
  - linearity assumptions
  - relevant range considerations
  - multiple causes of behaviour.
- Other classification systems include:
  - direct and indirect costs
  - prime cost and overheads
  - departmental costs.

Bibliography and further reading

Biggs C and Benjamin D, *Management Accounting Techniques*, 2nd edition, Butterworth Heinemann 1993, (Chapter 1)

Drury C, *Management and Cost Accounting*, 3rd edition, Chapman & Hall 1992, (Chapter 2)

Lucey T, *Management Accounting*, 3rd edition, DP Publications 1992, (Chapters 2 and 3)

Sizer J, *An Insight Into Management Accounting*, 3rd edition, Penguin 1989, (Chapter 2)

Self-review questions

1 Name three reasons for the classification of costs and give appropriate methods of classification for each.
   (See page 26.)

2 Distinguish between prime cost, manufacturing cost and total cost.
   (See page 36.)

3 What is the purpose of departmental costing?
   (See page 36.)

4 Why is it necessary to critically examine predictions of cost based upon the current behaviour of costs?
   (See page 31.)

5 What is a stepped cost?
   (See page 31.)

6 For cost prediction purposes what are the essential classifications of cost?
   (See page 26.)

Additional questions

3.1 The Handtool Company Ltd produces screwdrivers. From the following information calculate the prime cost and total cost of its products:

	£
Direct labour	8,000
Direct materials	
– steel	4,000
– plastic	1,800
– other	750
Factory rent	2,500
Administration	800
Insurance	350
Factory cleaning materials	75

3.2 Classify the following into direct and indirect costs:
- floppy discs for the office computer
- steel used in product manufacture
- wages of machine operators
- wages of factory security guards
- patent royalties on products manufactured
- tools for maintenance mechanics
- painting of the factory gates
- tyre replacement on delivery vehicles
- telephone rental
- overtime payments for machine operators.

3.3 From the following information calculate the variable cost of production of Company X:
- direct materials – 4 metres @ £5.00 per metre
- direct wages in the cutting department – 3 hours @ 6.70 per hour
- direct wages in the finishing department – 2 hours @ £7.50 per hour
- variable overheads – £15.00
- fixed overheads – £25.00.

3.4 The Bramley Apple Co makes fruit pies and incurs the following costs in making
each apple pie which it produces:

	£
Fruit	0.21
Flour	0.06
Other ingredients	0.12
Labour – 5 minutes @ £6 per hour	0.50
Fuel for cooking	0.08
Other manufacturing expenses	0.15

The owner of the business has asked you to calculate the prime cost and manufacturing
cost of producing one apple pie.

4 Establishing the cost of a product

Objectives

After studying this chapter you should be able to:

- explain the purpose of product costing
- distinguish between direct and indirect costs
- allocate costs to departments appropriately and allocate service department costs to production departments
- calculate overhead absorption rates using suitable bases
- explain the consequences of using different measures of capacity.

Walker Ltd – domestic kitchen unit production

Joan Palfreyman is the cost accountant of the company, Walker Ltd, which produces high quality domestic kitchen units. It sells these units directly to individual customers and the products are made to order.

The company is organised into five departments, three of which are involved in the production of the units – machining department, assembly department and finishing department – and two which support the production departments – maintenance department and stores.

The company has received an order from a customer for a particular set of kitchen units and Joan has been asked to calculate the cost of production of the units. Bill Wilson, the production manager, has estimated that the following materials and time will be involved in the production of each unit:

Materials	£500
Labour – machining department	5 hours
Labour – assembly department	3 hours
Labour – finishing department	2 hours

Joan has already worked out the budget for Walker Ltd. for the coming month and has the following information in front of her:

	Machining £000s	Assembly £000s	Finishing £000s	Maintenance £000s	Stores £000s	Total £000s
Direct materials	20,000	2,000	2,000			24,000
Direct labour	5,000	6,000	3,000			14,000
Indirect materials	2,000	1,000	1,000	500	1,500	6,000

	Machining £000s	Assembly £000s	Finishing £000s	Maintenance £000s	Stores £000s	Total £000s
Indirect labour	2,000	2,000	1,000	3,000	1,000	9,000
Power	3,000	2,000	3,000	500	200	8,700
Rent and rates						6,000
Administration						4,200
Machine insurance						500

Her assistant, John Woods, has also provided her with the following additional information:

	Machining £000s	Assembly £000s	Finishing £000s	Maintenance £000s	Stores £000s	Total £000s
Floor area (m²)	10,000	8,000	5,000	1,000	6,000	30,000
Machine hours (000s)	1,500	300	200			2,000
Direct labour hours (000s)	1,000	1,400	600			3,000
No. of employees	1,000	1,200	600			2,800
Value of machinery	2,500	1,500	1,000			5,000

Direct material only is issued from stores.

Joan knows that she needs to use this information in order to calculate the cost of production of the kitchen units ordered.

Introduction

We have seen how the behaviour of costs helps to determine the future level of costs for a business, and we now turn to an examination of the method of determining the costs of production for a manufactured product. In the case of Walker Ltd, the products manufactured are kitchen units and the problem facing Joan Palfreyman is that of determining the cost of production of the particular units for which an order has been received. We have seen how the costs incurred by a company can be divided into those costs directly associated with the production of a particular product and those which are concerned with the operation of the business. In order for it to be worthwhile for a business to produce a product the price at which it can sell the product must at least equal the cost of its production. If not the business would be better off by not producing the product and by concentrating its efforts on the production of other items. (There are exceptions to this which we will consider in later chapters.) This leads us however to a consideration of why the establishment of the cost of production of a product is so important to a business, and how this can help a manager of the business.

The value of product costing

In a company which manufactures a variety of products, such as Walker Ltd, the ability to determine the cost of production for each type of product is essential to enable managers of the business to be able to plan the business and its activities. Knowledge of the cost of production of a product is necessary to determine a price for the product as, in general, the price must exceed the cost of production. The product will then contribute towards the general costs of the business and towards the profit made by the business. If this is not the case then the company may well be better off by not making the product and concentrating instead upon the manufacture of other products.

The resources of a business are finite and there is a limit to how much it is able to produce. One reason for product costing therefore is to enable the allocation of the scarce resources of the business in the way which is most advantageous to it.

> Thus Walker Ltd needs to know whether it should make the kinds of units ordered by this particular customer and sell them at the agreed price, or whether it would be better off to stop making these units and concentrate upon other kinds of kitchen furniture.

If a calculation of the costs of production of individual products within the product range is not undertaken then it is possible that the company is operating profitably because some of its products are highly profitable and some are being produced at a loss. This would be disguised by the overall profitability of the business but some products would be subsidising others. This is known as *cross-subsidy*. In practice, not all products are equally profitable and some will be more profitable than others. Statistical techniques have been employed in businesses making many different products which show that generally speaking 20 per cent of the product range generates 80 per cent of the profit of the business. This is known as the Pareto Rule (after the inventor of this statistical technique) and is commonly called the 80:20 rule.

Businesses are constantly seeking to improve their production methods and to expand capacity, or to produce goods at a lower cost. To do so generally involves some capital investment, and we will look at this in detail in Chapter 14. In deciding whether or not to invest however the business naturally wants to undertake investment which is most beneficial to it. It makes sense for the business to concentrate its investment in the areas of production from which it will derive the most benefit. Product costing will help it to decide which areas these are.

The basic reasons why product costing is important therefore can be summarised as follows:

- to help make pricing decisions
- to allocate scarce resources
- to help make decisions concerning investment.

The components of the cost of production

We have seen in the last chapter that the cost of a product is made up of direct and indirect costs and that these can be broken down as follows:

- *direct costs –*
  materials
  labour
- *indirect costs –*
  overheads.

The total direct costs of materials and labour will equal the *prime cost* of the product.

We will now look at each of these in turn and consider the way in which they are accumulated in order to determine the cost of a product.

Materials

We have seen previously how materials can be categorised into *direct materials*, which go directly into producing the product, and *indirect materials*, which help the production process but do not go into the product.

> For Walker Ltd direct materials would include wood, paint and laminates while indirect materials would include such things as saw blades and sanding discs. All these raw materials are held in stock to be used as needed and we will look at the control of stock in detail in Chapter 17. Suffice it to say at this point that materials can be held centrally in a stores, such as the direct materials for Walker Ltd, and this needs a control and issuing procedure. Alternatively, they can be allocated directly to a production department to be used as needed. This is the case with the indirect materials of Walker Ltd.

We will look at the costing implications of this in more detail in Chapters 5 and 6 but the decision will be made to a large extent on the value of the materials in relation to the cost of the products being made.

> Thus saw blades are low-cost items and are used frequently in the machining department, but probably nowhere else, and so it is not worth the expense to the company of having a formal control and issuing procedure for these items.

One feature of manufacturing which is of increasing importance at present, and which affects the treatment of stocks and of raw materials used in the production process, is known as *just in time (JIT)*. This endeavours to eliminate stocks of raw materials entirely. The aim of this approach is to ensure that the ordering procedure enables materials to be ordered and delivered just in time for when they are needed rather than being delivered in advance and held in stock. This system, together with *materials requirements planning (MRP) systems*, is changing the nature of stock control, and therefore product costing. These advanced manufacturing technologies (AMTs), as they are known, will be considered in greater detail in Chapter 7.

At this point however if we consider Walker Ltd we can see that the direct materials are delivered into stock and are issued as required to each of the production departments and charged to those departments as part of the costs of production. Indirect materials however are delivered directly to the individual departments and form part of the costs of those departments. This is reflected in the budget which Joan Palfreyman has worked out for the company as follows:

	Machining £000s	Assembly £000s	Finishing £000s	Maintenance £000s	Stores £000s	Total £000s
Direct materials	20,000	2,000	2,000			24,000
Indirect materials	2,000	1,000	1,000	500	1,500	6,000

Labour

Labour costs also can be categorised into direct labour costs and indirect labour costs.

For Walker Ltd the *direct labour costs* are charged directly to the production department and consist of the costs of the people working in those departments directly involved in the production process. Thus direct labour costs can only occur in a production department and the labour costs of support departments are considered to be *indirect labour costs* because they do not directly relate to the production of any particular product. Indirect labour costs can however be incurred in both production and service departments, and this is the case for Walker Ltd.

In the stores and maintenance departments the indirect labour costs will be all the staff of the departments – storekeepers, engineers, repair staff, etc. In the production departments the indirect labour costs will be made up of those people who do not directly participate in the production process – foremen and women and supervisory staff, wages clerks, ordering clerks and other administrative staff.

In some businesses, supervisory staff are involved in the production process and so would form part of the direct labour costs. Whether or not this is the case is normally dependent upon the processes involved and upon the job specification of the individual supervisor concerned.

The budget for Walker Ltd can be seen therefore as follows:

	Machining £000s	Assembly £000s	Finishing £000s	Maintenance £000s	Stores £000s	Total £000s
Direct labour	5,000	6,000	3,000			14,000
Indirect labour	2,000	2,000	1,000	3,000	1,000	9,000

Labour costs can be classified into the direct costs of labour and the indirect costs of labour regardless of whether or not they are considered to be direct or indirect labour, and it is important to distinguish between these two classifications. The *direct costs of labour* are the wages, salaries, bonuses and overtime paid to the people themselves. The *indirect costs of labour* are such things as employer's national insurance and pension contributions, sick pay and the costs of calculating and operating the payroll system. This distinction is important as far as financial accounting is concerned but to the business manager the indirect and direct costs of labour are unimportant and it is just the total cost of labour which is of concern. This is the figure which is used in product costing, classified into direct and indirect labour.

When overtime is worked by members of the labour force this is often paid at a premium rate. Also when shift working is in operation some shifts attract a premium rate. Thus the cost of labour varies according to its timing. It therefore costs more to manufacture a product when overtime is being worked than it does during normal time. It is not however reasonable to suggest that the cost of production of any individual product depends upon when it is manufactured, although there are exceptions to this in special cases which will be considered in later chapters.

The precise time of manufacture depends upon the production scheduling process and what is important for calculating labour cost is the average cost of labour. Labour rates are therefore calculated as an average of the total cost of labour divided by the total productive hours worked, regardless of the rate paid for any particular time period or to any particular person.

From the information Joan Palfreyman has she is able to calculate the average cost of direct labour in each of the production departments and express this as a direct labour hour rate which can be used in establishing the costs of production for any particular product. This calculation is as follows:

	Machining £000s	Assembly £000s	Finishing £000s	Total £000s
Direct labour	5,000	6,000	3,000	14,000
Direct labour hours (000s)	1,000	1,400	600	3,000
Direct labour hour rate	5.00	4.29	5.00	

Overheads

All materials and labour expenditure, as well as all other expenditure which cannot be directly identified with the product itself, is classed as *indirect expenditure* and in total this is known as overhead. Overheads can be considered in total but it is more usual to separate them into categories according to the function which has caused the overhead to be incurred. Thus production, selling, distribution and administration are common categories of overhead, in a traditional manufacturing environment.

We will consider different treatments of overheads and the ways in which costs can be divided into direct and indirect costs in Chapters 6 and 7.

> In the case of Walker Ltd however the categories of overhead will be production overhead and administration overhead.

Some overhead comprises expenditure which is attributable directly to specific departments and, for Walker Ltd, indirect materials. Indirect labour and power can be attributable directly to departments. Other expenditure however, such as rent, rates and administration, is incurred in total and is not readily related to any specific department. In order to determine product cost however it is necessary that all expenditure be allocated to a particular department, whether it be a production department or a service department.

> Thus all centrally incurred expenditure for Walker Ltd which Joan Palfreyman has budgeted for she must allocate to one of the five departments of the company. Part of her task is to allocate this expenditure in some way and to find a reasonable basis for her allocation. For example, rent and rates expenditure is obviously incurred in part by each of the five departments and therefore needs to be charged partly to each department. This process of splitting common costs over individual departments is known as *apportionment* (see below) and the means of dividing up the common costs is known as the *basis of apportionment*.

The apportionment of expenditure

The objective of cost accounting is ultimately to be able to calculate the cost of production of individual products or services which a company provides. Classifying costs is the starting point for this exercise but it is necessary to go on from this to be able to charge the indirect costs (i.e. overheads) of production to individual products. This process is known as *apportionment*. The steps which need to be undertaken to arrive at this apportionment procedure are summarised in Figure 4.1.

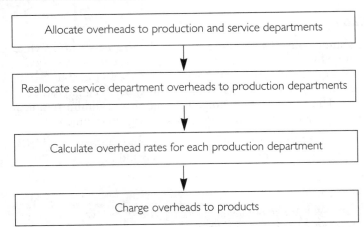

Figure 4.1 Overhead allocation procedure

One of the skills of a cost accountant, such as Joan Palfreyman, is to find a basis of apportionment for each type of cost she comes across, which is a reasonable representation of the way in which the cost arises. Departmental managers are naturally interested in these bases and are keen to ensure that the costs of their department are not higher than they need to be because of a basis of apportionment which disadvantages their department for the benefit of another department. Thus the apportionment of cost is a matter of particular interest in a business.

The basis of apportionment of a cost can be anything which is a reasonable representation of the way in which a cost is incurred. Obviously, however, a certain limited range of bases are common, but this does not mean that a different basis should not be considered and used, if appropriate to the circumstances. If we look at the expenses which Joan has to allocate to the five departments of Walker Ltd we can see illustrations of the way in which suitable bases are identified and used.

Rent and rates

Rent and rates are incurred for the existence and use of a building and its size. Size in this context is often considered to equate to floor area and this is a common basis of apportionment. In some circumstances, volume may be more appropriate and therefore used for apportioning costs.

In this case however floor area is considered appropriate and the rent and rates charge would thus be related to the floor area occupied by each department and apportioned as follows:

	Machining £000s	Assembly £000s	Finishing £000s	Maintenance £000s	Stores £000s	Total £000s
Rent and rates						6,000
Floor area (m²)	10,000	8,000	5,000	1,000	6,000	30,000
Departmental apportionment	2,000	1,600	1,000	200	1,200	6,000

Administration

Administration expenses are generally incurred because of the existence of employees in the business, and relate to those employees and their management. At least this is one of the causes of the expenditure, and it is reasonable therefore to suggest that a department incurs administration expenditure in relation to its size in term of number of employees. Alternative bases which could be considered would be number of orders received or computing hours involved for each department, or any other reasonable basis.

In this case, number of employees seems to be a reasonable basis for apportionment of administration expenses and can be calculated as follows:

	Machining £000s	Assembly £000s	Finishing £000s	Maintenance £000s	Stores £000s	Total £000s
Administration						4,200
No. of employees	1,000	1,200	600			2,800
Departmental apportionment	1,500	1,800	900			4,200

Machine insurance

This expenditure is obviously related to the machinery itself and more specifically to the value of that machinery.

Thus machinery value provides a suitable basis for apportionment, and can be calculated as follows:

	Machining £000s	Assembly £000s	Finishing £000s	Maintenance £000s	Stores £000s	Total £000s
Machine insurance						500
Value of machinery	2,500	1,500	1,000			5,000
Departmental apportionment	250	150	100			500

Once all expenses have been apportioned over the departments then the cost of operation for each department can be calculated.

For Walker Ltd the cost of each of the five departments is calculated as follows:

	Machining £000s	Assembly £000s	Finishing £000s	Maintenance £000s	Stores £000s	Total £000s
Indirect materials	2,000	1,000	1,000	500	1,500	6,000
Indirect labour	2,000	2,000	1,000	3,000	1,000	9,000
Power	3,000	2,000	3,000	500	200	8,700
Rent and rates	2,000	1,600	1,000	200	1,200	6,000
Administration	1,500	1,800	900			4,200
Machine insurance	250	150	100			500
Total cost	10,750	8,550	7,000	4,200	3,900	34,000

Relating departmental costs to production

The overhead costs of production departments can be directly related to the cost of production of the goods. The costs of support departments are equally related to the cost of production but cannot be directly related. It is however necessary to include them in the costing of products as they are part of the cost of production and we need to find a way in which to do so. The way in which this is done is to reallocate the service department costs to the production departments using a suitable basis which reflects the service provided by each service department to the production departments.

Thus Joan Palfreyman needs to reallocate the costs of the maintenance and stores departments to the three production departments using a suitable basis. She can do this as follows.

Maintenance department

This department is concerned with the maintenance of the machinery used by the three production departments. The level of maintenance required by machinery can be expected to be proportional to the usage of that machinery. The number of machine hours used by each department can therefore be considered a suitable basis for apportionment.

This department's costs can be reallocated as follows:

	Machining £000s	Assembly £000s	Finishing £000s	Maintenance £000s	Stores £000s	Total £000s
Total cost	10,750	8,550	7,000	4,200	3,900	34,000
Machine hours (000s)	1,500	300	200			2,000
Reallocated cost	3,150	630	420	(4,200)		

Stores department

The stores department handles the stores and issues the direct materials to the three production departments. The activity of this department is therefore related to the volume of materials used by each department.

In this case, the volume of materials is expressed in terms of value rather than physical volume and this provides a basis for reallocating the costs of the stores department. The calculation is as follows:

	Machining £000s	Assembly £000s	Finishing £000s	Maintenance £000s	Stores £000s	Total £000s
Total cost	10,750	8,550	7,000	4,200	3,900	34,000
Direct materials	20,000	2,000	2,000			24,000
Reallocated cost	3,150	325	325		(3,900)	

Once the costs of the service departments have been reallocated to the production departments then the total costs of those production departments, in terms of overhead costs involved in production, can be ascertained.

These are as follows:

	Machining £000s	Assembly £000s	Finishing £000s	Maintenance £000s	Stores £000s	Total £000s
Total cost	10,750	8,550	7,000	4,200	3,900	34,000
Reallocated cost (maintenance)	3,150	630	420	(4,200)		
Reallocated cost (stores)	3,150	325	325		(3,900)	
Total cost	17,150	9,505	7,745			34,000

Calculating overhead recovery rates

It is now possible to calculate the cost of production for each individual product which Walker Ltd makes within its range.

Overhead costs are part of the costs of production of each department and Joan Palfreyman needs to find a way of relating these costs to the actual production. The way in which this is done is to calculate an overhead recovery rate related to one of the direct costs of production. Again any suitable basis can be used but the two most common are:

- direct labour hour rate
- direct machine hour rate.

Labour and machine time are the chief components of any product in a manufacturing environment and this is the reason why they are used as the bases for recovering overheads. This has the result of spreading the overheads over the greatest individual direct cost, and the one selected tends to be the greater of the two in any particular process. In a service industry, labour cost tends to be the greatest direct cost in providing a service and so overhead again tends to be apportioned according to direct labour hours.

Each of these two bases relates to the number of hours of each factor of production which goes into the product.

For Walker Ltd the cost of production of the kitchen units which it manufactures is more directly related to the labour involved in their manufacture, particularly for the assembly and finishing departments. This therefore is the basis which Joan has selected for the recovery of overheads. The calculation is as follows:

Overhead rates for: *Total cost/Total direct labour hours*

Machining	17,150/1,000	= £17.15 per hour
Assembly	9,505/1,400	= £6.79 per hour
Finishing	7,745/600	= £12.91 per hour

If machine hours were used instead, the following overhead rates would be calculated:

Overhead rates for: *Total cost/total machine hours*

Machining	17,150/1,500	= £11.43 per hour
Assembly	9,505/300	= £31.68 per hour
Finishing	7,745/200	= £38.72 per hour

The total cost of production therefore consists of the direct materials used in the product and the direct labour and overheads used in the product. Total costs can therefore be expressed as:

Total cost = Direct materials + Direct labour (rate)

The calculation of the direct labour rate is arrived at by totalling the labour cost per hour and the overhead recovery rate:

Direct labour charging rate = Labour rate + Overhead rate

The calculation for each of the three departments of Walker Ltd, using the direct labour hour rate, is as follows:

Charging rate for:	Labour rate + Overhead rate
Machining	£5.00 + £17.15 = £22.15
Assembly	£4.29 + £6.79 = £11.08
Finishing	£5.00 + £12.91 = £17.91

Capacity measurement

It should be noted that overhead recovery rates are calculated from the budgets prepared at the start of the period and are therefore based upon expected levels of activity. In setting the budget for the level of activity expected for a period it is necessary to estimate activity levels and this is dependent upon an assessment of capacity. Capacity can be considered to be the level of activity which the company can undertake in the period. This can be expressed in a variety of ways:

- maximum capacity – the maximum level of activity which can be undertaken
- maximum practical capacity – the maximum practical level of activity which can be undertaken taking into account the needs of retooling, maintenance etc
- normal capacity – the level of activity normally achieved allowing for the above and downtime, sickness, etc.

It can be seen that these three measures will each give a different measurement of capacity and so a different level of activity expected. This will result in different overhead recovery rates being charged and so different costs of production being calculated. The basis of capacity measurement is therefore important in the determination of the cost of production of a product.

Additionally, the fact that the recovery rates are based upon budgets means that the actual costs are likely to be different and so the true costs of production will be different to those calculated in advance. The actual costs will not be known until after the event and so it is necessary to calculate based upon budgets so that the business can plan its operations. The implications of the difference between budgeted costs and those costs actually arising are considered in detail in later chapters.

Calculating the cost of a product

Once the indirect costs of production have been ascertained and a basis for adding them to the product cost has been arrived at it is then possible to combine these costs with the direct costs in order to arrive at the cost of production of a product.

Thus Joan Palfreyman is able to calculate the cost of production of the units which have been ordered by the customer. The calculation is as follows:

Direct materials	£500
Direct labour – machining department	5 hours
Direct labour – assembly department	3 hours
Direct labour – finishing department	2 hours

Calculation of cost:

	£
Direct materials	500.00
Machining cost – 5 hours x £22.15	110.75
Assembly cost – 3 hours x £11.08	33.24
Finishing cost – 2 hours x £17.91	35.82
Cost of production	679.81

Summary

- Product costing is needed for:
  pricing decisions
  allocating scarce resources
  investment decisions.
- Product costs comprise direct and indirect costs.
- Product cost comprise materials, labour and overheads.
- Departments can be classed as production or service departments.
- Indirect costs (overheads) are allocated to departments.
- Service department costs are reallocated to production departments using a suitable basis.
- Suitable bases are needed to allocate costs to departments and should reflect how the individual cost arises.
- Overhead recovery rates provide a basis of allocating overheads to products.
- Capacity measurement can affect product costing.

Bibliography and further reading

Drury C, *Management and Cost Accounting*, 3rd edition, Chapman & Hall 1992, (Chapters 3 and 4)

Lucey T, *Management Accounting*, 3rd edition, DP Publications 1992, (Chapters 2 and 3)

Sizer J, *An Insight Into Management Accounting*, 3rd edition, Penguin 1989, (Chapter 3)

Wilson R M S and Chua W F, *Managerial Accounting*, 2nd edition, Chapman & Hall 1992, (Chapter 4)

Self-review questions

1 Suggest four different bases for apportioning overheads and an expense type for which each is suitable.
(See page 45.)

2 Distinguish between direct labour costs, indirect labour costs and the indirect costs of labour.
(See page 44.)

3 Explain the meaning of basis of apportionment.
(See page 46.)

4 Name the most common bases for calculating overhead recovery rates.
(See page 50.)

5 Name the two most typical bases for allocating service department costs to production departments.
(See page 48.)

6 Define and distinguish between the three main methods of measuring capacity.
(See page 51.)

7 Explain the benefits of product costing to a business manager.
(See page 40.)

Additional questions

4.1 Calculate four different overhead absorption rates based on the following data:

Total overheads for the period	£25,800
Units produce in the period	1,075
Labour hours for the period	2,600
Direct materials for the period	£12,800
Direct wages for the period	£7,200

4.2 Warburton Ltd produces several products which pass through two production departments in its factory. These two departments are concerned with cutting and finishing. The company also has two service departments, maintenance and canteen.

Service department costs are allocated as follows:

	%
Maintenance:	
cutting	75
finishing	20
canteen	5
Canteen:	
cutting	60
finishing	30
maintenance	10

During the period just ended, actual overheads were as follows:

	£
Cutting	71,500
Finishing	47,300
Maintenance	25,100
Canteen	24,300

Allocate all overheads in order to calculate the overheads absorbed by the production departments.

4.3 Calculate the cost of production of one machine tool produced by Machine Tools Ltd, based upon the following information:

Unit cost:
Direct materials   £650
Direct labour –
    machining department   6 hours @ £7.40 per hour
    assembly department   3 hours @ £8.00 per hour
    painting department   2 hours @ £6.50 per hour

Production overheads are absorbed on the basis of direct labour hours, at the following rates:

Machining department   £8.75 per hour
Assembly department   £12.10 per hour
Painting department   £9.45 per hour

4.4 Bull Engineering is a small engineering company which manufactures two products. The company is organised into two manufacturing departments – machining and assembly – and also operates a canteen as a separate department.

Direct costs of its two products are as follows:

	Product A	**Product B**
Materials	£7	£5

Labour –
    machining (@ £8 per hour)   3 hours   4 hours
    assembly (@ £6 per hour)   4 hours   2 hours
Machining –
    machining department   3 hours   6 hours
    assembly department   1 hour   –
Production level (units)   2,500   2,000

Overhead costs are as follows:

	Machining £	**Assembly** £	**Canteen** £	**Total** £
Variable	28,000	18,000	16,000	62,000
Fixed	35,000	24,000	8,000	67,000
Total	63,000	42,000	24,000	129,000
Number of employees	16	8	2	26

As management accountant you have been asked to calculate an overhead absorption rate for each department using a suitable basis and to calculate the cost of production for one unit of each product.

5 Absorption costing

Objectives

After studying this chapter you should be able to:

- explain the purpose of absorption costing
- discuss the advantages and disadvantages of absorption costing as a means of arriving at a product cost
- explain the meaning of, and treatment of, over- and under-recoveries of costs
- calculate a product cost using absorption costing.

The Office Furniture Company – a manufacturer

As part of its product range the Office Furniture Company manufactures and sells one design of free standing coat rack for use in offices. Jill Reeves, the management accountant of the company, has been asked to prepare an income statement for the company's operations for the past year and a projected income statement for the forthcoming year. She has collected the following information:

Direct cost of manufacture	£8.00 per unit
Fixed costs incurred last year	£50,000
Projected fixed cost for next year	£51,000
Sales price	£15.00 per unit
Selling expenses for last year	£3,000
Projected selling expenses for next year	£3,200
Administration expenses associated with production (each year)	£1,400

Bill Johnson, the production manager, has confirmed to her that fixed factory overhead is based upon an estimated activity level of 20,000 units in each year. He has also provided her with the following sales and production data:

	Actual (last year) (units)	Estimated (next year) (units)
Opening stock of finished goods	1,000	6,000
Production	22,000	18,000
Sales	17,000	22,000
Closing stock	6,000	2,000

Jill Reeves knows that she has all the information she needs to produce the required income statements in time for the forthcoming board meeting.

The absorption of overheads

We have seen that overheads form part of the cost of production of a product but that they cannot be directly identified with any particular product. Instead they are general costs associated with the production process and therefore cannot be directly charged as a cost of production in the same way that direct costs can be. We have seen that it is however necessary to charge overheads as a cost of production in order that the full cost of a product can be calculated. The way in which this is done is to spread the overheads over a cost unit by a process which is known as *overhead recovery* or *overhead absorption.*

Overhead absorption is normally done by calculating an overhead absorption rate which is based upon an estimate of overhead costs for the period and an estimate of the level of activity during the period. Dividing the costs by the activity level therefore provides an overhead recovery rate and this is the rate at which overheads are recovered during the period depending upon the production achieved during the period.

For Office Furniture Company therefore the calculation of the overhead absorption rate for each year is as follows:

	Last year	Next year
Projected fixed costs	£60,000*	£51,000
Divided by:		
expected production level (units)	20,000	18,000
Equals:		
overhead rate (per unit)	£3.00	£2.83

* Projected costs = 20,000 units x £3.00

This rate will be added to the direct costs of manufacture to arrive at a calculation of the total costs of manufacture.

Thus for Office Furniture Company we can see that the cost of manufacture of the coat rack will change for next year as compared with last year due to the changed overhead absorption rate. The comparison is as follows:

	Last year £ per unit	Next year £ per unit
Direct cost	8.00	8.00
Overheads absorbed	3.00	2.83
Production cost	11.00	10.83

We can see that the overhead absorption rate is based upon estimates, both of future costs and of future activity levels. It can be expected therefore that the actual overhead absorption rate, calculated by using actual costs and actual activity, will be different from the predetermined rate used.

For Office Furniture Company, this is as follows:

Comparison of estimated and actual overhead absorption rates for this year

	Estimate	Actual
Fixed costs	£60,000*	£50,000
Production (units)	20,000	22,000
Overhead recovery rate (per unit)	£3.00	£2.27
(i.e. costs/production)		

* Estimated fixed costs calculated as:

Number of production units x Overhead recovery rate

For Office Furniture Company therefore we can see that the costs of manufacture of goods charged in the accounts has been higher than it actually should have been, based upon actual costs. Thus more overheads have been recovered through the overhead absorption rate than were actually incurred. This has resulted in what is known as an over-recovery of overheads and the accounts need to be adjusted to reflect the actual cost.

The treatment of over- and under-recoveries will be considered later in this chapter.

This over-recovery of overheads does however illustrate one problem with treating overheads in this manner. This is that the calculation of the overhead absorption rate is based upon estimates of both cost and activity level. These estimates are made based largely upon past and current performance, adjusted for known factors, and so a company is using past data to predict future performance. Using such estimates of costs can obviously affect the performance of the company and hence its decision making regarding such things as price setting, investment and the product mix. There is a danger using this method that these decisions are made upon inaccurate data as the true cost of production is not known until after the event – at the end of the period.

Office Furniture Company makes this calculation at the end of its year but most manufacturing companies, particularly those in which this information is crucial to decision making, will operate overhead absorption rates on a month by month basis, recalculating as necessary in the light of actual data.

We can see that the calculation of the overhead absorption rate is crucial to a company and it needs to get this rate as close to the actual as possible. This rate is of significance to business managers in all areas of the company who will be making decisions relating to product mix, pricing or sales forecasting, based upon the cost of manufacture of the product. It is important therefore that these managers understand the basis of product costing as used in their company and the possible consequences of using this method of treating overheads.

Absorption costing

This procedure, by which overheads are absorbed into the costs of production of a product, is known as *absorption costing*. The procedure operates through the calculation of an overhead absorption rate, which we considered in the last chapter. You will remember that it can be explained as shown in Figure 5.1.

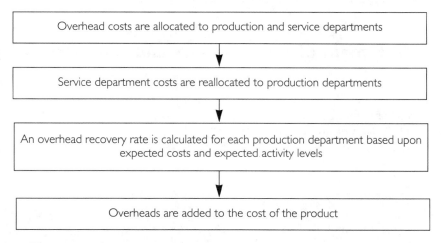

Figure 5.1 Steps in the absorption costing process

The total overheads absorbed in this manner include:

- fixed costs, i.e. those costs which are not dependent upon the level of activity of the company, such as rent or supervisory salaries
- variable costs, i.e. those which vary roughly in proportion to the level of activity undertaken, such as power or consumables for machines.

Absorption costing therefore has implications as far as stock valuation and performance measurement are concerned. The weakness of absorption costing in these respects has been recognised and has been the subject of criticism by both accountants and by business managers. These weaknesses are considered later in this chapter. An alternative method of costing exists which excludes fixed costs from the absorption process and charges them in total against the results of the period. This method is known as *marginal costing* and will be considered in detail in Chapter 9.

A more modern method of costing, known as activity based costing, has been developed and this will be considered in detail in Chapter 8.

Absorption costing by its very nature implies that indirect costs are related to products in proportion to the time consumed in their manufacture. Thus the most common bases for absorbing overheads are either direct labour hours or direct machine hours. Each provides a basis for allocation based upon time taken in the manufacture of the product, as we considered in Chapter 4. However, in an environment in which a range of products is manufactured it has been argued that this time basis does not accurately reflect the way in which costs are incurred. It is for this reason that the development of activity based costing has taken place and this method of costing provides a more accurate representation of the cost of manufacture of individual products within a range.

A variation of absorption costing is the technique known as standard costing. In this technique, standards are set for activities which basically are predetermined estimates of costs and activities based upon what the company expects to achieve in normal operating conditions. Performance is therefore evaluated against these standards. Standard costing is considered in detail in Chapter 20.

The treatment of over-recovery and under-recovery of costs

We have seen how the use of absorption costing can lead to an over-recovery or an under-recovery of indirect costs because of the need to estimate both costs and levels of activity at the start of the accounting period.

In the case of Office Furniture Company this has led to an over-recovery of costs in the last year amounting to £16,000. Thus:

Statement of overheads incurred and absorbed

	£
Overheads absorbed (£3.00 per unit x 22,000 units)	66,000
Overheads incurred	50,000
Over-absorption of overheads	16,000

The result of this is that more cost has been charged to the accounts than has actually been incurred and the manufacturing account for the company for the last year shows a higher cost of production for the goods produced than has actually been incurred. This also means that the cost of production of each coat rack, as shown in the accounts, is higher than it actually was and so the valuation of stock (which is shown as cost of production) is higher than it should be because of this over-recovery of overheads.

We can therefore see that stock valuation for a company is affected by the overhead recovery rate and this is another problem with absorption costing.

It is necessary that the accounts of a company reflect the actual cost incurred by that company relating to the period in question. The fact that there has been an over-statement of cost in the manufacturing of coat racks by Office Furniture Company due to the over-recovery of overheads therefore means that there needs to be an adjustment in the accounts. This is needed to ensure that the accounts reflect the actual costs of manufacture. The way in which this adjustment is effected is to consider the over- or under-recovery of overheads in total as a period cost and to show the net figure as an entry in the profit and loss account.

This can be illustrated for Office Furniture Company by examining the income statement which Jill Reeves has been asked to prepare for the company which parallels the profit and loss account. This statement will appear as follows:

Office Furniture Company

Income statement

	This year (actual)		Next year (estimated)	
	£	£	£	£
Sales		255,000		330,000
Less cost of goods sold:				
Opening stock	11,000		66,000	
Production	242,000		195,000	
Cost of goods available	252,000		261,000	
Less closing stock	66,000	187,000	21,660	239,340
Gross profit		**68,000**		**90,660**
Less period costs:				
Administration costs	1,400		1,400	
Selling costs	3,000		3,200	
Over-absorption of overheads	(16,000)	(11,600)		4,600
Net profit		79,600		86,060

Absorption costing in a multi-product environment

Most manufacturing companies produce more than one product and in such an environment there is a need to absorb overheads over the whole range of products. This is done in exactly the same way as Office Furniture Company absorbs overheads. In other words, whatever basis is chosen for the absorption of any particular overhead this is applied throughout the product range. Thus, for example, if overheads were to be absorbed on the basis of direct labour hours then an overhead absorption rate would be calculated and this would be applied to all products, based upon the number of direct labour hours which went into the production of each individual product.

Absorption costing in service industries

In service industries, absorption costing is used for the recovery of overheads in much the same way as it is used in manufacturing industry. In this case, there are no products produced but instead services are provided. These can be equated however to products and overhead absorption rates calculated and applied in a similar manner.

Reasons for using absorption costing

We have seen that there are a variety of problems in a company using absorption costing which the business manager must be aware of. Given the existence of these problems and the existence of the other methods of costing which have been mentioned it might be thought that absorption costing should not be used by a company and that another method would be preferable. Unfortunately, these other costing methods too have their disadvantages as well as their advantages. Despite the problems in its use there are some compelling arguments for using absorption costing. The advantages and disadvantages of absorption costing therefore need to be recognised.

Advantages of absorption costing

SSAP9: stocks and work in progress
The Accounting Standards Committee, which consists of members of the UK accounting bodies, has issued a set of Statements of Standard Accounting Practice (SSAPs) which UK companies are required to adhere to in completing their accounts. SSAP9 requires that costs and revenues are matched in the period in which the revenue arises rather than the period in which the costs are incurred. It also recommends that stock valuation must include all the production overheads which are incurred in the normal course of business even if such costs are time related (i.e. fixed in nature). These production overheads must be based upon normal activity levels. This SSAP therefore has the effect of requiring that absorption costing be used by a company as far as the production of its final accounts is concerned and thus provides the reason for the widespread use of absorption costing in industry. The value of marginal costing as an alternative method of costing is thus relegated to purely internal use within the company (see Chapter 9).

Reducing profit fluctuations
Where production levels are fairly constant but sales fluctuate, absorption costing has the effect of reducing fluctuations in net profit. Similarly, where stock building is an

essential part of the operating of the company (e.g. whisky maturing) absorption costing is both necessary and desirable in order to include fixed costs in the stock valuation. Otherwise the accounts of the business would show a series of losses which would be followed by a very large profit when the stock was eventually sold.

Ensures all costs are covered
The inclusion of fixed costs in the cost of production recognises that these are an essential part of the cost of producing the product and that the assets represented by these costs are an essential part of the production process. Failure to recognise this could lead to pricing decisions, particularly in an environment in which a variety of products are manufactured, which did not ensure that all the costs of production were covered in the prices charged for the various products.

Avoids cost separation
The split between fixed and variable costs is often arbitrary and many costs are mixed, containing an element of both types. The use of absorption costing in charging all production overheads to product cost simplifies the accounting procedures and reduces argument by eliminating the need to split costs into fixed and variable, and to split mixed costs into their fixed and variable components. This has the effect of reducing subjectivity in the cost allocation process.

Creates an awareness of resources used
Fixed costs are a significant proportion of the costs of a business and without the buildings, machinery, etc. which cause the fixed costs to be incurred the product could not be manufactured. The inclusion of fixed costs in the production overhead, and therefore in the production cost and stock valuation, provides a signal to managers in the business that these items are utilised in the manufacture of the product, thereby reminding them that the resources used include more than those represented by the variable costs. It therefore provides a reminder to those managers not involved in the production process of all the resources that are used in production and need to be considered in the planning of the business.

SSAP2: accounting policies
This statement requires the implementation of the accruals concept of accounting by requiring that costs be charged to the accounts in the time period to which they relate rather than the time period in which they are incurred. As fixed costs are an essential part of the cost of production of a company's product this statement therefore implies that these costs should be accrued during production and charged when stock is sold. This SSAP has therefore been interpreted as requiring the use of absorption costing by a manufacturing company.

Reveals inefficient use of resources
As the full cost of overheads is charged to production in each period using the overhead absorption rate this then implies that the lower the level of activity in any area of the business the higher will be the overhead absorption rate. Consideration of this rate and examination of changes to the rate over time, or by comparing the actual rate calculated at the end of the period with the estimated rate calculated at the beginning of the period, will indicate to the managers of the business where activity levels are not as planned or costs are not as expected. This can indicate problems in production and can also indicate where the resources of the business are not being used as efficiently as possible.

The search for the most efficient means of production possible will cause managers to seek to drive this overhead absorption rate down to as low a level as possible. Absorption costing therefore provides a means of indicating possible inefficiencies in the use of resources within the business.

Disadvantages of absorption costing

Profit varies with production

Using absorption costing, costs are charged to production and incorporated within the stock valuation and this occurs whether or not the product is actually sold. It is therefore possible to make a profit as far as the books of the business are concerned just by producing for stock. It is also possible to increase profits merely by increasing the level of production, even if the level of sales does not increase, and this increased production is represented only by increased stock holding of finished goods. In some businesses with irregular sales patterns (e.g. toy manufacturing) or long production cycles (e.g. forestry and timber production) this technique can be used to even out profit fluctuations. It must be recognised however that for all businesses using absorption costing, profits are to some extent dependent upon production levels and a business manger needs to ensure that profits are related to sales rather than production by concerning him or herself with stock levels as well as production levels and sales levels.

Allocation is arbitrary

The apportionment of fixed costs to departments and ultimately to the product itself is frequently on an arbitrary basis as no reasonable basis exists for such apportionment. Thus in a company such as Office Furniture Company, the salary of Jill Reeves can be readily charged to the cost of production of the sole product. If several products were made however there is no correct basis of apportioning her salary which is essentially indivisible. Any apportionment which will need to be made therefore will be on the basis of an allocation which is by its nature arbitrary. The need to apportion all costs leads to the need to find a basis for each allocation and the resources of the business are used in determining a suitable basis for the allocation of each cost type.

These bases of allocation can also be a source of tension within an organisation as each departmental manager seeks to reduce the allocation made to his or her department by arguing about the suitability of any basis of allocation for that particular cost. Absorption costing therefore can consume the time not just of the accountants in the business but also of the managers of the business and can lead to increased cost and an inefficient use of managerial time.

Conclusion

We have seen therefore that there are problems in the use of absorption costing within a business but also that there are compelling reasons why it should be used. It is therefore used in one form or another throughout manufacturing industry, and throughout service industries. We have also seen that the use of this costing method has implications for the business which affect not just the accountants within the business but also the managers of the business whether or not they are involved in the production process.

It is important to a business manager to understand the principles of the costing system used by the business in which he or she is employed and the effects which this might have upon his or her areas of responsibility. We have seen however that there are problems in using absorption costing and in Part 2 we will consider some alternative methods of costing which a business might use.

Summary

- Overheads are absorbed into the cost of a product by the calculation of an overhead absorption rate.
- Absorption costing is a method of including the full cost of overheads in the cost of production of a product.
- Absorption costing is based upon estimates of costs and activity levels. This can result in the over- or under-recovery of costs.
- Over- and under-recovery of costs are treated as period costs for adjustment purposes.
- The advantages of using absorption costing are:
  - compliance with SSAP9
  - it reduces profit fluctuations
  - it ensures that all costs are covered
  - it avoids cost separation
  - it creates an awareness of resources used
  - compliance with SSAP2
  - it can reveal the inefficient use of resources.
- The disadvantages of absorption costing are:
  - profit varies with level of production
  - the allocation of overhead costs is arbitrary.

Bibliography and further reading

Biggs C and Benjamin D, *Management Accounting Techniques*, 2nd edition, Butterworth Heinemann 1993

Drury C, *Management and Cost Accounting*, 3rd edition, Chapman & Hall 1992, (Chapter 8)

Lucey T, *Management Accounting*, 3rd edition, DP Publications 1992, (Chapter 2)

Sizer J, *An Insight Into Management Accounting*, 3rd edition, Penguin 1989, (Chapter 3)

Self-review questions

1 What are the main steps in the calculation of an overhead absorption rate? (See page 59.)

2 Explain why the cost of a product varies with the level of production. (See page 64.)

3 Why is absorption costing a requirement for UK companies? (See page 62.)

4 Identify five advantages of using absorption costing. (See page 62.)

5 Identify two disadvantages of using absorption costing. (See page 64.)

6 Explain how the use of absorption costing might help a business manager identify inefficiencies in the use of resources within a business. (See page 63.)

Additional questions

5.1 Galbraith Manufacturing Co Ltd manufactures a single product with the following variable costs per unit:

Direct materials	£6.00
Direct labour	£6.50
Manufacturing overheads	£3.00

The selling price of the product is £40.00 per unit.
Fixed manufacturing costs are expected to amount to £1,265,000 for the period.
Fixed non-manufacturing costs are expected to be £920,000. Fixed manufacturing costs can be analyzed as follows:

Production departments		Service	General factory
1	2	department	overheads
£	£	£	£
360,000	455,000	220,000	230,000

General factory costs represent space costs (e.g. lighting, heating and rent). Space utilisation is as follows:

Production department 1	45%
Production department 2	35%
Service department	20%

Service department costs are related to labour activity (50 per cent) and to machine activity (50 per cent). Normal production department activity is as follows:

	Direct labour hours	Machine hours	Production units
Department 1	70,000	3,200	150,000
Department 2	110,000	2,600	150,000

Fixed manufacturing overheads are absorbed at a predetermined rate per unit of production for each production department, based upon normal activity levels. The company operates a full absorption costing system.

Actual costs were as per expectations except for additional expenditure of £25,000 on fixed manufacturing overheads in Department 1. Actual production level achieved and level of sales were 146,000 units.

Prepare a profit statement for the period.

5.2 Two factories are operating in the same area and making similar products. Each factory calculates its production overhead absorption rate using a similar method. However the rate used by one factory is significantly lower than that of the other. Can this be taken to indicate that one factory is more efficient than the other?

5.3 Metal Products Ltd has budgeted for the following production overheads for its departments for the coming period:

Production departments:
machining	£180,000
assembly	£150,000

Service departments:
stores	£80,000
maintenance	£60,000

The following data relate to these departments:

	Machining	Assembly	Stores	Maintenance
No. of employees	75	36	12	8
Stores orders	120	85		26
Maintenance hours	30,000	26,000		

Budgeted data for the production cost centres was as follows:

	Machining	Assembly
Machine hours	8,400	6,800
Labour hours	9,000	12,000
Labour cost	£55,000	£90,000

Actual results for the production cost centres were as follows:

	Machining	Assembly
Machine hours	8,600	7,200
Labour hours	8,500	12,400
Labour cost	£52,000	£98,000
Actual overheads	£240,000	£210,000

Overhead rates are calculated on the following basis:
for machining – machine hours
for assembly – labour hours.

Prepare a statement showing the extent of over/under-absorption of overheads for each department for the period concerned.

5.4 The Abacus Co Ltd produces a variety of office equipment. Among its product range is the Abacalc. Data regarding the product for the last two months is as follows:

	Month 1	Month 2
Sales (units)	6,000	8,000
Production (units)	8,000	7,000
Selling price (£ per unit)	100	100
Variable production costs (£ per unit)	50	50
Fixed production overheads	£108,000	£108,000
Overhead absorption rate (per unit)	£13.50	£13.50
Selling and administration costs (fixed)	£32,000	£32,000

You have been asked, as management accountant to the company, to produce a profit statement for each of these two months. The company operates a full absorption costing system.

6 The different costing methods used in industry

Objectives

After studying this chapter you should be able to:

- explain the difference between the main costing methods used in industry
- identify an appropriate method to calculate the cost of any particular product
- calculate product costs using appropriate methods
- critically evaluate costing methods in the light of modern production methods.

Jones & Andrews Ltd – buildings repair and maintenance service

Joseph Gibson is the cost accountant of Jones & Andrews Ltd, a company which provides a building repairs and maintenance service. The company operates a job costing system in order to identify the cost and profit for each job carried out. Several jobs tend to be in progress at any one time. One such job is number 3152, for the repair of a local office block. This job was started and finished completely during one quarter.

Joseph has the task of preparing a statement of costs associated with this job and the resulting profit arising from its completion. He has collected the following information concerning the job:

- Issues of the main material, cement, were 960 kilos and issues of all other materials were costed at £2,120. Of the total materials issued to the job, wastage cost £38 and materials used for rectification work cost £36. Materials are issued from stores to the job as required.
- The hours of direct personnel working on the job were 494, including 35 hours of overtime, 14 hours of idle time and 8 hours spent on rectification work. Overtime is worked as necessary to meet the general requirements of the business and is paid at a premium of 30 per cent over the basic rate. The basic rate for direct personnel is £6 per hour.

Joseph has also collected the following information concerning all work carried out during the quarter:

- The opening stock of cement was 3,225 kilos valued at £5,822. Purchases during the month were 3,600 kilos at £1.81 per kilo and 3,800 kilos at £1.82 per kilo. Issues from stores amounted to 7,160 kilos for all jobs, including 60 kilos which were subsequently wasted and 340 kilos which were used for rectification work. Raw materials are priced at the end of the period using a weighted average basis (see later).

- Other materials issued to jobs were costed at £19,396, including £228 wastage and £197 for rectification.
- Direct personnel were paid at basic rate for 3,660 hours with a further 310 hours paid at overtime rate. These hours include 81 hours of idle time and 38 hours spent on rectification work.

Other costs incurred during the period were:

	£
Supervisory labour	3,760
Depreciation on plant	590
Cleaning materials	67
Telephone and stationery	281
Rent and rates	969
Vehicle running costs	318
Other administration	716

Overheads are absorbed into job costs at the end of each quarter at an actual rate per direct labour hour. Idle time, wastage and rectification work, after the completion of jobs, are normal features of the business. The company policy is that idle time is not expected to exceed 2 per cent of total hours, wastage is not expected to exceed 1 per cent of the costs of materials issued to a job, and rectification costs are not expected to exceed 1.5 per cent of direct costs. Such costs are not charged as direct costs of individual jobs.

The price for the job was £11,000.

Joseph knows that he is expected to produce a costing and profitability statement for job number 3152 and to comment upon the amount of idle time and rectification work associated with the job.

Introduction

Although the basic principles of costing relating to the classification, allocation, apportionment and absorption of costs are common to all types of manufacturing there are nevertheless differences in the way in which products are manufactured or processed. It is for this reason that different methods of costing have been developed which are designed to suit the particular production methods of an individual company. The main costing methods used by industry are:

- job costing
- batch costing
- contract costing
- process costing.

Each of these costing methods provides a basis upon which costs can be classified and absorbed into product costs, and so each can be considered to be a variant of absorption costing. The principal difference between them is the way in which cost accumulation is related to the operating methods of the business.

Job costing

Job costing is used where the nature of the business is such that each individual job is separate and individual in nature. This type of costing is used by a company which makes products to order (e.g. a specialist iron foundry) and is particularly suitable for a building contractor working on individual repairs and maintenance contracts, such as Jones & Andrews Ltd The main purpose of job costing is to enable a company to establish the profit (or loss) made on each individual job and to provide a valuation of work in progress for each job in the process of completion.

Job costing can be illustrated as shown in Figure 6.1.

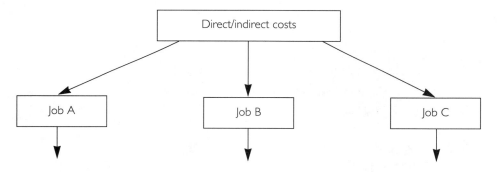

Figure 6.1 Job costing

Job costing is undertaken by creating an individual job cost card for each job and so job number 3152 would be one such job cost card. This card (a computer record most probably now) would contain details of the following:

- direct labour costs – including time based and piecework costs
- direct materials costs – based on stores issued and special purchases
- direct expenses – expenses incurred specifically for that particular job (e.g. tool hire).

For job 3152 the following details would be entered:

Job card	Job 3152
Direct labour hours	
Standard rate*	$496 - 35 - 14 - 8 = 437$
Overtime rate	38

*Direct labour hours at standard rate =
Total hours – (Overtime + Idle time + Rectification time)

Direct labour cost

Standard rate	437 x 6.00 =	2,622
Overtime rate	35 x 7.80 =	273
Total cost		2,895

Direct materials

Cement 960 kilos @ 1.81* =	1,738	*price calculation	
Other materials	= 2,120	3,225 in stock = 5594	
Less wastage	38	3,600 @ 1.81 = 6,516	
Less rectification	36	3,800 @ 1.82 = 6,916	
Total cost	3,784	Total 10,625	
		@ cost 19,254	
		average price: £1.81	

For job 3152 this calculation would be as follows:

Calculation of overhead recovery rate

Overhead costs incurred:

	£
Supervisory labour	3,760
Depreciation on plant	590
Cleaning materials	67
Telephone and stationery	281
Rent and rates	964
Vehicle running costs	318
Other administration	716
Total costs	6,701

Direct labour hours:
  3,660 + 310 − 81 − 38 = 3,851
Overhead recovery rate:
  £6,701/3,851 = £1.74 per direct labour hour

Using these details the production overheads would be added to the job by means of the calculation of an overhead recovery rate.

A job is normally valued at works cost until it is completed and it is at this point that administration and selling expenses are added to the job cost, as a percentage of works cost. Until this point the job represents work in progress and the total of all the job cost cards represents the total value of work in progress.

Once the job is finished all costs can be accumulated and the total cost of the job computed.

For job 3152 a statement of costs would be as follows:

	£
Direct labour	2,895
Direct materials	3,784
Prime cost	6,679
Overheads [1.74 x (437 + 35)]	821
Total cost	7,500

From this it is possible for Joseph Gibson to produce a costing and profitability statement for job 3152 which would be as follows:

Profitability statement for job no 3152

	£
Revenue	11,000
Cost	7,500
Profit	3,500

Joseph Gibson also needs to comment on the amount of idle time and rectification work associated with the job and in a job costing environment it is normal to consider such performance data for each individual job.

Idle time is defined as the amount of time spent between jobs in not performing any function. Rectification work is caused by faulty initial work. In a manufacturing environment this may well result in scrap products but in this environment it requires time to be spent in reworking the initial work to an acceptable standard.

Joseph Gibson's calculations and comments would be as follows:

	Job 3152	All jobs
Idle time	2.83%	2.04%
	(14/494)	(81/3970)

	Job 3152	All jobs
Wastage	1.00%	0.87%
	(38/3784)	*60 x 1.81 + 228
		19,254 + 19,396

* Materials wastage:
    cement 60 kilos x £1.81: total cement cost £19,254
    other £228: total cost £19,396

	Job 3152	All jobs
Rectification work	1.57%	1.65%
	8 x 6 + 36	[†]38 x 6 + 340 x 1.81 + 197
	6679	19,254 + 19,396 + 3,660
		x 6.00 + 310 x 7.80)

[†] Labour: rectification work 38 hours @ £6.00 per hour
            total cost 3,660 hours @ 36.00 + 310 hours @ £7.80
    Cement: rectification work 340 kilos @ £1.81
            total cost £19,254 (calculated previously)
    Other materials: rectification work £197
            total cost £19,396

For job 3152 performance was below expectation as far as idle time and rectification work was concerned but met the target for wastage. For all jobs completed during the quarter, performance was below expectation as far as idle time was concerned but exceeded expectations as far as wastage and rectification work were concerned. Performance for job 3152 was below the average for all three measures.

Batch costing

This is a variation of job costing which is appropriate when a quantity of identical items are produced together as a *batch*. In this case the batch would be treated as a job and costs accumulated for the batch. When the batch has been completed the total costs of the batch would be divided by the number of successfully completed items in the batch to provide the cost per unit. This method of costing therefore simplifies the production costing by enabling all units completed together to be costed together, rather than attempting to cost each item individually. Batch costing is commonly used in a variety of industries such as engineering components and clothing.

Contract costing

Contract costing also is a variation of job costing but is usually adopted for work which is of long-term duration, based at a particular site, and undertaken as an individual contract to meet the particular requirements of the customer. It is a method of costing which is employed within the construction industry for major projects such as the construction of a housing estate, office block, new motorway or railway.

Contract costing differs from job costing in that as the project takes place on a self-contained site more costs can be identified as direct costs and therefore charged to the contract. Thus costs such as telephones on site, supervision, site vehicle direct costs, and planning salaries can be identified as specific to the contract and treated a direct costs rather than as overheads as is the case in a job costing environment. Also because of the lengthy nature of a typical contract, extending over several years, and the value involved in a contract, it is normal for the contractor to receive payments at stages throughout the project (known as *stage payments* or *progress payments*) and to estimate a profit made on work completed to date.

This estimation of profit made year by year is necessary to avoid undue fluctuations in the profit of the company. Interim payments are generally made on the certification by an architect or surveyor of work completed to date and will be to a formula agreed between the customer and the contractor which allows for some retention by the customer (a percentage of value of work certificated as completed) which will be paid upon completion of the whole contract. These contract normally include a time scale for completion of the work, details of when payments will be made upon completion of agreed stages of the work, and what penalties or forfeitures will be required for unsatisfactory work or late completion.

Profits taken during the course of the contract will need to be conservative to allow for unforeseen difficulties and costs, and there tend to be industry norms which suggest the amount of profit to be taken in stages throughout the contract.

Process costing

Process costing is appropriate in an industry where the product in course of manufacture follows a series of sequential processes and the transfer from one process to another is frequently automatic. Examples of such automatic sequential processing industries include brewing, oil refining, food processing and glass making. In this type of manufacturing process it is not possible to divide the product into discrete units (i.e. jobs or batches) and *process costing* therefore is concerned with collecting the total costs of each process and averaging these costs over the total throughput of the process. *Throughput* in this environment will also include work in progress and partly completed products will be treated as equivalent units of completed products. Thus 100 litres of beer which is 80 per cent completed as far as processing is concerned will be treated as 80 litres equivalent of fully processed beer.

In this environment, the cost of the output of one process is charged as the raw material input of the next process and cost is added process by process throughout production until the product is fully complete. The cost of production of each unit therefore is an accumulation of the average cost of each process through which the product has passed.

Process costing can be illustrated as shown in Figure 6.2.

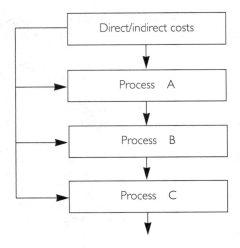

Figure 6.2 Process costing

With many processes in this type of production environment it is common that the quantity of output, in terms of weight or volume, is less than the quantity of the raw materials input. There is therefore a norm for the quantity of finished product which can be expected from any specific quantity of raw materials. Losses in materials arise from such factors as evaporation, imperfect use of raw materials or shrinkage. When differences such as this occur there are three possibilities:

- *normal process losses* – the losses are as expected in this type of process
- *abnormal process losses* – the losses are greater than expected in this type of process
- *abnormal process gains* – the losses are less than expected in this type of process.

When there are normal losses in the production process these are treated as overheads and the costs are spread over the good production. Abnormal losses or gains however are excluded from such routine reporting. These abnormal items are treated a separate items in the process account. Such abnormal gains or losses would be of interest to the manager of the process and would be the subject of investigation for possible problems in the same way that the performance data for Jones & Andrews Ltd in a job costing environment is subject to investigation.

It is normal in a manufacturing environment that part of the direct materials issued into production end up as scrap. Examples include offcuts of wood, cloth or metal. In some cases this scrap has a realisable value and when sold the revenue can be used to reduce the overall cost of production, rather than to reduce the cost of individual products. In other cases, a business must pay for the disposal of scrap (e.g. toxic material) and this will increase the overall cost of production. The small value of scrap means that a business will treat scrap in this way rather than accounting separately for it.

Although losses in the production process are treated as overheads, and a certain proportion of loss is expected, this represents wasteage and inefficiency in the production process. This is considered further, in terms of quality in the production process, in Chapter 7.

The treatment of joint products

Joint products are those which undergo the same processing together as one product for part of their processing. At some point in the manufacturing process these products are then split and processed separately until completed and at this split off point they then become separately identified products. An example of joint products can be found in the oil refining industry where crude oil is refined as a product but at certain points the product is split and treated separately to become aviation fuel, petrol, kerosene, etc.

For costing purposes it is normal to treat all costs together for a joint process and to treat costs separately for each product from the split off point at which the products can be identified as distinct products. Common costs – i.e. those incurred during the joint processing – are then apportioned to the individual products to arrive at a total cost of production for each product. Two alternative methods are used for apportioning joint costs and these are:

- the *physical unit basis* – where costs are apportioned in proportion to the weight or volume of each of the products produced
- the *sales value basis* – where costs are apportioned according to the sales value of each of the products produced.

These alternative methods of apportioning joint costs are based upon the accounting conventions of the company concerned rather than any underlying rationale, but the two alternatives can produce significantly different costs of production for the joint products concerned. The cost apportionment mechanism therefore needs to be understood by the business manager as these costs can affect product profitability and business decisions associated with pricing and investment.

The treatment of by-products

A *by-product* is one which is produced incidentally during the course of manufacture of the main product and tends to have relatively little sales value. Examples are spent yeast from the brewing industry (sold for use in animal food production) and sawdust and bark from the timber processing industry. As these products tend to have relatively little value compared with the main products being produced, and arise as a result of that processing rather than being specifically manufactured in their own right, it is not usual to cost the production separately from the cost of production of the main product. The normal method of costing therefore is to cost the production of the main product and to credit against this the net realisable value of the by-product, thereby effectively reducing the total cost of production of the main product.

Although by-products are incidental to the production of the main product it sometimes happens that these by-products become desirable products in their own right and hence have high value. If this happens then the product will need to cease being treated as a by-product and the two products will be treated a joint products. It is therefore important for managers to pay due regard to the by-products of their company and to look for market opportunities for these products, where they can add value to the production process and add to the profitability of the company.

Joint and by-product costing can be illustrated as in Figure 6.3.

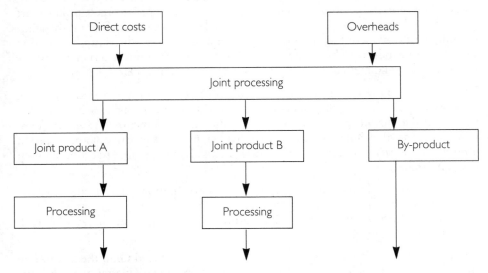

Figure 6.3 Joint and by-product costing

Costing in a service environment

These costing techniques have been developed within a production environment and have tended to be considered less relevant to a service environment. In a service environment however the processes which the company undergoes in the provision of its service can be considered similar to production processes. The difference is that generally a service has no value until it is complete and delivered to the customer. There is thus no question of value attached to work in progress. In a restaurant, for example, a meal has no value until it is supplied to a customer and any not supplied will be wasted. Similarly, the work of a travel agent has no value until a holiday can be provided to a customer.

Until the service is complete therefore no value is attached to it, although costs are incurred. It is thus possible to accumulate costs for the various parts of the company involved in the provision of the service. For a restaurant the cost of cooking meals can be accumulated, as can the costs of serving meals and the costs of cleaning up afterwards. Thus a restaurant could be treated as a form of job costing as far as cost accumulation is concerned, while process costing might be more appropriate for a travel agency.

The costing methods we have considered above represent methods of accumulating costs and so can be equally appropriate to service businesses.

An appraisal of product costing

Costing systems such as described above are widely used in industry. Such methods of costing however were developed during the early part of this century to deal with product costing in the typical factory which then existed. Since these techniques were developed, the typical production environment has changed significantly and this has led to a questioning of the appropriateness of these methods of product costing.

The techniques of product costing were designed for the type of environment which existed at that time. This was an environment in which:

- the direct costs of production (i.e. materials and labour) formed a very high proportion of the total cost
- the support functions were few in number and overheads were therefore relatively low
- the production environment was one of low levels of mechanisation
- larger runs of standardised products were manufactured
- there was a slow rate of change in terms of production methods and product development.

In such an environment, the apportioning of overheads to products in proportion to direct costs seemed a reasonable costing basis and the method of apportionment and the development of suitable bases made little difference to the overall cost of production of any product. Costing methods were therefore relatively uncontroversial and provided merely a means of accumulating costs.

In a modern environment, cost patterns have changed significantly. The features of a modern production environment are:

- direct costs, particularly labour in a highly automated environment, form a much lower proportion of the total cost of production
- overheads however form a much higher proportion of total costs
- a growth in the cost and extent of service functions needed to support the efficient production of high-quality products and to market them to customers.

Examples of these new functions include product design, machine tool setting using CNC (computer numerically controlled) machines, data processing, O&M (organisation and methods), production control and scheduling. The significant feature of these new types of overhead is that they do not vary according to production volume but tend to vary over the long term according to the range and complexity of products manufactured, rather than according to volume. This factor, together with the increased automation of production processes, has tended to mean that a much higher proportion of production overheads are fixed rather than variable. The implications for cost accumulation and for product costing will be considered in detail in Chapter 7.

The basis of apportionment of overheads is therefore a significant factor to a modern business and of much more importance then when these costing methods were developed. One effect of the changing nature of overheads and their changing importance in terms of the proportion of total cost has been that these traditional costing methods, based upon apportioning overheads based upon volume, have tended to overstate the production cost of high-volume products while understating the production costs of low-volume products. This can have a significant effect upon product profitability and upon the decisions made by business managers based upon product costing. A recognition of this type of problem has led to the discussion, amongst accountant and business managers, of the suitability of these costing methods to a modern business and to the development of new costing techniques which attempt to address these problems. The most successful of these new techniques of costing has been *activity based costing* which is considered in Chapter 8.

A further change in business which is concerned with product costing has been the increasing use of costing data, not just to provide information about the production costs of products, but also to provide data for performance measurement, such as the data produced by Joseph Gibson of Jones & Andrews Ltd regarding idle time and rectification work. The increasing use of this data for performance measurement has called into question the appropriateness of costing data, particularly by people such as Johnson and Kaplan (1987), who suggest that the changing use of this data means that decisions are made within the business based upon inappropriate data. The changing use of this data has had implications for the behaviour of business managers and for decisions taken within a company. These implications are considered in detail in Chapters 15, 18 and 22.

Summary

- The main costing methods used by industry are:
  - job costing
  - batch costing
  - contract costing
  - process costing.
- Job costing involves costing each job separately and calculating the profit on each job completed.
- Batch costing involves treating a whole batch as one job and finding product costs by dividing total batch cost by the number of completed units.
- Contract costing is concerned with long-term contracts and costs are accumulated during the contract but profit is taken at intervals during the contract.
- Process costing is concerned with continuous processes and costs are averaged over throughput. Losses during processing are subdivided into normal and abnormal and treated separately.
- Joint products are treated as one until the split-off point and costed together until this point.
- By-products are incidental to the main production and the net realisable value is credited against the product cost of the main product.
- The relevance of costing methods has been questioned in the light of modern production methods.

Bibliography and further reading

Drury C, *Management and Cost Accounting*, 3rd edition, Chapman & Hall 1992, (Chapters 5, 6 and 7)

Johnson H T and Kaplan R S, *Relevance Lost: The Rise and Fall of Management Accounting*, Harvard Business School Press 1987

Lucey T, *Management Accounting*, 3rd edition, DP Publications 1992, (Chapter 2)

Sizer J, *An Insight Into Management Accounting*, 3rd edition, Penguin 1989, (Chapter 3)

Self-review questions

1 What are the main costing methods used by industry?
(See page 70.)

2 Explain why traditional costing methods may no longer be appropriate.
(See page 79.)

3 When are overheads and profit added to the cost of a job?
(See page 72.)

4 Distinguish between a joint product and a by-product. How are product costs treated for each?
(See page 77.)

5 Identify two bases for apportioning costs of joint products between the products.
(See page 77.)

6 Explain how normal and abnormal gains and losses are treated in a process costing environment.
(See page 76.)

Additional questions

6.1 Although one of the main functions of cost accounting is the determination of product costs, in a situation in which joint products are produced, the treatment of joint process and the resulting apportionment of their costs depends upon the method of apportionment selected. This makes the product costs difficult to define absolutely and prevents managers from making decisions about the future of the products based upon the certainty of information. This problem is exacerbated when a by-product is involved. Discuss.

6.2 Total Engineering Co makes brackets which are fitted into motor vehicles. It manufactures these brackets in batches of 400. Batch number 36 was produced and machined at the rate of 20 per hour but 50 brackets failed to pass the final inspection. Of these 20 were scrapped, and the scrap value credited to the batch cost account. The remaining brackets were considered to be rectifiable and rectification work took 10 hours.

Data for batch 36 is as follows:

	£
Raw materials per bracket	2.40
Scrap value per bracket	0.80
Hourly rate of machine operators	6.80
Machine overhead rate (per running hour)	2.50
Setting up cost of machine:	
normal	32.00
rectification	36.00

Calculate:
(a) the cost per unit of units actually produced
(b) the cost of defective work.

6.3 Products A, B and C are manufactured by Associated Conclomerates Ltd from the same raw materials in a single process. Costs for the period were as follows:

Raw materials	£10,000
Processing costs	£8,000

Production for the period was:

Product A	8,000 lbs
Product B	8,000 lbs
Product C	4,000 lbs

Sales for the period were:

Product A	6,400 lbs @ £1.50 per lb
Product B	6,000 lbs @ £2.00 per lb
Product C	3,200 lbs @ £1.00 per lb

Products A and B are the main products of the process, while product C is treated as a by-product and accounted for as reducing production costs of the main products. Joint costs are apportioned using a sales value basis.

Assuming no opening stock, calculate the costs of production of each product and the value of closing stock at the end of the period.

7 Manufacturing technology and accounting systems

Objectives

After studying this chapter you should be able to:

- describe the various manufacturing methods which are included in advanced manufacturing technology (AMT)
- describe the changes in accounting methods resulting from AMT
- identify and explain new developments in accounting resulting from the new environment
- outline the features of total quality management (TQM)
- explain the significance of AMT for performance measurement.

Mckenna Manufacturing Ltd – a manufacturer of high-quality ceramics

Mckenna Manufacturing Ltd is a manufacturer of high-quality ceramics. It has recently employed a firm of consultants to complete an appraisal of its manufacturing systems. One of the findings of the consultants' report is that it identified a general weakness in the quality of the products of the company. The board considers that product quality is one of the critical factors for the success of the company and is determined to improve it.

One of the problems for the company is that the management accounting system does not explicitly report on product quality. Sandra Michaels, the management accountant, has been requested to produce a report to the board on this issue and has been given the following brief:

- to consider what part the management accounting system can play in supporting the aim of improved product quality
- to consider how the management accounting system can ensure that the control information produced is relevant to the aim of the company

- to consider how the analyses produced by the system can contribute towards improved product quality
- to indicate what features might be built into the management accounting system so that it can report upon product quality

Introduction

Management accounting and its various techniques of costing have evolved in order to provide business managers with data concerning the operating of their business; in particular that concerning product costing and stock valuation. These techniques have however been designed to help the manager working in a traditional manufacturing environment. Increasingly however new technology has changed and is continuing to change the nature of the manufacturing environment – changing the way products are made, increasing the flexibility of companies' operations and affecting stock holding practices. These various techniques together are known as *advanced manufacturing technology (AMT)*. There is also in the modern business an increasing emphasis upon quality in the product manufactured and an increasing pace of product development and innovation. These changes have affected the manufacturing environment and changed it dramatically over recent years, and this change is still continuing.

This scenario has presented many challenges to a business manager involved in production but has also affected other areas such as marketing and planning. In addition, it has led to a questioning of the value of traditional costing techniques in meeting the information needs of a business manager working in such an environment.

Management accounting has had to adapt to these new production methods and information needs and to develop techniques which meet these new needs of the manager of a business. This has led to the development of new techniques of costing and management accounting. At the same time however the traditional techniques have been maintained and continue to be used because it has been recognised that they provide data which is needed by managers.

In this chapter therefore we shall look at a variety of techniques included within advanced manufacturing technology and the changes in accounting techniques which have evolved to meet the changing information needs of the manager.

Advanced manufacturing technology (AMT)

Rather than being a technique itself AMT is an expression which encompasses a variety of techniques which have been introduced into manufacturing. The use of AMT enables a company:

- to be more responsive
- to produce high-quality goods at low cost
- to be innovative and flexible

- to be able to deal with shortening product life cycles
- to reduce levels of stock holding.

These techniques thereby enable a company to provide increasing levels of customer satisfaction. They are based upon the consideration of the process of manufacturing rather than a consideration of the products. This approach enables a company to be more responsive to the market needs and flexible in its product mix and production processes. Techniques which make up AMT include the following.

Computer aided manufacturing (CAM)

Computers have increasingly been introduced into manufacturing for the control of production machinery and this has taken the form of computer numerically controlled (CNC) machines and increasingly the use of robots. These machines have the advantage of being able to perform many functions and have therefore increased the flexibility of manufacturing and reduced the need for direct labour. CAM has introduced greater control into the manufacturing process which has led to better and more consistent quality, and less wastage through scrap and the need for the reworking of items of output. It has also resulted in fewer machines being needed to perform the various production processes and in reduced machine set-up times, thereby increasing productivity.

Flexible manufacturing systems (FMS)

A *flexible manufacturing system (FMS)* is a highly automated manufacturing process which is capable of producing components in an automated manner, moving these components from tool to tool as needed, and assembling them to form finished products. Such a system contains a combination of CNC machines and robots which are linked together by automated materials handling equipment. In a FMS environment therefore there is less need for human intervention and the direct labour component of a product made in this environment is extremely low. The ultimate aim of FMS is the complete automation of a whole factory, known as *computer integrated manufacturing*. Although major steps have been taken in this direction this ultimate system has not yet been implemented in any production environment.

Computer aided design (CAD)

Computers are increasingly being used to design products and the components which make up the final product. This speeds up the design process by allowing the design to be modified as needed throughout the process without the need to start again. It also enables a database of standard parts to be incorporated into the design process. This in turn can lead to simplified design and reduced costs by the use of standard components, thereby minimising stock holding. *Computer aided design (CAD)* thus speeds up the design process, simplifies product development and speeds up the rate at which new products can be introduced. It also increases the range of variations which can be designed into the product range to meet the individual needs of customers. It is common for companies to integrate CAD with CAM (known as CAD/CAM) thereby reducing the lead time from product design to its manufacture and introduction into the market.

Just in time manufacturing (JIT)

Just in time manufacturing (JIT) aims to match the usage of raw materials with their delivery from suppliers, thereby reducing the levels of raw materials and work in progress stocks to a minimum with the ultimate aim of reducing such stock holding to zero. JIT production works on a demand pull basis which seeks to ensure that components are not made until required by the next process, working backwards from the finished product through the various processes to the raw materials. This method eliminates (or at least almost eliminates) work in progress as it ensures that components are not completed until needed for the next process and reduces the need for raw materials held in stock to a minimum. Reduced costs are incurred by a company using JIT due to the reduced investment in stock, space savings from inventory reduction and reduced manufacturing time through the elimination of waste at intermediary stages in the production system. JIT is an approach which attempts to move the manufacturing environment away from a job or batch processing environment towards a repetitive processing environment. Hence it is only appropriate when this type of environment exists.

Materials requirement planning (MRP)

Materials requirement planning (MRP) is a computerised scheduling tool which has the objective of maintaining a smooth flow of production. Its aim is to schedule the production of components and the ordering of raw materials by ordering the schedule of processing for each machine tool within the factory so that the final output is maximised from minimal stock levels and with maximum speed. It thereby ensures that the various machines used in production are utilised to best effect. At the same time, MRP has the effect of reducing work in progress as components are not manufactured and left waiting for the next stage in the processing cycle for the completion of other jobs. It also has the effect of reducing stock holding by maximising the efficiency of the timing of orders for parts and raw materials from external suppliers. MRP is designed to be used in any manufacturing environment rather than merely the continuous processing environment for which JIT is suitable. It is therefore more flexible and suitable to job and batch processing environments.

Manufacturing resources planning (MRPII)

MRP has been extended by MRPII which is designed to integrate the materials resource planning with machine capacity planning, factory capacity and labour scheduling. Its aim is to schedule the whole resources of the factory to achieve maximum output from the resources available and to minimise wastage, work in progress and cost, while maintaining quality. Therefore, MRP and MRPII are techniques which are particularly suitable to complex manufacturing environments, such as job processing or made to order environments, where the simplifications of JIT techniques are not appropriate.

Optimised production technology (OPT)

Optimised production technology (OPT) is a technique which recognises that some processes in the production cycle cause bottlenecks and limit the production capacity of the company while others are not so critical as they do not affect production capacity. OPT concentrate upon the critical bottleneck processes in the production cycle and attempts to manage the operations of the factory to best effect by managing the scheduling of work within the bottleneck processes. The objective is to manage the operations in these processes by scheduling the order of work to be processed in such a way that it enables work flow through the other production processes, and hence total output of the company, to be maximised.

The importance of quality

In traditional manufacturing processes and their associated management accounting practices the quality of production – or rather the lack of quality in production – has been disguised by conventions which include within the process costs an allowance for 'normal' wastage, scrap and the cost of reworking. The emphasis has been upon high volume and as long as the wastage was kept within acceptable limits then all was considered well with the production processing. Indeed the product costing methods used have encouraged high volume even when such production has been merely to increase the level of stocks of finished goods. The emphasis has changed in modern manufacturing companies using AMT towards a constant production of high-quality output and an aim of zero defects, thereby eliminating wastage.

> Mckenna Manufacturing Ltd consider that the quality of their production is one of the critical factors for the success of the company. Increasingly, quality has become not a feature which gives a competitive advantage to a business but an essential feature of products; one necessary to enable a company to compete in the market place and ultimately to ensure its survival.

Total quality management (TQM) therefore has become an integral feature of a modern business which affects all its areas. In a business which is practising TQM this requires a change in the culture of the organisation from one of accepting the status quo to one in which every department and every person involved in the production process is geared towards a continuous improvement in quality. The philosophy of *total quality* is that quality is designed and built into the product at every stage during its manufacture and not ensured by inspection after completion. Quality control as the final process in manufacturing has disappeared in such an environment and has been replaced by continuous inspection throughout all the stages of manufacture to ensure that the product meets the required standards of quality.

When total quality is applied in an organisation the incidence of defects decreases and cost savings result from the avoidance of scrap and reworking. TQM therefore has the effect of reducing total manufacturing cost for a company and improving the standard of manufacturing. If a British company meets the necessary standards of quality throughout its organisation then it can be accredited under ISO 9000 (an International Standard) and such accreditation is becoming an essential requirement for a company seeking to conduct business, particularly abroad.

This changing emphasis on quality in a business needs to be reflected in a change to the management accounting system of the business. There is a need for the accounting to be used not just as a method of allocating costs of production but also as a means of reporting upon the effectiveness of the production methods and systems. The accounting system therefore needs to report on the issues which are of significance to the business and quality is one of these issues.

The report produced by Sandra Michaels for the board of Mckenna Manufacturing Ltd is likely to include the following key points:

- It is a major deficiency of the management accounting system that it does not report on quality. The system has the weakness, in common with most management accounting systems, that it concentrates on costs rather than factors such as quality which are vital to the success of the company. With a factor such as quality, non-financial indicators are likely to be more important than financial factors. Thus such factors need to be built into the reporting system. Key indicators might include:
  - reject rates
  - number of reworks
  - machine failure rates
  - design to production timescale.
- In order to be relevant to the aim of quality the control information needs to satisfy the following criteria:
  - important factors reported on
  - information should be specific to individual managers and their needs
  - information needs to be complete, accurate and reliable
  - time scales of production of information must meet the needs of individual managers
  - information should not encourage short-term behaviour but rather the company's objectives.
- Analysis of variance tends to encourage a cost minimisation attitude and a production maximisation environment. This fails to meet the needs of the company so analysis needs to be changed to focus upon the quality objective of the company
- Product quality needs to be designed and built into the products and not achieved by inspection. Reporting should therefore take place on the various stages of the production process rather than upon the product itself. Techniques such as *target costing* and *backflush accounting* (see below) might therefore be considered.

Changing accounting methods

The changing production methods used by a modern business have meant that management accounting and costing systems have needed to adapt in order to more accurately reflect the changing business needs for information. This has led to the introduction of new accounting and costing methods which, rather than replacing the traditional method of absorption costing, have adapted it to more effectively meet the needs of the business and its managers. Such new methods of accounting include the following.

Activity based costing (ABC)

The principles of ABC are considered in Chapter 8. Here it is sufficient to say that the choosing of appropriate cost drivers (i.e. those factors in the production process which cause costs to be incurred) enables costs to be allocated to products in a manner which better reflects their association with individual product lines. ABC also enables more costs which have traditionally been identified as overheads to be related specifically to products and therefore to be treated as direct costs. This technique therefore enables the production costs of individual products in a multi-product environment to be more accurately identified.

Throughput accounting

This technique is based upon the facts that the output of a company is determined by the throughput of the bottleneck operations in its production processing and that profitability is determined by how quickly goods can be produced to meet customer orders rather than by producing goods for stock. Like JIT it is based on the assumption that the ideal inventory level is zero and products should not be made unless a customer is waiting for them. It is therefore a type of accounting which is particularly appropriate to a JIT method of production.

Throughput accounting identifies all costs (including direct costs such as labour which are traditionally considered to be variable), except the cost of raw materials, as fixed in the short term, and groups them together as total factory costs. Throughput accounting is also based on the concept that overheads should be allocated to products based upon their usage of the bottleneck resources. Product cost is therefore measured in terms of the number of hours usage of the bottleneck resource included in the product with total factory cost being converted into a cost per hour of this resource.

Throughput accounting therefore concentrates upon maximising the profit to a company by means of maximising the use of its scarce resources (i.e. the bottleneck processes).

Backflush accounting

Backflush accounting is defined by the Chartered Institute of Management Accountants as:

> a cost accounting system which focuses upon the output of the organisation and then works backwards to allocate costs between goods sold and inventory.

When using backflush accounting therefore costs are not accumulated by the product as it progresses through the various manufacturing processes but instead are merely accumulated in total by the company. When a product is sold the standard cost of manufacture (see Chapter 9 for a definition of standard cost) is credited against this total cost of manufacture.

Backflush accounting is simple to operate as production units do not need to be tracked through the factory with associated costs being attached as the production processes are undergone. It also has the advantage of providing no incentive for increasing volumes of production and thereby increasing stock levels. However, its disadvantage is that it relies upon standard costs (see Chapter 20) and therefore requires accounting control and effort to ensure that standard and actual costs remain in alignment.

Target costing

Target costing is a technique which is widely used by Japanese manufacturers and which is particularly appropriate to new product development, or to diversification whereby an existing product is developed for new markets. It is a market driven approach to product development. Market research is used to identify the need for new products, the performance requirements that the product needs in order to be successful and the target price at which the product must be launched to gain the desired volume of sales. From the target selling price a profit margin is deducted in order to arrive at the target cost of production for the product. This target cost is the cost of production which needs to be met in the long term for the product to be successful. The company then organises its product design and manufacturing processes to meet this target and enable the product to be produced at or below this target cost. Thus the manufacturing processes and the accounting systems of the company when it is using target costing are driven by the requirements of the market rather than the needs of the company.

Performance measurement

AMT makes considerable demands upon accounting systems for information which is appropriate not just for operational control but also for the measurement of performance. We have seen that management accounting has developed to meet these needs. In an AMT environment a much greater proportion of costs are fixed in nature and regarded as overheads rather than being variable direct costs. This has meant that the traditional methods of allocating overheads according to volume is inappropriate. Equally, there is a danger that conventional management accounting encourages behaviour, such as production for stock and output maximisation, which is inconsistent with the aims of AMT, such as inventory minimisation and production to order.

Production methods such as OPT and JIT however lend themselves to the production of performance data which is not financially related and can be used to measure performance along with the traditional financial data produced by the management accounting system. The changing manufacturing environment therefore is leading to a change in the measurement of performance which is placing less reliance upon financial data for the measurement of performance and using such data together with other non-financial data to provides measures of performance which are appropriate to the new environment.

Summary

- Modern production is concerned with product innovation, product development and short product life cycles. Its emphasis is on short product runs and rapid changes in manufacturing times.
- As the manufacturing environment has changed, so accounting techniques used have needed to change to meet the changed business needs.
- Advanced manufacturing technology (AMT) is a term used to describe a range of manufacturing methods which have been introduced into modern businesses. Such techniques include:
  - computer aided manufacture (CAM)
  - flexible manufacturing systems (FMS)
  - computer aided design (CAD)
  - just in time manufacturing (JIT)
  - materials requirement planning (MRP)
  - manufacturing resources planning (MRPII)
  - optimised production technology (OPT).
- The importance of quality has led to the introduction of total quality management (TQM). British companies which meet the necessary standards can be accredited under ISO 9000.
- Changed production methods have led to the introduction of new accounting techniques. Such techniques include:
  - activity based costing (ABC)
  - throughput accounting
  - backflush accounting
  - target costing.
- In an AMT environment a greater proportion of costs are fixed and treated as overheads rather than direct costs. Conventional management accounting focuses upon the wrong aspects of performance. It is for this reason that greater emphasis is being placed on non-financial measures of performance.

Bibliography and further reading

Clutterbuck D and Crainer S, *The Decline and Rise of British Industry*, W H Allen & Co 1988, (Chapters 18 and 19)

Drury C, *Management and Cost Accounting*, 3rd edition, Chapman & Hall 1992, (Chapter 21)

Lee J Y, *Managerial Accounting Changes for the 1990s*, Addison-Wesley 1987

Lucey T, *Management Accounting*, 3rd edition, DP Publications 1992 (Chapter 22)

Monden Y and Sakurai M, *Japanese Management Accounting*, Productivity Press 1989

Self-review questions

1 Describe the changed production environment which has led to the introduction of AMT.
(See page 84.)

2 List and describe five different techniques that can be considered as part of AMT.
(See page 87.)

3 What is ISO 9000 and why is it important to British industry?
(See page 88.)

4 Explain the term TQM and its importance to manufacturing industry.
(See page 87.)

5 Describe four new accounting techniques used in an AMT environment.
(See page 89.)

6 Describe a manufacturing technique to cope with production bottlenecks and an accounting technique appropriate for use with this production technique.
(See page 87 and 89.)

7 Describe the changed nature of product costs in an AMT environment. What effect has this had upon measures used to evaluate performance?
(See page 90.)

Additional questions

7.1 It has been suggested that the introduction of advanced manufacturing technology has changed the nature of product costing and brought about a change from labour intensive to capital intensive manufacturing. How has this affected management accounting and what new techniques have been developed to cope with this change in the manufacturing environment?

7.2 Modern manufacturing is based upon an emphasis upon quality of production, upon speed of product development and upon rapid response to market needs. Identify advanced manufacturing technologies which accommodate these needs and the way in which target costing can assist a manufacturer in meeting these needs.

8 Activity based costing

Objectives

After studying this chapter you should be able to:

- describe how activity based costing (ABC) differs from traditional costing
- explain the meaning of cost drivers and identify appropriate cost drivers
- discuss the advantages and disadvantages of activity based costing
- calculate product costs using activity based costing.

Reid Manufacturing Ltd – an industrial batteries manufacturer

Sunanda Singh is the management accountant of Reid Manufacturing Ltd, a small company which manufactures industrial batteries. The managing director has become aware of activity based costing as a technique which more accurately reflects the cost of manufacture of products. He considers that this information may be of significance to the company in setting its prices for its products. Therefore he asked Sunanda to prepare a comparative statement of product costs using traditional absorption costing and activity based costing.

Reid Manufacturing Ltd makes four different types of batteries:
X432, X467, Y145 and Z359.

Sunanda has collected the following information which she needs for her comparative analysis of product costing:

Product	Volume (units)	Material cost per unit (£)	Direct labour per unit (hours)	Machine time per unit (hours)	Labour cost per unit (£)
X432	600	6	0.5	0.4	4
X467	6000	5	0.5	0.2	4
Y145	700	18	1.5	1.0	12
Z359	8000	20	2.0	1.2	16

Factory overheads recovered over machine hours	£35,220
Set-up costs	£4,096
Cost of ordering materials	£2,304
Material handling costs	£6,440
Administration for spare parts	£10.024

These overheads costs are currently absorbed by products on the basis of machine hours at a rate of £4.95 per hour.

Sunanda has investigated the production activities of the company for the last period. Her investigations have revealed the following:

	Product			
	X432	**X467**	**Y145**	**Z359**
Number of set-ups required	2	5	2	7
Number of materials orders	1	5	2	4
Number of times materials were handled	2	8	4	9
Number of spare parts required	1	6	2	5

Sunanda knows that she has all the information she needs to complete her analysis of product costs using the two methods – absorption costing and activity based costing.

Costing a product

Traditional methods of costing are based upon the assumption that costs are related to the volume of production of each of the products made by a business. Thus costs are absorbed in relation to volume and it is assumed that all costs are related to a product in this manner. There is a tendency, using this traditional method of product costing, that the cost of production of high-volume products is overstated while the cost of low-volume products is understated. This is because economies of scale in the production process are not recognised in traditional methods of costing, which assume that volume is the sole determinant of cost.

It has also been argued that not all overhead costs relate in equal proportions to the volume of production of each product and that the costs of production are therefore not as accurately calculated as is desirable. This has obvious implications for a business where pricing decisions are based to some extent upon the calculated costs of production of each product in the range.

We have seen (in Chapter 7) how changes in manufacturing techniques have tended to result in a smaller proportion of the cost of manufacture of a product being attributable to direct costs and a correspondingly greater proportion being attributable to overhead costs. Any inequality in overhead cost apportionment using absorption costing is therefore exaggerated in a modern production environment. It is for this reason that more attention has been given to the way in which overhead costs arise in relation to the manufacture of a product. This investigation has led to the development of activity based costing (ABC) which seeks to allocate overhead costs to products on a more realistic basis than that of production volume.

The philosophy of activity based costing

Activity based costing is based upon the philosophy that costs arise when an activity is performed rather than when a product is produced. Thus, for example, costs are incurred every time a machine set-up takes place and therefore a product which takes seven machine set-ups is more costly to produce than a product that only requires one. ABC attempts to reflect this cost difference in the product costing by identifying those activities in the production process which cause cost to be incurred. These activities are known as *cost drivers*.

A *cost driver* can therefore be defined as:

an activity or transaction which is a significant determinant of cost.

For Reid Manufacturing Ltd, Sunanda Singh has identified the following activities as causing costs to be incurred in the battery manufacturing process:

- machine set-up
- ordering of materials
- handling of materials
- administration of spare parts.

There are no simple rules for identifying cost drivers and these depend upon the individual business and the way in which it operates. Kaplan (1990), one of the main proponents of ABC, suggests that the best approach is to identify those resources which constitute a significant proportion of the cost of a product and to determine their cost behaviour.

In order for ABC to be of value to a business in determining product costing it is necessary for the cost drivers selected to be a realistic representation of the way in which costs are incurred in the production process. In other words, the product costs produced from the use of ABC are only as realistic as the cost drivers identified as contributing to costs. It is necessary therefore that the production process is understood in detail when the cost drivers are selected and the managers of the production process must be involved to a large extent in defining the ABC system in order for it to be of value in better identifying the cost of production of individual products within the product range.

The steps in activity based costing

In order to develop an ABC system the following steps need to be undertaken:

- Identify the main activities in the organisation which relate to the production process. Such activities can include materials ordering and handling, machining, and assembly.

- Identify the factors which determine the cost of an activity. These are known as *cost drivers* and include such things as number of purchase orders made, number of machine set-ups, and number of times materials are handled.
- Collect the costs of each activity in a cost pool. This *cost pool* is equivalent to a cost centre in a conventional absorption costing system.
- Estimate an appropriate cost absorption rate for each cost driver based upon estimated costs and estimated usage. This is the *application rate* for the cost driver.
- Use the application rate for each use of the cost driver in order to apply activity costs to the products being produced.

This can be summarised in Figure 8.1. The principles of ABC can be seen in Figure 8.2 which can be compared with the principles of conventional product costing in Figure 8.3.

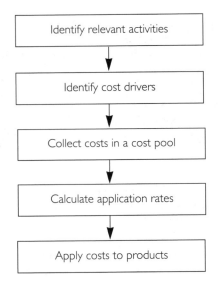

Figure 8.1 Attributing costs using ABC

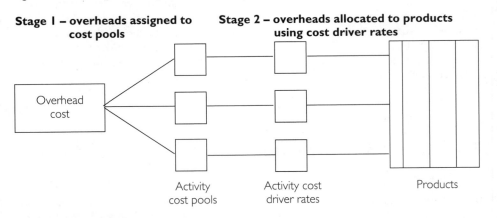

Figure 8.2 Activity based costing

Stage 1 – overheads assigned to production departments

Stage 2 – overheads allocated to products

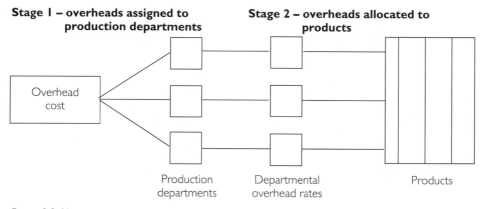

Figure 8.3 Absorption costing

The calculation of product costs using ABC

Once the cost drivers have been identified in the manufacturing process the next step in the calculation of product costs is to calculate the cost driver application rates.

For Reid Manufacturing Ltd these can be calculated as follows:

Machine related cost driver (factory overheads)
(i.e. using the same basis as for the absorption costing system)

Cost of factory overheads	£35220
Number of machine hours	600 × 0.4 (X432)
	+ 6,000 × 0.2 (X467)
	+ 700 × 1 (Y145)
	+ 8,000 × 1.2 (Z359)
	= 11,740
Cost per machine hour	£35,220/11,740 = £3.00

Set-up cost driver

Cost of machine set-ups	£4,096
Number of set-ups	2 (X432) + 5 (X467) + 2 (Y145)
	+ 7 (Z359) = 16
Cost per set-up	£4,096/16 = £256

Materials order cost driver

Cost of ordering materials	£2,304
Number of orders	1 (X432) + 5 (X467) + 2 (Y145)
	+ 4 (Z359) = 12
Cost per set-up	£2,304/12 = £192

Materials handling cost driver

Cost of handling materials	£6,440
Number of handlings	2 (X432) + 8 (X467) + 4 (Y145) + 9 (Z359) = 23
Cost per set-up	£6,440/23 = £280

Spare parts cost driver

Cost of administering spare parts	£10,024
Number of orders	1 (X432) + 6 (X467) + 2 (Y145) + 5 (Z359) = 14
Cost per set-up	£10,024/14 = £716

These application rates are then used to apply the costs of each of the activities to the products being produced.

For Reid Manufacturing Ltd these would be applied as follows:

Machine related overhead cost per unit of output
(number of hours x cost per hour)

X432	0.4 x £3.00	= £1.20
X467	0.2 x £3.00	= £0.60
Y145	1.0 x £3.00	= £3.00
Z359	1.2 x £3.00	= £3.60

Set-up cost per unit of output
(number of set-ups x cost per set-up)/number of units produced

X432	(2 x £256)/600	= £0.85
X467	(5 x £256)/6,000	= £0.21
Y145	(2 x £256)/700	= £0.73
Z359	(7 x £256)/8,000	= £0.22

Materials ordering cost per unit of output
(number of orders x cost per order)/number of units produced

X432	(1 x £192)/600	= £0.32
X467	(5 x £192)/6,000	= £0.16
Y145	(2 x £192)/700	= £0.55
Z359	(4 x £192)/8,000	= £0.10

Materials handling cost per unit of output
(number of handlings x cost per handling)/number of units produced

X432	(2 x £280)/600	= £0.93
X467	(8 x £280)/6,000	= £0.37
Y145	(4 x £280)/700	= £1.60
Z359	(9 x £280)/8,000	= £0.37

Spare parts administration cost per unit of output
(number of spare parts x cost per part)/number of units produced

X432	(1 x £716)/600	= £1.19
X467	(6 x £716)/6,000	= £0.72
Y145	(2 x £716)/700	= £2.05
Z359	(45 x £716)/8,000	= £0.45

It is then possible to calculate the total overhead cost for each product, as follows:

	X432 £	X467 £	Y145 £	Z359 £
Overhead costs				
Factory overheads	1.20	0.60	3.00	3.60
Set-up costs	0.85	0.21	0.73	0.22
Material ordering costs	0.32	0.16	0.55	0.10
Material handling costs	0.93	0.37	1.60	0.37
Spare parts costs	1.19	0.72	2.05	0.45
Total overhead cost	4.49	2.06	7.93	4.74

The total cost of production for each of the four products which Reid manufacturing Ltd produces is then as follows:

	X432 £	X467 £	Y145 £	Z359 £
Product cost				
Direct materials	6.00	5.00	18.00	20.00
Direct labour costs	4.00	4.00	12.00	16.00
Total overhead cost	4.49	2.06	7.93	4.74
Total product cost	14.49	11.06	37.93	40.74

A traditional absorbtion costing approach would produce product costs as follows:

Overhead cost per unit of output
(number of hours x cost per hour)

X432	0.4 x £4.95	= £1.98
X467	0.2 x £4.95	= £0.99
Y145	1 x £4.95	= £4.95
Z359	1.2 x £4.95	= £5.94

	X432 £	X467 £	Y145 £	Z359 £
Product cost				
Direct materials	6.00	5.00	18.00	20.00
Direct labour costs	4.00	4.00	12.00	16.00
Total overhead cost	1.98	0.99	4.95	5.94
Total product cost	11.98	9.99	34.95	41.94

It is therefore possible for Sunanda Singh to produce a statement comparing the cost of production using ABC and absorption costing. Her statement would be as follows:

	X432 £	X467 £	Y145 £	Z359 £
Product cost				
Absorption costing	11.98	9.99	34.95	41.94
Activity based costing	14.49	11.06	37.93	40.74
Difference	+2.51	+1.07	+2.98	−1.20

Here + means that ABC leads to an increased product cost and − means that ABC leads to a reduced product cost.

It can be seen that the two product costing systems produce very different costs for the four products and this can have a significant impact upon the business and upon the prices charged for each product. Therefore the product costing system used by a company is not merely an impartial reporting mechanism but can significantly shape the performance of the business and can affect the prices charged for the various products, the quantities sold based upon these prices, and ultimately the viability of producing some of the products in the product range.

The effect of the product costing system upon the behaviour of the company is considered in greater detail in Chapters 18 and 19.

Activity based costing in service organisations

This discussion of activity based costing has been set in a manufacturing environment but the use of ABC is equally appropriate in a service environment. The principle of linking costs to activities in the service process would assist in providing more accurate costs of individual services just as much as providing costs of individual products in a manufacturing environment. Thus ABC has been used successfully in service industries such as banking, where cost drivers can be related to the volume of activity on a customer's account rather than to the number of accounts which a person possesses or the size of any particular balance.

The variable–fixed cost dichotomy

The traditional method of cost classification is to divide costs into variable costs and fixed costs. *Variable costs* are those which vary with the volume of production and include direct costs. *Fixed costs* are those which are not dependent upon the production volume and this includes the majority of overhead costs. Activity based costing however attributes costs to activities and this requires a different classification of costs. This different classification is needed because some overhead costs are related to production volumes while other overhead costs are related to the production process. There is a need, when using ABC, to consider not just whether costs are variable but also why they may vary.

Kaplan (1990) has proposed classifying costs into the following three categories.

Short-term variable costs

These costs do vary with production volumes, such as power costs which are directly related to machine hours used. It is suggested that such costs are traced to product cost using production-volume related cost drivers, such as machine hours or direct labour hours, in the manner of traditional absorption costing. In most organisations, only a relatively small proportion of overhead costs will be classified as short-term variable costs.

Long-term variable costs

These costs do not vary in accordance with production volume but rather with other measures of activity. Examples would include stock purchasing and handling, machine set-up costs, and general support activities. Such costs can be regarded as fixed in the short term but variable in the longer term, depending upon the range and complexity of products manufactured and changes in product mix or production methods. In traditional costing systems, such costs would be regarded as fixed and recovered through a general overhead recovery rate. With activity based costing however they are regarded as variable and can be recovered through the transaction based cost drivers identified within the system. These costs are likely to include the majority of overhead costs, particularly in an advanced manufacturing technology environment.

Fixed costs

Such costs do not vary with any activity indicator and are therefore classified as fixed. They would include such things as directors' salaries and it is suggested that these costs will form a relatively small proportion of total costs.

Activity based costing therefore requires that costs be looked at differently to the way in which they are viewed in traditional costing systems. It has the advantage that a much greater proportion of overheads can be regarded as variable, rather than fixed, and allocated to product costs in relation to how they are incurred. This is particularly important in a modern production environment and is one of the main reasons why it is claimed that ABC enables more accurate product costings to be calculated.

The advantages of activity based costing

The following can be considered to be the main advantages of activity based costing:

- *Better product costing* ABC enables more overheads to be traced to product costs and provides a more realistic assessment of how costs are incurred. It therefore leads to more realistic product costing, particularly in a modern AMT environment where support costs comprise a high proportion of total costs.
- *Control of costs* ABC recognises that it is activities which cause costs to arise rather than production volume. It therefore focuses attention on the real nature of cost behaviour. This makes it possible to control costs better, by controlling the activities which cause costs. This will lead to better use of managerial time.
- *Supports cost reduction efforts* ABC enables the recognition of the value added by the various activities in the production process by comparing costs with benefits. It therefore facilitates the identification of non-value adding activities which can be reduced in scope, as part of the cost reduction efforts of the management process, thereby leading to a better use of managerial time. This can also lead to job redesign as the activities which do not add value are eliminated and workers are able to concentrate their efforts on the value adding parts of the company's activities. A recognition of the value added by certain functions can also increase motivation for those performing those functions – they realise that the value of their work is recognised by the company.
- *Facilitates performance measurement* ABC provides a variety of measures of performance which includes financial measures, such as the cost driver application rates, as well as non-financial measures, such as transaction volumes. These measures together give a better means for managers to measure and evaluate performance than do the measures provided by traditional costing systems.
- *Facilitates strategic decisions* More realistic product costs enable the managers of a business to make strategic decisions based upon better information. Such decisions will include not just pricing decisions and investment decisions but also decisions involving product mix changes and introducing or discontinuing products. Competitiveness with other businesses making similar products is also more accurately evaluated for all of the products in the range on an individual product basis.

The disadvantages of activity based costing

Activity based costing however also has some disadvantages in comparison with traditional costing systems, as follows:

- *Costly to operate* The need to collect costs in a variety of cost pools and to operate a variety of cost driver application rates is more complex to administer than a simple overhead absorption rate. Thus ABC is inevitably more expensive to operate than traditional costing systems.

- *Use of managerial time* ABC requires the selection of appropriate cost drivers and realistic product costing is dependent upon the selection of these cost drivers. Such cost drivers are pertinent only to an individual company and therefore managerial effort is required to identify them. This identification of appropriate cost drivers requires a detailed knowledge of the production processes and a constant review of operations to ensure that relevant and realistic cost drivers continue to be used. This managerial effort can be offset against the reduction in managerial time spent in controlling costs and activities but nevertheless represents a change in emphasis for managers of the business rather than a reduction in managerial effort.
- *Based on historical cost* Like all costing systems, ABC is based upon historical costs and activities and these may not represent a sound basis for planning future activity. ABC therefore has the disadvantage of a historical base which limits its appropriateness to an AMT environment in the same way as more traditional costing systems (see Chapter 7). This has a tendency to negate one of the claimed advantages of ABC in its appropriateness for such environments.

Conclusion

Activity based costing is one of a range of accounting techniques which have been developed in order to provide a better basis for controlling a business operating in a modern manufacturing environment. We have seen that it addresses some of the problems discussed previously concerning product costing and decision making but we have also seen that it has limitations. The heavy investment of time involved in setting up such a system is perhaps one reason why it has not been universally adopted by businesses. The costs of running such a system make it only practical for larger, multi-product businesses but its limitations for an AMT environment tend to preclude it from being adopted by such businesses.

It is perhaps for these reasons that its adoption is more widespread in the USA, where it was developed as a technique, than in the rest of the world where it remains something of a rarity. Nevertheless, as a costing system it does offer advantages to a business manager who understands the principles underlying it and is sufficiently widespread in use for a business manager to need to understand it as a method of product costing.

Summary

- Traditional costing relates overhead costs to volume of production. Activity based costing (ABC) relates costs to activities.
- ABC is based upon the philosophy that costs are only incurred when an activity takes place. This activity is known as a cost driver.
- The steps in ABC are:
  - identify relevant activities
  - identify cost drivers

  - collect costs in cost pools
  - calculate application rates
  - apply costs to products.
- ABC can provide very different product costs to those from traditional costing systems. This can have important implications for an organisation.
- ABC means that the classification of costs into fixed and variable costs is no longer appropriate. The following alternative is proposed:
  - short-term variable costs
  - long-term variable costs
  - fixed costs.
- ABC enables more costs to be classified as variable and allocated directly to products.
- ABC has the following advantages:
  - more realistic product costing
  - supports cost control and cost reduction
  - facilitates performance measurement
  - facilitates strategic decisions.
- ABC has the following disadvantages:
  - costly to operate
  - uses managerial time
  - based on historical cost.

Bibliography and further reading

Atkinson A A, Banker R D, Kaplan R S and Young S M, *Management Accounting*, Prentice Hall 1995, (Chapters 3 and 7)

Drury C, *Management and Cost Accounting*, 3rd edition, Chapman & Hall 1992, (Chapter 11)

Kaplan R S, 'Contribution margin analysis: no longer relevant', in *Journal of Management Accounting* (US), Fall 1990, pages 2–15

Lucey T, *Management Accounting*, 3rd edition, DP Publications 1992, (Chapters 2 and 22)

Self-review questions

1 How does activity based costing differ in concept from traditional costing?
   (See page 95.)

2 What is a cost driver?
   (See page 95.)

3 Explain how a cost driver application rate is derived in a production environment.
   (See page 96.)

4 Describe the different cost classifications which have been suggested as appropriate for activity based costing.
(See page 101.)

5 Explain why activity based costing is claimed to provide more realistic product costs.
(See page 102.)

6 Why might the different product costs arrived at by using activity based costing be of significance to a business?
(See page 100.)

7 Suggest four advantages to a business in using activity based costing.
(See page 102.)

8 What limitations to activity based costing might have resulted in its use not being wide-spread?
(See page 103.)

Additional questions

8.1 Production data for the company in which you are the management accountant is as follows for the last period:

	Product		
	A	B	C
Output (units)	100	120	80
Cost per unit (£)			
Direct materials	40	50	40
Direct labour	21	27	18
Machine hours per unit	3	4	2

Production overhead is currently absorbed using a machine hour basis and costs for the last period are as follows:

	£
Machine department costs	8,430
Stores department costs	5,350
Materials handling costs	2,100

Investigation reveals that machine department costs are related to set-ups. All products are produced in batches of 20 units and the machines need to be set-up after each batch has been produced. Stores department costs are driven by orders from the production department. The number of orders for each product was as follows:

Product A	2 orders per batch
Product B	3 order per batch
Product C	3 orders per batch

Materials handling costs are related equally to each batch produced.

Calculate the total cost of each product:
(a) if all overhead costs are absorbed on the basis of machine hours
(b) if all costs are absorbed using activity based costing.

8.2 Changing technology means that the traditional methods of absorbing costs tend to cause problems in cost allocation and lead to unrealistic estimates of cost of production. It is for this reason that activity based costing has become more popular as it tends to lead to more accurate product costing. Discuss.

8.3 Hall Products Ltd makes three main products and uses basically similar equipment and production methods for each. At present, a traditional absorption costing system is used by the company but the managing director is interested in the use of activity based costing. She has therefore asked you, as management accountant, to evaluate the two methods of product costing by calculating the unit cost of each of the three products the company makes using both traditional and activity based costing methods.

The following information is available to you:

	Product A	Product B	Product C
Labour hours per unit	0.5	1.0	1.3
Machine hours per unit	1.0	1.5	2.5
Materials cost per unit (£)	17	12	20
Annual volume (units)	1,000	1,500	6,000

Production overheads are absorbed on the basis of machine hours at a rate of £24 per machine hour. Direct labour is paid at a rate of £8 per hour.

Analysis of production overheads has shown that they can be classified as follows:

Machining costs	35%
Set-up costs	30%
Materials handling costs	15%
Inspection costs	20%

Activities in respect of these classifications relate to the total production volume and have been established as follows:

	Product A	Product B	Product C
Number of set-ups	100	120	350
Number of materials movements	15	12	65
Number of inspections	100	240	500

9 Marginal costing

Objectives

After studying this chapter you should be able to:

- explain the concept of marginal costing
- calculate the marginal cost of a product or service
- contrast marginal costing with absorption costing
- outline the advantages and disadvantages of marginal costing.

Franklin Technology Ltd – high-technology electronic components manufacturer

Franklin Technology Ltd is a manufacturer of high-technology electronic components. The products manufactured, due to the pace of technological development in this area, have a short product life cycle. The average life of a product is one year. Competition amongst manufacturers in this industry is intense leading to very high marketing costs. The technological nature of the products also makes their development costs substantial.

The company has just developed a new product for the market which has the following cost profile:

	£	£
Direct costs:		
Materials	123	
Labour	28	
Expenses	57	208
Absorbed manufacturing overheads:		
Fixed	40	
Variable	30	70
		278
Absorbed non-manufacturing overheads:		
General administrative costs	37	
Development costs	240	
Marketing costs	110	387
Total product cost		665

The absorbed non-manufacturing costs and fixed manufacturing costs have been arrived at by dividing the total costs in each category by the total number of products planned to be produced during the year.

The board of Franklin Technology Ltd are concerned that it cannot launch this product onto the market at a price which will enable the product cost to be covered due to the competitive nature of the market for this product. It has therefore asked David Smith, the management accountant, to investigate the product costs calculated to see if this cost is correct.

Introduction

We have looked in detail at the costing of products and services (Chapters 4 to 6) and the way in which these costs are built up through the activities of the company. We have seen that both direct costs and indirect costs form part of the cost of a product or service. *Indirect costs* include all the fixed costs of the company and, as these too form part of the cost of production. They are included in the product or service cost and are charged to the cost of the product or service in the form of *overheads*. We have identified the basic method of product costing as absorption costing and have seen that this method of costing enables us to value stock at its full cost of production and to calculate the profit of the business which is derived from its trading. This costing method also enables the company to satisfy its legal reporting requirements and comply with accounting conventions as specified in the appropriate Statements of Standard Accounting Practice (SSAPs).

When we have looked at the internal operations of a business however we have seen that the use of absorption costing causes problems within the company by the way in which costs are allocated to the various products or services. This allocation is often arbitrary and so it has been argued that the costs of production do not necessarily represent the true cost of delivering a particular service or producing a particular product. We have seen examples, particularly through the use of activity based costing, whereby the allocation of costs to products in a different way results in quite different product costings.

Given this problem of identifying the costs of a product or service therefore it is difficult for a company to plan efficiently for its operations, decide upon the optimum mix of products or services to deliver, and to price those products or services in accordance with market conditions. This problem also makes it difficult for a company to decide upon the allocation of its resources in such a way that the use of any additional resources available to the business can be utilised to best effect in terms of performance improvement.

It is for these reasons that a company uses a different method of costing when considering its internal reporting and the making of operational and investment decisions, while continuing to use absorption costing for stock valuation and profit accounting purposes. This different method of costing is known as *marginal costing*, or alternatively as *variable costing* or *direct costing*. As decisions are made on the basis of marginal costing it is important that business managers understand the principles of this method of costing, its benefits and limitations, and can distinguish between the use of costs for decisions making and the use of costs for stock valuation and reporting.

In this chapter we will consider the principles of marginal costing in detail, while in subsequent chapters we will consider the way costing and accounting information can be used by managers to help in the decision-making process.

Marginal costing defined

Marginal costing is concerned with the marginal cost of production of an extra unit of the product or service. *Marginal cost* can be defined as:

> the sum of the additional or incremental costs which are incurred as a result of production and distribution of one extra unit.

As it is not practical to identify the marginal cost of one extra unit of production in this manner, in a normal production environment, the technique focuses upon the variable cost of production, hence the alternative term variable costing.

Thus:

Marginal cost = Variable cost

Marginal costing is concerned with all the costs that are incurred in the production process, both direct and indirect costs, just as absorption costing and activity based costing are. In Chapter 3 however we distinguished between product costs and period costs. Marginal costing considers *fixed costs* to be period costs, which continue to be incurred whatever the level of production. Marginal costing tries to measure the relative impact of changes in production levels upon a business and therefore is only concerned with variable costs as far as product cost calculations are concerned. Thus:

Marginal cost = Direct labour cost + Direct materials cost + direct expenses + variable overheads

For Franklin Technology Ltd the marginal cost of the new product can be calculated as follows:

Marginal cost of the new product

	£	£
Direct costs		
Materials	123	
Labour	28	
Expenses	57	208
Absorbed manufacturing overheads		
Variable		30
Marginal cost		238

Marginal costing therefore traces all variable costs to products or services and treats all fixed costs, both manufacturing and non-manufacturing, as *period costs* rather than as overheads. However, we considered in Chapter 3 that fixed costs are only fixed within a particular range, and we will consider in detail the relationship between costs and production volume in Chapter 10. It therefore follows that in certain circumstances the marginal cost of changes to production might involve additional fixed costs. We will consider this further in Chapter 12 when we consider the relevant costs for making any particular decision.

Figure 9.1 explains the marginal costing approach.

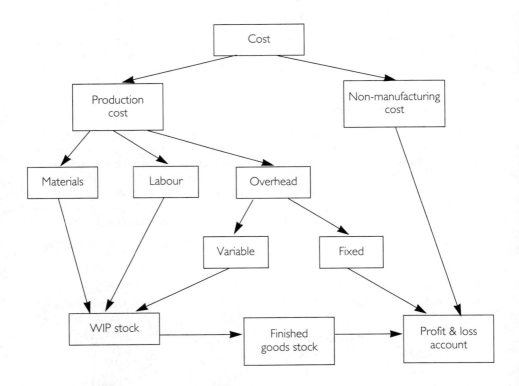

Figure 9.1 Cost accumulation using marginal costing

A comparison of marginal costing with absorption costing can be seen from Figures 9.2 and 9.3.

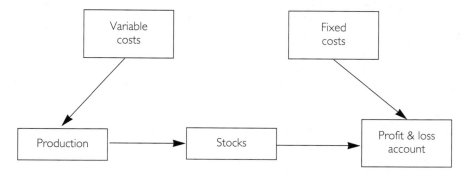

Figure 9.2 Marginal costing

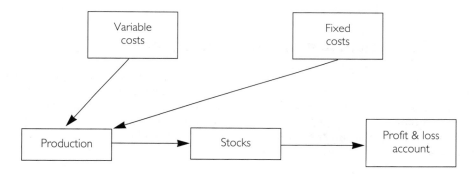

Figure 9.3 Absorption costing

Marginal costing is defined by the Chartered Institute of Management Accountants as follows:

> the accounting system in which variable costs are charged to cost units and fixed costs of the period are written off in full against the aggregate contribution. Its special value is in decision making.

The term *contribution* in this definition is calculated as the difference between selling price and marginal cost and is the contribution made by the unit of production towards fixed costs and profit. Thus:

Contribution = Selling price – Marginal cost

and the relationship between marginal cost and profit can be explained as:

Selling price – Marginal cost = Contribution

and:

Contribution – Fixed cost = Profit

Because marginal costing makes use of variable costs as the equivalent of marginal costs and bases product or service costs on average variable cost, three important assumptions are made in the calculations. These are as follows.

- *Linearity* It is assumed that all costs have a linear relationship with production volume so that the variable cost of each unit is identical with that of each other unit.
- *No step costs* It is assumed that no step costs exist in the variable costs of production so that the linear relationship exists throughout the range of the activity under consideration.
- *Relevant range* It is assumed that the relationship between costs and production holds throughout the range under consideration and so the analysis is restricted to the relevant range.

In subsequent chapters we will examine the effects of these assumptions not being true as far as decision making is concerned but for now we will assume that they remain true.

The theoretical argument for marginal costing

The principal difference between absorption costing and marginal costing is in the treatment of fixed costs. In absorption costing they are treated as product costs whereas in marginal costing they are treated as period costs. The argument for treating fixed costs as product costs is based upon the revenue production concept while the argument for treating them as period costs is based upon the cost obviation concept. These two concepts can be explained as follows.

Revenue production concept

This concept distinguishes the costs of producing stock between assets and expenses by defining an asset in terms of its ability to contribute towards the production of revenue in the future. All costs which cannot contribute in this way are defined as *expenses*. These expenses should be matched against the revenue obtained when the stock is sold, and therefore included in the stock valuation as part of the production costs. Fixed costs of a company must be classified as expenses according to this definition because they do not contribute towards future revenue production. This concept therefore implies that absorption costing must be used.

Cost obviation concept

This concept defines assets differently and identifies an asset in terms of its potential to save future costs. Thus Horngren and Sorter (1962) state:

> If the total future cost of an enterprise will be decreased because of the presence of a given cost, the cost is relevant to the future and is an asset.

Using this definition it can be seen that stock is defined as an asset because it saves future costs. On the other hand, the fixed costs of a business will not save costs in the future and will need to be incurred again in future periods. This implies that fixed costs should not be included in stock valuation but should be treated as period costs. Thus marginal costing should be used.

Therefore theoretical arguments exist for the use of both absorption costing and marginal costing, but in practical terms absorption costing must be used by a company in valuing stock in order to comply with the appropriate SSAPs (see Chapter 5). Any use of marginal costing therefore is restricted to the internal reporting of a company. For it to be used in addition to absorption costing it must fulfil a function which justifies its use as an additional costing method. This use is for decision making and in Chapters 12 and 13 we will look in detail at decision relevant costing. In this chapter however we will consider the benefits of using marginal costing for decision making.

The advantages of marginal costing

In making decisions the use of marginal costing can be seen to give the following advantages to business managers who need to make those decisions.

Avoids arbitrary apportionment of fixed costs

Under marginal costing, fixed costs are treated as a whole and charged to revenue rather than being absorbed into product costs. The absorption of fixed costs into product costs involves, as we have seen, some arbitrary allocations of those costs to products. These allocations can cause argument and conflict within the company between different managers and can also lead to different product costs depending upon how the costs are allocated.

Marginal costing however only charges variable costs to products and these are inevitably directly attributable to those products. Marginal costing split costs into fixed and variable and enables projections to be made, which are dependent upon this split (see Chapter 10) and therefore provides information relevant to decision making.

Avoids the need for determining suitable bases

For fixed costs to be charged to products or services there needs to be a suitable basis for absorbing each of these costs into the various products or services. This requires the development of a basis for each type of fixed cost incurred; one which is based upon an approximation of the relationship of this cost to the various products. This is a time consuming operation which can be subject to much argument and revision, and needs to be followed by calculation to apportion the cost for allocation purposes. We can see that this takes time and effort for absorption costing and even more so for activity based costing.

The time involved is managerial time and that of accountants, in activities which do not add to the overall performance of the organisation. Marginal costing avoids this and is much simpler to operate.

Avoids the time element of fixed cost

Fixed costs are incurred due to the passage of time and do not relate to the level of activity of the company. Thus salaries are incurred monthly, rates annually and telephone charges quarterly, regardless of the level of activity of the period concerned, and regardless of when a product is made or when it is sold. Under absorption costing the overhead charge for fixed costs is dependent on the level of activity and so production costs increase when the level of activity decreases, and vice versa.

These overhead charges do not however represent changes in the level of costs of the business. Also the fixed costs need to be incurred with the passage of time and absorption costing absorbs them into stock costs and recovers them when the product is sold, even in a future time period when the fixed costs are being incurred again for that period. These cost however relate to the company in the period in which they are incurred, and are incurred due to the existence of the company in that period. It can therefore be argued that it is logical to write them off to revenue in that period and marginal costing does so.

Restricts costs to controllable ones

Variable costs of production are controllable within the production process whereas fixed costs are not. Thus using marginal costing as a means of measuring production costs restricts the costs of production to those which are controllable by the managers responsible for production. The costs which are not controllable by them are treated as period costs. This helps the managers concerned with their planning and also enables responsibility to be restricted to those costs which can be influenced by the relevant managers. This in turn helps the company and its managers to measure and evaluate the performance of particular operations within the company.

Profits not dependent upon production levels

We have seen in Chapter 5 that when absorption costing is used profit is dependent upon the level of sales and also the level of production. Thus when it is used profit can be earned in any particular period merely by producing more goods which are not sold but instead increase stock levels. This is because the fixed costs are absorbed into stock valuation and only charged to revenue when the stock is sold. Conversely, when sales increase and this increased demand is satisfied by a reduction in stock levels, the profit earned does not increase in relation to the increased sales volume. Thus profit levels of the company can be distorted by changing stock levels. When marginal costing is used however profit is entirely dependent upon the level of sales achieved and varies in accordance with these sales.

No under- or over-absorption of overheads

Under- or over-absorption of costs is due to the absorption of fixed costs into product costs. The overhead absorption rate is set based upon expected levels of costs and expected levels of activity. When the actual costs or activity levels differ from the planned level this will result in an under- or over-absorption of these costs. Marginal costing, by contrast, is based entirely upon variable costs and so this situation cannot arise. Thus marginal costing avoids this complication and makes the accounting simpler to operate and to understand.

Cash flow comparisons

Profit, as we have seen, is dependent upon the accounting methods used and does not necessarily relate to cash flow. Cash flow is dependent upon the level of sales achieved and the level of costs incurred in any particular time period. Marginal costing accounts for costs on the basis of those actually incurred and therefore marginal costing provides a closer approximation to the cash flow position of the company than does absorption costing. Cash flow is important to a business and is more directly relevant to a company's success and short-term survival than is its measurement of profit over the short term. A method of costing which approximates to the cash flow position of the company has benefits for planning future operations.

Helps pricing decisions

We will see in Chapter 11 how product costs can influence the prices set by a company and so influence the sales of the company and hence its production planning. We have however seen (Chapter 8) how changing the method of absorbing costs can influence the product costings and hence the prices set by the company. Marginal costing determines the variable costs of producing a product or delivering a service, and any price set needs to at least cover the variable costs of production in order for it to be worthwhile for the company to produce the product. The price need not however cover the full cost of the product in order for the company to benefit from its production, and we shall examine situations in which this might be the case in Chapter 13.

Marginal costing determines the contribution made by a product towards fixed costs and profit, and this provides the basis for deciding whether a product is worth producing. Generally speaking, a product is worth producing if its selling price exceeds its marginal cost and it therefore makes a contribution; this is provided that there is no better alternative use for the resources employed in producing the product. Maximising the total contribution from the product mix can be seen as the way for a company to maximise its profit.

The disadvantages of marginal costing

We have already seen that marginal costing cannot be used by a company for its external reporting and stock valuation because of its failure to comply with SSAP9 and so one disadvantage of a company using marginal costing in its decision making is that it still needs to have an absorption costing system. This therefore necessitates a company operating two costing systems, absorption costing for its external reporting and marginal costing for its decision making. The use of information technology (IT) in business however means that this is not an insuperable problem and computers make it realistic to operate two costing systems.

There are however other disadvantages in using marginal costing, as follows.

Pricing may not cover total costs

While it may be advantageous for a company to produce a product if its selling price exceeds its marginal cost and it thereby makes a contribution to fixed costs, this only applies to individual products and only in the short term. Within the total product mix of the company it is necessary that the contributions from all the products at least cover the total fixed costs, as well as each product covering its individual variable costs. Otherwise the company will not be making a profit and will be operating at a loss. While a company can survive in the short term by operating at a loss, in order to do so it is utilising some of its net value (i.e. capital). Many companies do manage to survive in this manner for some time, particularly in a period of recession. The long-term survival of a business however is dependent upon it making a profit, and so decisions made based upon marginal costs need to ensure that over the whole product range and in the long term this leads to the company making a profit.

Distorts revenue when stocks fluctuate

Although we have seen that marginal costing can eliminate profit fluctuations based upon stock level changes and production level changes, this can be a disadvantage for some businesses. For example, a manufacturer of seasonal goods will produce those goods throughout the year but only sell them at a particular time of year. Such a manufacturer will wish to ensure that the profit earned will be spread over the various periods of the accounting year. A marginal costing approach would show the company making a loss throughout the year until the season in which the sales were made even though an overall profit would eventually be made from the production and sale of such products. This profit needs to be spread throughout the year in order to more truly represent the operating positions of the company and prevent excessive fluctuations in profit. This problem would be even more severe if the production cycle ran throughout more than one year.

Absorption costing on the other hand can take into account these irregular production and sales patterns and reflect a more steady profit for the business which provides a better reflection of its actual operating situation.

Understates the importance of fixed costs

Marginal costing separates fixed costs from the production process and charges them as period costs, thereby implying that the fixed costs are not relevant to the production process. In a modern manufacturing environment however fixed costs form an increasing part of production costs (see Chapter 7) and in no situation can a company produce products or deliver a service without incurring some fixed costs, such as the costs of buildings or plant and equipment. The exclusion of such fixed costs from a decision-making context based upon marginal costing ignores the importance of these fixed costs to the decision and can mean that the implications of any decision, as far as fixed costs are concerned, are ignored in the making of that decision. It is thus unwise to assume that fixed costs are not related to production but are merely time based costs, and marginal costing tends to give this impression. Techniques such as activity based costing (see Chapter 8) have also addressed this problem and seek to define costs differently.

Product costing for Franklin Technology Ltd

Franklin Technology Ltd has calculated the cost of production of its new product by using absorption costing. If we analyse its cost of production we can see that it is made up as follows:

Analysis of product cost

	£	%
Direct costs	208	31
Absorbed manufacturing overheads		
Fixed	40	6
Variable	30	5
Absorbed non-manufacturing overheads		
General administrative costs	37	5
Development costs	240	36
Marketing costs	110	17
Total product cost	665	100

The company is concerned that its cost of production is higher than the market price for the product and so the product cannot be sold profitably. However, if we consider the components of this cost of production we can see the following:

- The marginal cost of producing this new product is £238 (i.e. direct costs of £208 plus variable overheads of £30) and so any price which could be charged for the product in excess of this amount would mean that the product would make a contribution towards fixed costs and profit, even if that price was below the calculated full cost of production of £665. It may therefore be worthwhile for Franklin Technology Ltd to produce and sell this product at a price exceeding marginal cost if no alternative use is available for the resources of the company. (We will consider further the implications of alternative uses for resources when making decisions in Chapter 13.)
- Fixed manufacturing costs and general administrative costs are costs which need to be incurred for the operating of the business, regardless of whether or not this product is manufactured. The basis of apportionment has been arrived at entirely based upon the planned level of production for the year and this may well not be the most appropriate basis for apportionment for all costs included under these headings. Thus the problem of allocation of costs is a feature of the costing method used, which would be eliminated by the use of marginal costing. We have considered previously the effect of using a different basis of apportionment and how this could result in a different cost of production. In the case of this product, 12 per cent of the calculated cost of production of this new product is caused by these overheads and so a recalculation based upon different bases may make a significant difference to its cost.

- Development costs account for 36 per cent of the total product cost but this calculated cost of £240 has again been arrived at by spreading the total development costs over the total planned production. It is probable that the development costs differ between products quite considerably and it would be reasonable to suggest that development costs be identified specifically to individual products. We do not however know what effect this would have upon the calculated cost of this particular product. Also this particular product has been developed already and so its development costs have already been incurred. We will consider the significance of this for decision making in detail in Chapters 12 and 13.
- Marketing costs account for 17 per cent of the total product cost and again this has been calculated by spreading total marketing costs over the total planned production, and the marketing costs may well be different for different products. Indeed, if this product does not go into production because it cannot be sold profitably there will be no marketing costs for it and the costs will need to be absorbed by the other products made by Franklin Technology Ltd. The marketing costs have been treated by the company as fixed costs but in reality some costs will be fixed, such as staff costs, while others will be variable, such as advertising. The variable costs can be attributed to particular products and treated as part of the marginal cost of that product.

We can see therefore the problems that arise from using absorption costing by Franklin Technology Ltd and how this gives them no basis upon which to make a decision about whether or not to launch this particular product. Using marginal costing, as calculated but revised to take into account the variable marketing costs, would provide the company with a basis from which to make this decision.

The relative merits of absorption and marginal costing

The advantages of marginal costing are roughly the same as the disadvantages of absorption costing and vice versa, and so neither method of costing is superior to the other in all circumstances. We have seen in Chapter 5 that certain SSAPs have the effect of requiring the use of absorption costing in the production of published accounts, although absorption costing can be modified through the use of activity based costing to give more accurate product costs. Nevertheless, there still remains a place for marginal costing in business. Indeed marginal costing is of particular relevance to a business manager in planning the activities of the business, measuring performance and appraising projects. We shall see in Part 3 how this is so. At this point however we should understand that a business manager needs to understand the principles of all the differing methods of arriving at product costs which we have considered so far but that marginal costing is a technique which has been developed specifically for decision making.

Marginal costing for decision making

Marginal costing can therefore be seen to provide a basis for making decisions as to whether to launch a product and at what price. Examples of decisions which can best be made by considering the marginal cost of production will be considered in detail in Chapter 13. Decisions which we will consider include:

- changing the product mix, adding a product or dropping a product
- accepting or rejecting a special order
- making or buying in components
- expanding or contracting the market segments which a company trades in.

These decisions need to be made using marginal costing as the basis for them but they also need to be made in the context of decision relevant costs. This we will consider in detail in Chapter 12.

Summary

- Marginal costing is concerned with the incremental cost of making one extra unit of a product. It is also known as variable costing or direct costing
- The marginal cost of a product or service is the sum of the direct costs and variable overheads. The difference between selling price and marginal cost is known as the contribution.
- The theoretical argument for marginal costing is based on the cost obviation concept while the theoretical argument for absorption costing is based on the revenue production concept.
- Absorption costing must be used by a company for stock valuation and external reporting in order to comply with SSAPs.
- Marginal costing is the basis for decision making by business managers but needs to be applied within a context of decision relevant costing.
- The advantages of marginal costing are:
  - it avoids arbitrary apportionment of fixed costs
  - it avoids the need to determine bases for allocation
  - it avoids the time element of fixed costs
  - it restricts costs to controllable ones
  - it avoids under- or over-absorptions
  - it reduces the dependence of profit on production
  - it aids cash flow comparisons
  - it helps pricing decisions.
- Marginal costing has the following disadvantages:
  - its use requires a duplication of costing
  - pricing may not cover total costs
  - it distorts revenue when stocks fluctuate
  - it understates the importance of fixed costs to production.

Bibliography and further reading

Drury C, *Management and Cost Accounting*, 3rd edition, Chapman and Hall 1992, (Chapter 8)

Emmanuel C, Otley D and Merchant K, *Accounting for Management Control*, 2nd edition, Chapman & Hall 1990, (Chapter 6)

Lucey T, *Management Accounting*, 3rd edition, DP Publications 1992, (Chapter 14)

Horngren C T and Sorter G H, 'Asset Recognition and Economic Attributes – The Relevant Costing Approach', The *Accounting Review*, 37 (July 1962)

Self-review questions

1 Define marginal cost and distinguish between marginal costing and absorption costing.
(See page 109.)

2 What is meant by the term contribution? How is it calculated?
(See page 111.)

3 Explain why absorption costing must be used by a company even when marginal costing is also used.
(See page 115.)

4 Distinguish between cost obviation and revenue production and explain the significance of these arguments for product costing.
(See page 112.)

5 Describe and explain six advantages of using marginal costing.
(See page 113.)

6 What is the main advantage of a company using marginal costing?
(See page 118.)

7 Outline the main disadvantages of marginal costing.
(See page 115.)

8 Explain the effect of different costing methods on stock valuation and profit recording.
(See page 116.)

Additional questions

9.1 The Mobile Lighting Company manufactures and sells one design of standard lamp. The costs of production of this lamp are:

Direct cost	£5.00 per unit
Fixed factory overhead absorption rate	£3.00 per unit
Fixed costs incurred year 1	£90,000
Fixed costs incurred year 2	£90,000

The fixed factory overhead rate is based upon an estimated activity level of 30,000 units.

The sales price is £16.00 per unit.

Sales and production data for years 1 and 2 are:

	Year 1 (Units)	Year 2 (Units)
Opening stock of finished goods	2,000	6,000
Production	32,000	27,000
Sales	28,000	31,000
Closing stock of finished goods	6,000	2,000

During the years, selling expenses were £3,500 in year 1 and £3,800 in year 2, while administrative expenses not associated with production were £2,100 in each year.

Prepare income statements for years 1 and 2 using both absorption and marginal costing methods. Explain any differences there may be in reported profit between the two methods.

9.2 A company manufactures a single product with the following variable costs per unit:

Direct materials	£6.00
Direct labour	£7.50
Manufacturing overheads	£2.40

The selling price of the product is £35.00 per unit. Fixed manufacturing costs are expected to be £1,240,000 for the period. Fixed non-manufacturing costs are expected to be £765,000. Fixed manufacturing costs can be analyzed as follows:

Production departments		**Maintenance department**	**Stores department**
1	**2**		
£360,000	£470,000	£240,000	£170,000

Stores department costs are related to materials issued. Issues are as follows:

Production department 1	35%
Production department 2	50%
Maintenance department	15%

40 per cent of the maintenance department costs are labour related and the remaining 60 per cent are machine related. Normal production department activity is:

	Direct labour hours	Machine hours	Production units
Department 1	90,000	3,600	150,000
Department 2	120,000	3,400	150,000

Fixed manufacturing overheads are absorbed on a per unit of production basis for each production department, based on normal activity.

Prepare a profit statement for the period using the full cost absorption costing system as described above, and showing each element of cost separately. Costs for the period were as per expectation, except for additional expenditure of £20,000 on fixed manufacturing overheads in production department 1. Production and sales were £146,000 and £144,000 respectively for the period.

Prepare a profit statement for the period using marginal costing principles instead.

9.3 A company has a manufacturing capacity of 15,000 units per month of its single product and is currently operating at full capacity. Due to changed economic conditions however the management team is expecting a large reduction in sales volume during the coming month. The managing director therefore instructed the production director to cut capacity during the last month to 75 per cent of normal volume.

The company operates a standard absorption costing system and summarised results for the last three months are as follows:

	Month 1 £000s	Month 2 £000s	Month 3 £000s
Sales revenue (@ £30 per unit)	600	600	600
Standard cost of goods sold	400	400	400
Fixed costs	120	120	120
Overhead volume variance	–	–	(100)
Net income	80	80	(20)

The managing director suggests that the loss in the third month is due to excessive costs being incurred.

You are asked to evaluate this opinion, suggest other causes for this reduction in income and comment upon the effect of using a marginal costing approach.

9.4 Smith & Co produces a fruit based fizzy drink which they bottle and then sell in cases of one dozen bottles. Costs of production for their product are as follows:

	£
Selling price per case	8.00
Production costs per case:	
Direct materials	1.60
Direct labour	1.00
Variable overheads	0.80
Total fixed overheads budgeted and incurred	22,000
Selling and administration expenses:	
Fixed	12,000
Variable	15% of sales revenue

Normal production level on which fixed overheads are absorbed is 44,000 cases.

Actual data for the last period was:
Production   46,000 cases
Sales   40,000 cases

The managing director has asked you to produce a profit statement for the period. He is interested in marginal costing and has asked you to explain any differences in profit resulting from using marginal costing instead of absorption costing.

10 Planning of profit and volume

Objectives

After studying this chapter you should be able to:

- explain the relationship between profit, cost and production volume
- identify the assumption underlying the analysis
- solve cost–volume–profit (CVP) problems either graphically or algebraically
- discuss the limitations of this type of analysis
- identify business problems for which this type of analysis is useful.

Anytown District Council – a local authority

Anytown District Council is a local authority situated on the east coast and whose area includes the holiday resort of Anytown. The authority operates a holiday home which is let to visiting parties of children in care from other authorities. The home is open during the summer season for 30 weeks each year.

The visiting parties of children are accompanied by their own house mothers who supervise the children throughout their holiday. The home accommodates up to 16 guests and is let for at least six people at a time. The charge made is £100 per person and the same charge is applied to both adults and children.

The weekly costs per guest incurred by Anytown District Council are:

	£
Food	18
Electricity	4
Domestic cleaning	6
Use of minibus	15

Seasonal staff supervise and carry out all necessary duties at the home at a cost of £12,000 for the 30 week season. This provides sufficient staffing for between six and 10 guests but if 11 or more guests are to be accommodated additional staff are required at a total cost of £200 per week. Such additional staff need to be recruited for the whole 30 week season.

Rent of the property amounts to £2,500 per annum and the garden of the home is maintained by the council's recreation department which charges a nominal fee of £1,500 per annum.

The chief executive of the council is concerned about the viability of this home and has asked Fred Davis, a member of the accounts team, to provide a report to him showing the level of occupancy needed for the home to cover its costs.

Introduction

Any business, whether it be a manufacturing company or a local authority operating a holiday home, needs to understand the nature of its cost and revenues and the way in which these change as the volume of output or level of activity changes. This is necessary in order that the business manager can make operating decisions about the business and plan the level of production in the short term. A technique which examines the relationship between changes in volume and changes in total cost and total revenue is that of *cost–volume–profit (CVP) analysis*. This technique is also known as *break even analysis*. It is intended to be a guide for a business manager for short-term decision making and planning by considering the effects of business decisions on these three interrelated aspects of cost, profit and volume.

The kinds of short-term decisions which can be helped by an understanding of the CVP relationship for a business include pricing decisions, planned levels of output, shift working patterns and special order acceptance/rejection decisions.

For Anytown District Council the technique can be used to help make decisions regarding the planned level of occupancy for the holiday home.

The assumptions of CVP analysis

CVP analysis is a mathematical technique devised to explain the relationship between costs, profit and level of activity, and the technique is open to both graphical and algebraic solutions. Both will be examined in this chapter. As a mathematical technique however there are several assumptions which are made about the behaviour of costs and revenue as the level of activity changes. We will consider the limitations to this technique caused by these assumptions later in the chapter but first we must consider the nature of these assumptions.

Costs

It is assumed that all costs can be readily divided into fixed and variable costs although we have seen previously that this is by no means a simple process. For *fixed costs* it is assumed that these costs remain constant over the different levels of activity which are under consideration. For *variable costs* it is assumed that these vary with the changing level of activity but that they remain constant per unit of output. It is therefore assumed that for both fixed and variable costs there is a linear relationship between the total cost level and the total activity level as illustrated in Figure 10.1.

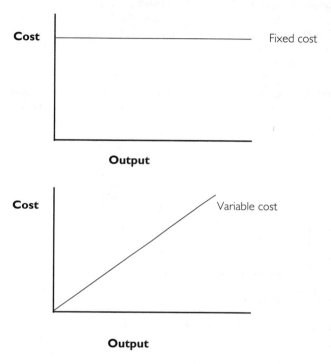

Therefore total cost:

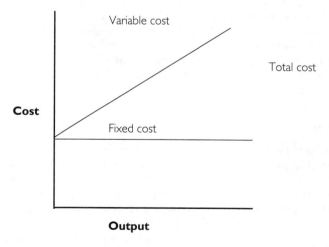

Figure 10.1 The relationship between total cost level and total activity level

The technique therefore assumes that efficiency and productivity remain constant and do not vary in accordance with the level of activity. This assumption is at variance with economic theory which suggests that returns to scale (i.e. economies of scale) will reduce unit costs up to a certain level before diminishing returns than cause an increase in unit costs. The technique further assumes that the behaviour of costs can be explained in terms of the single variable of changing level of activity.

Revenue

It is assumed that revenue per unit remains constant and that there is therefore a linear relationship between total revenue and total output as shown in Figure 10.2.

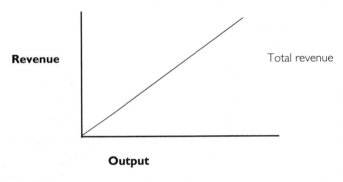

Figure 10.2 *The relationship between total revenue and total output*

Relevant range

The assumptions of the linearity of the relationship between costs and revenue and output do not hold true whatever the level of activity which the business undertakes. Nevertheless, it is reasonable to assume that these relationships do hold true within a certain range of activity and this range is known as the *relevant range*. This range may be quite small in terms of the possible levels of activity of a business but nevertheless sufficient for a company to understand the CVP relationship for its business and to consider changes to its activity level in the short term.

The short term

The assumptions are based upon the situation as it exists within the business at the time in which the analysis is undertaken and the analysis therefore assumes that these relationships will hold constant in the future. In the long run however these relationships do not hold true and such factors as economic conditions or competition can affect the revenue–volume relationship. Similarly technological changes or economic conditions can affect the cost–volume relationship. This analysis therefore is only appropriate for short-term decision making (i.e. within the next year) rather than for long-term planning.

CVP analysis is therefore suitable for Anytown District Council to plan its occupancy strategy for its holiday home for the forthcoming season but not for a consideration of the long-term future of the home.

Constant sales mix

If a business makes a variety of products within its business then a change in the mix by varying the respective proportions of each product will of necessity change the total revenue function and probably also the variable cost function. CVP analysis assumes therefore either a single product or a constant sales mix.

These assumptions may seem unnecessarily restrictive and to diminish the value of CVP analysis but they are made to ensure linear relationships which can be solved algebraically. It is possible to relax all these assumptions and explore the CVP relationships which exist in a business in this situation. Many businesses do indeed use this technique in this way, but this requires complicated mathematical techniques of modelling which are outside the scope of this book. The use of computers however means that in business a manager who understands the principles explained concerning CVP analysis can build a computer model which enables him or her to explore these relationships as they exist within the relevant business.

Comparison of economic theory and the accounting approach

Economic theory suggests that the total cost function and the total revenue function of a company are both curvilinear (as shown in Figure 10.3) rather than linear as assumed by the accountant's model of CVP analysis.

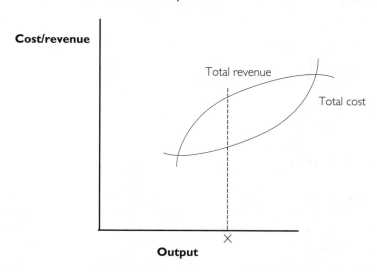

Figure 10.3 The curvilinear relationship between total cost and total revenue

This means that in the economist's model there are two break even points with the optimal level of activity being at point X between the two points. The economist's model however attempts to predict the behaviour of costs and revenues over the whole possible range of activity rather then the smaller range of the accountant's model (i.e. the relevant range). Economic theory attempts to produce a model which is designed to enable prediction to be made about the behaviour of market variables (i.e. price, output, etc.) whereas the accountant's model of CVP relationships merely attempts to provide assistance to business managers for short-term decision making within a particular company. The two alternative views of CVP relationships therefore should not be considered to be competing but merely to be showing different approaches to differing aspects of the same situation.

The graphical approach to CVP analysis

The graphical approach to CVP analysis provides a simple overview of the relationships for a business and illustrates the effects which decisions will have on these relationships. It is not however suitable when precise figures are required and for this an algebraic solution is required. The chart drawn is known as a break-even chart (see Figure 10.4).

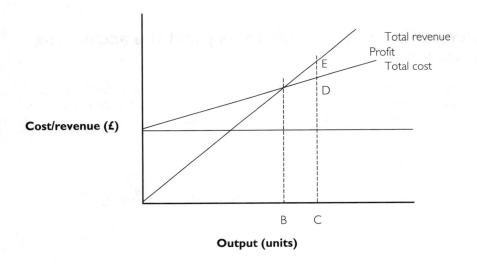

Figure 10.4 A break-even chart

From this chart it can be seen that up to the level of output B the company is operating at a loss and for levels of output in excess of B the company is operating at a profit. This point is known as the *break-even point* – that is the point at which neither a loss nor a profit is being made.

Point C represents the planned level of activity and at this point the expected profit level is represented by E – D. The difference between the planned level of activity and the break-even level of activity (i.e. C – B) is known as the *margin of safety* and represents the amount by which actual output may fall short of that planned without a loss being incurred. The margin of safety is expressed as a percentage of sales, and can be calculated either in terms of number of units or in terms of revenue.

It can be seen from Figure 10.7 (later) that the margin of safety is dependent upon the respective proportions of fixed and variable costs that are involved in producing a product and that the higher the level of fixed costs in relation to variable costs the lower will be the margin of safety at any given sales level.

It is important for a business manager to understand the concept of margin of safety and how it can vary from one business to another as it is an important part of understanding budgeting and planning and the effect that shortfalls against budgeted activity can have upon the profitability of the business.

An alternative form of break-even chart is known as the *contribution break-even chart* (see Figure 10.5).

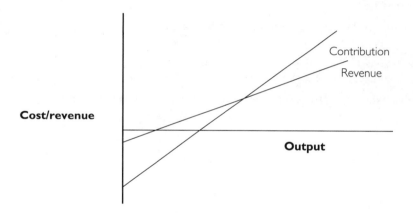

Figure 10.5 A contribution break-even chart

From Figure 10.5 it is possible to establish the contribution made by the product, given by the following formula:

Contribution = Sales – Variable costs

The revenue therefore can be seen to contribute first to the fixed costs of the business and then to profit, once the fixed costs are covered. This approach is of particular relevance when a marginal costing approach is used (see Chapter 16).

It is possible for Fred Davis to use this graphical approach to CVP analysis to understand the nature of the cost–occupancy relationship for the Anytown District Council holiday home. The cost and income relationships are calculated as follows.

No. of guests	Income £ p.a.	Fixed costs £ p.a.	Variable costs £ p.a.	Total costs £ p.a.	Net revenue £ p.a.
6	18,000	16,000	7,740	23,740	(5,740)
7	21,000	16,000	9,030	25,030	(4,030)
8	24,000	16,000	10,320	26,320	(2,320)
9	27,000	16,000	11,610	27,610	(610)
10	30,000	16,000	12,900	28,900	1,100
11	33,000	22,000	14,190	36,190	(3,190)
12	36,000	22,000	15,480	37,480	(1,480)
13	39,000	22,000	16,770	38,770	230
14	42,000	22,000	18,060	40,060	1,940
15	45,000	22,000	19,350	41,350	3,650
16	48,000	22,000	20,640	42,640	7,360

Calculations

Income: 100 per week x 30 weeks x Number of guests

Fixed costs:
Up to 10 guests   12,000 + 2,500 + 1,500
Over 10 guests   12,000 + 2,500 + 1,500 + (200 per week x 30 weeks)

Variable cost: (18 + 4 + 6 + 15) x 30 weeks x Number of guests

From this a break-even chart can be produced similar to that shown in Figure 10.6.

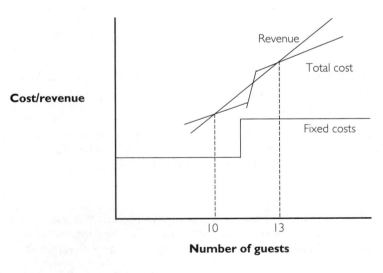

Figure 10.6 Break-even chart for the holiday home

From Figure 10.6 it can be seen that, due to the stepped nature of the fixed costs, there are two break-even points for the holiday home. These are at approximately nine and 13 guests per week. For more precise figures an algebraic solution is required.

The algebraic solution of CVP analysis

The algebraic approach enables the precise calculation of figures for break-even point, profit and contribution margin at any level of activity, and the margin of safety. These can be obtained using the following formulae:

Break-even point (in terms of revenue) = $f/[(p - v)/p]$

Break-even point (in terms of number of units) = $f/(p - v)$

Profit = $y(p - v) - f$

Contribution margin ratio = $(p - v)/p$

Margin of safety = $\dfrac{\text{Planned sales} - \text{Break-even point sales}}{\text{Break-even point sales}} \times 100\%$

Where:
y = units produced and sold
p = price per unit
v = variable cost per unit
f = total fixed cost.

For Anytown District Council therefore the calculation of the break-even point (BEP) for the holiday home is as follows:

For fixed cost of £ 16,000 p.a.

$BEP = f/(p - v)$

$= 16,000/(100 \times 30 - 43 \times 30)$
$= 9.36$ guests

Therefore ten guests represents the break-even point (as part guests do not exist).

For fixed costs of £ 22,000 p.a.
$BEP = f/(p - v)$
$= 22,000 / (100 \times 30 - 43 \times 30)$
$= 12.87$ guests

Therefore 13 guests represents the break-even point (as part guests do not exist).

This shows that for the holiday home to break even each week of the season it needs to attract ten guests (nine or 11 would result in a loss) or 13 to 16 guests. In order to break even over the season, average occupancy needs to be considered and for this the average occupancy would need to be between 9.36 and ten (with a maximum of ten in any one week) or over 12.87 per week. An understanding of this CVP relationship would therefore enable the council to plan its occupancy levels for the holiday home for the forthcoming season.

This understanding of the CVP relationship for a business would help any manager to understand the implications of any decisions made in the business regarding selling price, costs or volume.

Margin of safety

In assessing the viability of the holiday home it is useful to be able not just to calculate the average occupancy needed per week but also to be able to assess the scope for failing to meet this average occupancy before a loss is incurred. This is known as the *margin of safety* and is the difference between the break-even level of sales and the expected level of sales. The margin of safety is expressed as a percentage and can be calculated from the following formula:

$$\text{Margin of safety} = \frac{\text{Expected sales} - \text{Break-even sales}}{\text{Break-even sales}} \times 100\%$$

This can be calculated in terms of sales value or in terms of number of units.

Margin of safety is related to the relative proportions of fixed and variable costs which

For Anytown District Council the margin of safety for the holiday home would be as follows:

Occupancy up to ten people:

$$\text{Margin of safety} = \frac{\text{Expected sales} - \text{Break-even sales}}{\text{Break-even sales}} \times 100\%$$

$$= \frac{10 - 9.36}{10} \times 100\%$$

$$= 7.6\%$$

Occupancy over ten people:

$$\text{Margin of safety} = \frac{\text{Expected sales} - \text{Break-even sales}}{\text{Break-even sales}} \times 100\%$$

$$= \frac{16 - 12.87}{16} \times 100\%$$

$$= 19.6\%$$

This shows that a small margin of safety exists for occupancies of up to ten people between the level of occupancy which makes a profit and the level of occupancy which causes additional costs to be incurred and the home to make a loss. For occupancies above ten people a higher margin of safety exists between the break-even point and the maximum occupancy of the home. The margin of safety is an indication of how much an estimate of levels of sales (in this case of occupancy) can vary before the operation ceases to make a profit and starts to make a loss. The smaller the margin of safety the closer is the possibility of making a loss.

a company incurs. In general terms, the higher the proportion of fixed costs for a given level of sales the smaller is the margin of safety (see Figure 10.7). At output P the margin of safety is the difference between the total line and the total cost line.

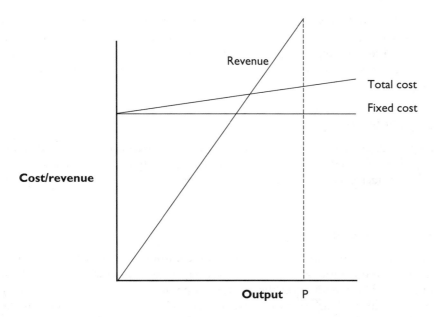

Figure 10.7 Showing how the margin of safety varies according to fixed costs

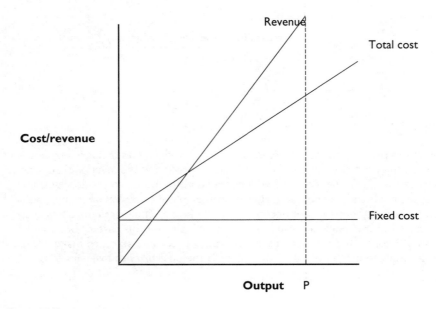

Figure 10.7 continued

Applications of CVP analysis

CVP analysis, as we have seen, is a useful technique for understanding a business and the relationship between costs, revenue, profit and level of activity. We have also seen that it is useful to a business manager in making decisions of a short-term rather than long-term nature. Decisions which can be facilitated by using CVP analysis include the following.

Pricing decisions

Changing the price of a product would change the total revenue function of the business and this would affect the break-even point and the margin of safety. These factors need to be considered along with market based factors such as the demand for the product.

Sales mix decisions

Altering the sales mix in a multi-product environment would tend to alter the total revenue function of the business and also the variable cost function (and hence the total cost function). This would affect the break-even point and margin of safety but by explaining the effects of different sales mixes it is possible to consider their effect on the profitability of the business and this will facilitate decisions regarding the sales mix.

Production capacity planning

We have seen that the cost and revenue relationships do not apply indefinitely but only within the relevant range. As activity is expanded it will eventually be constrained by a shortage of one of the factors of production (e.g. machine hours, factory space or skilled labour) and this factor is known as the *limiting factor*. While this limitation can be overcome in the long term, in the short term maximum profits can be made by maximising the contribution per unit of the limiting factor (see Chapter 18). CVP analysis can facilitate an understanding of the effects upon profit of the limiting factor.

Profit planning

CVP analysis provides an understanding of profit in relation to output levels and the way in which profit changes as the level of activity changes. The technique can therefore help in planning profit by planning the level of activity for the next period and also in revising profit plans if the actual activity level varies from that which has been planned.

Problems with CVP analysis

We have seen that there are a variety of problems with using CVP analysis which limit its effectiveness as a technique to help a business manager. These are as follows.

Relevant range

The assumptions of CVP analysis concerning linearity mean that the value of the analysis is restricted to the relevant range of activity. This range is the current level of activity plus or minus a certain amount (perhaps 20 per cent). While this might be appropriate for a business looking for a small change in its level of activity it means that the technique is inappropriate for a company seeking to change its activity level considerably, for example, one planning a rapid expansion programme. It also has the problem that it is difficult to determine exactly what is the relevant range within which the assumptions made actually do apply.

Short-term decisions

The assumptions of the CVP technique mean that it is appropriate for short-term decisions regarding production, pricing, etc. Companies normally plan for the long term however and wish to ensure that any short-term decisions also fit with the longer-term planning. The assumptions of CVP analysis mean that there are difficulties in reconciling decisions made from this analysis with any long-term planning.

Perfect knowledge

There is an assumption that the company has perfect knowledge of the behaviour of its cost and revenue functions. In practice, this is not the case and this reduces the reliability of any analysis undertaken using this technique.

Perfect market

It is assumed that a perfect market exists and that the company therefore accepts the price determined by the market. In reality a company can significantly affect market prices through its actions; this cannot be ignored in pricing and production decisions.

Technological change

Changing technology and production methods are a continuing feature of modern business and these changes cause continuous changes in the cost function of a company. CVP analysis ignores this and assumes that current production methods (and hence costs of production) will remain unchanged in the future. This makes the analysis less reliable the further into the future it is projected.

Risk and uncertainty

All companies operate under conditions of uncertainty and there is an element of risk attached to all planning and decision making. This risk and uncertainty has a cost to it for a business, which will expect rewards commensurate with the risks which it takes. CVP analysis ignores these elements and assumes that the future, in terms of returns and costs associated with different activity levels, is perfectly predictable.

Market change

In addition to changes within the company due to technology the market itself is constantly changing and is affected not just by the actions of the company but also by the actions of its competitors as well as by economic conditions, consumer preference, and taste and product developments. CVP analysis assumes that the market will remain unchanged.

Conclusion

CVP analysis is a technique which can be used by business managers to help understand the relationship between costs, revenue and level of activity for a particular business. It is designed to help in short-term decision making within the company and we have seen how this can be the case. Nevertheless, there are limitations to the value of CVP analysis which we have also considered and a business manager needs to be aware not just of how the technique can help in decision making but also of these limitations in order to be able to make best use of the technique in helping manage the business.

Summary

- CVP analysis (also known as break-even analysis) is a technique for understanding the relationship between the level of activity and the associated costs and revenues. It is useful as a planning tool.

- CVP analysis can be looked at from a graphical or algebraic viewpoint.
- The following assumptions are made in the analysis:
  - costs and revenues are linear relationships
  - there is a constant sales mix
  - relationships only hold within the relevant range
  - relationships only hold in the short term.
- This analysis is different from the analysis undertaken in economic theory, which is for different purposes.
- CVP analysis is useful in the following applications:
  - pricing decisions
  - sales mix decisions
  - production capacity planning
  - profit planning.
- This analysis has the following problems in its use:
  - relationships only apply within the relevant range
  - relationships only apply in the short term
  - a perfect market is assumed to exist
  - a perfect knowledge of cost and revenue functions is assumed
  - changes to market conditions and technological changes are ignored
  - the relationship of rewards to risk and uncertainty is ignored.

Bibliography and further reading

Drury C, *Management and Cost Accounting*, 3rd edition, Chapman & Hall 1992, (Chapter 9)

Lucey T, *Management Accounting*, 3rd edition, DP Publications 1992, (Chapter 14)

Sizer J, *An Insight Into Management Accounting*, 3rd edition Penguin 1989, (Chapters 4 and 12)

Storey R, *Introduction to Cost and Management Accounting*, Macmillan 1995, (Chapter 17)

Self-review questions

1 Explain what is meant by the break-even point.
   (See page 128.)

2 List and explain four different assumption on which CVP analysis is based.
   (See page 124.)

3 What is meant by the relevant range?
   (See page 126.)

4 Why is this type of analysis only appropriate to short-term decision making?
   (See page 126.)

5 Suggest three different applications for CVP analysis.
(See page 134.)

6 Explain why the different models of cost and revenue behaviour suggested by CVP analysis and economic theory do not conflict.
(See page 128.)

Additional questions

10.1 Gardening Ltd manufactures garden ornaments which it supplies to garden centres. Its results for the past 12 months have been as follows:

	£000s	£000s
Sales (100,000 units)	5,000	
Direct materials	1,000	
Direct labour	1,300	
Variable production overheads	750	
Variable selling and distribution overheads	450	
Fixed production overheads	700	
Fixed selling and distribution overheads	200	4,400
Net profit		600

Required:
(a) Calculate the contribution per unit and break-even level of production.
(b) The company is considering the purchase of new manufacturing equipment which will have the following effect:
  – fixed production costs will increase by £200,000 per annum
  – direct labour costs will reduce by £3 per unit
  – variable production overheads will decrease by 50p per unit.
  (i)   If the price is maintained what effect will this have on profit?
  (ii) If it is desired that profits should remain at the present level what price will need to be set for the product if sales volume is unaffected?
(c) If advertising expenditure were to be increased by £250,000 it is believed that the price could be increased by 6 per cent without affecting sales volume. What effect would this have on the profits of Gardening Ltd?
(d) If the current price is increased by 10 per cent it is believed that sales volume would reduce by 5 per cent. What effect would this have on net profit?

10.2 Alpha Production Ltd produces a single product which sells for £10 per unit. Variable costs amount to £8 per unit. If the break-even point in terms of sales revenue is £350,000, calculate the amount of fixed costs which the company incurs.

If the fixed costs incurred were reduced to £50,000 but sales revenue remained unchanged, calculate the new break-even point and the margin of safety from operating at this level of sales.

10.3 Caring Products Ltd sold 180,000 units of its product last year at a price of £20 each, out of a total production of 200,00 units, the capacity of the plant. Variable costs of production amount to £14 (£10 for manufacturing and £3 for selling). Fixed costs amounted to £500,000 for manufacturing costs and £292,000 for administrative costs, and were incurred evenly throughout the year.

Calculate the following:
(a) profit for the year
(b) break-even point in terms of units and sales value
(c) margin of safety at which the company is operating.

If labour costs amount to 50 per cent of variable costs and 20 per cent of fixed costs calculate the changed break-even point if wages are increased by 10 per cent.

10.4 Ryan Co Ltd produces a single product, an electric mixer. Currently, the mixer is selling at £20 per unit and has a variable cost of production of £14. Fixed costs are £65,000 and the company sold 20,000 units in the last year.

The sales director believes that sales can be increased significantly by reducing the price of the mixer. She has proposed three alternatives: reduce the price by 5 per cent, or 10 per cent, or 15 per cent.

She has asked you, as the management accountant, to evaluate her proposals and calculate the margin of safety under which the company would be operating at current volumes and the alternative price levels for the product. She has also asked you to calculate how many extra sales would be required at each price level in order to maintain existing levels of profit.

11   The pricing decision

Objectives

After studying this chapter you should be able to:

- describe the three pricing methods used by companies
- calculate prices based upon total cost or contribution margin
- explain the relationship between cost, price and demand
- outline the limitations of accounting information for pricing decisions.

DLK Ltd – a components manufacturer ————————

DLK Ltd is a company which manufactures several products which are components for other manufacturing companies, including the transunit. Production scheduling constraints mean that only one batch of transunits can be produced each month and the production of a batch of 20,000 units has been scheduled for next month. This production is expected to take place as planned and any surplus to demand requirements will be taken into stock.

Brian Jones, the financial accountant, has confirmed that the standard variable cost of production of the transunit will be £20 at the scheduled level of output and that the budgeted fixed costs associated with the production of transunits are £160,000 per month.

At present, DLK Ltd operates a 'cost plus' pricing policy and the selling price for each product is set by calculating its full cost and adding 25 per cent for profit.

Edith Jackson, the managing director, wishes to reconsider the pricing policy for the transunit and has called a meeting of the management team to discuss the future pricing policy. She has commissioned a market research report which she presents to the meeting. This report reveals the following relationship between price and expected demand for the transunit:

Price per unit £	Demand (units)
30	20,000
35	18,000
40	15,000
45	11,000
50	7,500

At the meeting a heated discussion takes place concerning the price to be charged for the transunit. David Carr, the production manager, maintains that the current cost plus pricing policy should be continued as this is the industry norm. Brian Jones, on the other hand, advocates a price of £45 per unit as this will lead to profit maximisation. Tony Cooper, the management accountant, intervenes suggesting a price of £40 as this will maximise the contribution made from sales of transunits.

Edith Jackson can see that all parties are determined on their proposed pricing suggestions and she needs to resolve the conflict and reach a pricing decision.

Introduction

The decision as to what price to charge for a product or service is one of the most crucial decisions which an organisation has to make. The economist's view of price is that it will be set by the market at a point where the supply curve and the demand curve intersect, but in reality the decision is not as simple as this. A company will understand the supply curve and will be able to determine its level of production, and the cost of producing the product or service at that level of production. It may also have an idea of the demand curve for the product and how much can be sold at different price levels and, if it does not have experience in producing and selling the product, normally undertakes some market research in order to gather this kind of information. From this information however the company needs to set a price for the product, produce it at an appropriate level, and then see if the its demand is in line with its expectations.

This is the dilemma facing DLK Ltd and we can see that several alternative prices have been proposed for the transunit, each argued to be the correct price. Edith Jackson needs to make a decision about the price to be charged and can draw upon the techniques of management accounting to help make that decision.

The pricing of a product is concerned with equating supply with demand and it is achieved through the setting of the price for the product. In the case of a manufacturing company supply is determined by the level of production of its products whereas for a service company supply is related to the amount of time available to supply the service. Thus an advertising agency is limited by the time of its employees and this determines supply. For a distribution company, such as a food retailer, supply is determined by the stocks which it carries. In all cases however the company is seeking to minimise stock by attempting to ensure that supply equals demand. Demand however is difficult to estimate accurately and is outside the direct control of the company. The company therefore determines supply and sets its price and is then forced to accept the demand resulting from these decisions. Thus pricing is crucial to the successful operating of the company.

The objectives of price setting

Although companies are in existence to make a profit it is not necessarily true that companies will set their prices so that profits are maximised. The company may be interested in maximising volume of sales rather than profit and increasing market share may therefore be an objective. This is particularly true for a new product or a new entrant into a new market. Thus a company such as Daewoo is a new entrant into the motor car market in the UK and is seeking to increase its market share, believing that this is a route into future profitability. In this case, the price Daewoo sets will not be dependent on the costs of production but will be determined by the prices of its competitors.

Similarly, a company such as Toyota has built a manufacturing plant in the UK, which was a costly exercise, and the first cars which came from the plant had very high costs of production. These costs will reduce per unit for the company as production increases towards the maximum capacity. Again a price has not been set according to costs of production and the millionth car produced will not be sold at a lower price than the first even though its cost of production will be lower than the first.

Thus pricing cannot be undertaken strictly in accordance with costs and other factors need to be taken into account. These other factors include such things as the objectives of the company, the level of competition and ease of substitution, the level of activity and of capacity usage, and the stage in the production life cycle which the product is at. These other factors will be reflected to some extent in the marketing strategy of the company and pricing will be determined not just by cost but also by the marketing plan. Pricing is therefore a strategic issue for a company and involves a variety of factors in making the decision. Management accounting has a part to play in this although other factors will also affect the pricing decision. One factor which is of obvious importance is the cost of production, as ultimately the selling price of the product must exceed its cost if the company is to remain in business.

Pricing methods

Many factors need to be taken into consideration when setting the price for a product or service and this leads to a variety of approaches to pricing. These can however be divided into three categories of pricing method:

- total cost pricing
- contribution margin pricing
- demand based pricing.

Each of these will be examined in turn using the problem facing Edith Jackson as a means of illustration.

Total cost pricing

Total cost pricing involves calculating the total cost of a product, i.e. using the absorption costing or standard costing method of allocating costs, and then adding a mark-up on this, for the profit margin, in order to determine selling price. This is known as *cost plus pricing*.

For the transunit therefore we can see that the total cost consists of two elements, variable cost and fixed cost, and 25 per cent is added to this to determine the selling price. The calculation of price therefore is as follows:

	Cost per unit £
Variable cost	20
Fixed cost	8*
Total cost	28
Profit mark up (25%)	7
Selling price	35

* Fixed cost per unit is calculated as follows: fixed cost of £160,000 divided by production level of 20,000 units.

This is the pricing method advocated by David Carr, the production manager, as it is the method commonly employed by this industry. It has the advantage that it is easy to calculate and provides a ready means of adjusting price when the cost of production changes.

This method however has several disadvantages:

- Price is determined by cost and this cost is determined by how the overhead costs are allocated to the products produced. We have seen previously how there are a variety of methods of allocating overheads to products and in a multi-product company it is possible to allocate costs in a variety of ways. This can result in the cost of production of a product varying according to the costing method used. It is thus difficult to argue that cost plus pricing reflects a mark-up on the true cost of a product.
- Cost predictions, as we have seen, are based upon past experience and so this method of pricing is based upon projecting past costs into the future. It is therefore difficult to take into account different situations, such as technological changes, in this method of pricing.
- The price determined by this method does not take into account the demand for the product, and it is sensible to recognise and take into account the fact that demand is determined to some extent by price. Demand for a product is determined not just by its price but also by how it is perceived by potential customers. Thus, for

example, a product which is perceived to be a luxury item will have a higher demand than a standard item in relation to its price, and this will not necessarily be dependant upon its cost of production.

● This method of pricing ignores the relationship between risk and reward. If the production of something has an element of risk attached to it, such as is the case in the introduction of a new product, then those taking that risk expect a higher reward for their risk than they would from making a safe product. This would suggest therefore that a new product with the same cost of production as an established product should have a higher price than the established product because of the higher level of risk. Cost plus pricing makes this relationship difficult to establish.

Brian Jones, the financial accountant, also advocates total cost pricing, but in his case he has related the cost to the expected demand at each price level to arrive at a calculation of the profit made at each price level. His calculation can be seen in the following table:

Demand (units)	Selling price £	Variable cost £	Fixed cost £	Profit per unit* £	Total profit** £
20,000	30	20	8	2	40,000
18,000	35	20	8	7	126,000
15,000	40	20	8	12	180,000
11,000	45	20	8	17	187,000
7,500	50	20	8	22	165,000

*   Profit per unit = Selling price – Variable cost – Fixed cost.
** Total profit = Profit per unit x Demand

In this case, we can see that a selling price of £45 does indeed result in the maximum profit from sales of the transunit and this therefore looks like an attractive price to charge. The problem with this however is that only 11,000 units of the 20,000 produced are expected to be sold at this price, leaving 9,000 carried forward as stock. The stock carried forward is valued at £28 per unit which includes £8 per unit of fixed costs. This means that £72,000 (£8 x 9,000 units) of fixed costs from the total of £160,000 have not been recovered during this period but have been carried forward in the stock valuation, to be recovered in the next period when the stock is sold. The same level of fixed costs can be expected to be incurred again during the next period and so the profit in the next period is likely to be lower.

In addition, only just over half the stock has been sold and so to meet the expected demand at this price less transunits will need to be produced (at a higher cost per unit because of the absorption of fixed costs over a smaller level of production). This illustrates therefore that profit maximisation in the short term does not necessarily lead to profit maximisation in the medium or longer term.

Contribution margin pricing

Contribution margin pricing is concerned with the contribution which a product makes towards fixed costs and profit, and is therefore concerned with the variable costs of production.

This is the basis for the price suggested by Tony Cooper, the management accountant. His calculation can be seen from the following table:

Demand (units)	Selling price £	Variable cost £	Contribution per unit* £	Total contribution £
20,000	30	20	10	200,000
18,000	35	20	15	270,000
15,000	40	20	20	300,000
11,000	45	20	25	275,000
7,500	50	20	30	225,000

* Contribution per unit = Selling price – Variable cost

From this it can be seen that a price of £40 does indeed maximise total contribution. In order to arrive at the profit made however it is necessary to deduct the fixed costs from the contribution and this can be seen from the following table:

Demand (units)	Selling price £	Total contribution £	Fixed cost £	Profit £
20,000	30	200,000	160,000	40,000
18,000	35	270,000	160,000	110,000
15,000	40	300,000	160,000	140,000
11,000	45	275,000	160,000	115,000
7,500	50	225,000	160,000	65,000

This method of pricing has the advantage over total cost pricing that all the fixed costs are charged in the period in which they occur. Against this however is the danger that considering contribution only in the pricing decision does not necessarily ensure that the fixed costs are covered. This is a particular danger in a multi-product environment where it is necessary to ensure that all the contributions from all the products do indeed cover all the fixed costs. While it is not necessary that each individual product covers a proportion of the fixed costs, or even that the fixed costs are fully covered in every single time period, it is essential for the survival of the business that in the long term all fixed cost are covered by the different contributions. Failure to do so would mean that the company would be operating at a loss and would eventually go out of business.

It can be seen therefore that contribution margin pricing is dangerous for a business to operate. It has the advantage of establishing the cost–volume–profit (CVP) relationship and relating it to price but as a pricing basis its use is essentially short-term in nature. It is a useful method to use in considering alternative uses of spare capacity or in considering whether to accept a particular contract at a particular price but is less useful as a means of deciding prices for a continuing business. Contribution margin pricing has the same disadvantage as total cost pricing in that it concentrates upon the supply side of the business and does not take into account demand.

Demand based pricing

Demand based pricing, as its name suggests, is concerned with the relationship between demand and price rather than any concern with supply. Production costs are largely irrelevant to this approach and the price set is determined by the objectives of the company. Different types of demand based pricing include the following.

Premium pricing

This is where the price of the product is set higher than that of its competitors (i.e. at a premium) on the basis that the product is of a superior nature. This may not necessarily reflect higher costs of production. For example, a Rolls Royce car is priced higher than its competitors, and while its costs of production may be higher, this is not the basis for the price setting.

Penetration pricing

This pricing policy is based upon setting a low price in order to gain rapid acceptance of a new product or rapid growth of market share. Again the price is set relative to the competition rather than relative to the costs of production.

Price skimming

This involves setting an initially high price for a new product in order to exploit those sections of the market for which demand is inelastic and for which the novelty value of a new product appeals. Price in this case will be expected to decrease once the initial demand has been met and the product is priced to appeal to a broader section of the market. Examples of this type of pricing can be found in the consumer electronics leisure market – products such as camcorders, CD players or multimedia computers – where the initial high prices are gradually lowered to broaden demand for the products.

Products made to order

If a product is made to a specific order then the product, or service, is unique and is not subject to competition. In this case, while costs are important, this is not the sole basis of pricing and uniqueness and time scale of delivery are important. Examples of this kind of product can be found in the *haute couture* part of the fashion industry or in a variety of personal service industries.

Conclusion

The pricing decision is important to the success of a company, which needs to ensure that the price set for a product or service reflects the objectives of the company. Price is set by the interaction of supply and demand but the company itself determines price, rather than market forces, and considers either supply or demand in its decision. It is not able to affect both supply and demand. While product costs are important in considering price these are not the only criterion for setting price and other factors need to be considered. Management accounting can aid the pricing decision by considering product costs and the affect of the decisions made concerning price, in terms of profit or contribution, but management accounting alone is not sufficient to determine pricing.

Summary

- Three categories of pricing method exist, namely:
    - total cost pricing
    - contribution margin pricing
    - demand based pricing.
- The objectives of the company play an important part in the determination of pricing policy.
- Pricing needs to consider not just cost but also demand and other factors such as the market and competition.
- Price equates supply with demand but the company can only manipulate price and either supply or demand.
- Management accounting has a role to play in pricing, but is not itself sufficient to enable pricing decisions to be made.

Bibliography and further reading

Drury C, *Management and Cost Accounting*, 3rd edition, Chapman & Hall 1992, (Chapter 12)

Kaplan R S and Atkinson A A, *Advanced Management Accounting*, 2nd edition, Prentice Hall 1989, (Chapter 6)

Pride W M and Ferrell O C, *Marketing*, 5th edition, Houghton Mifflin 1987, (Chapters 16 and 17)

Sizer J, *An Insight Into Management Accounting*, 3rd edition, Penguin 1989, (Chapter 12)

Self-review questions

1 What is cost plus pricing and what problems are associated with it?
(See page 143.)

2 How does the economist's view of pricing differ from the reality as applied by companies?
(See page 141.)

3 How does demand based pricing differ from other pricing methods?
(See page 146.)

4 List five possible objectives of a company in setting the price for a product.
(See page 142.)

5 When is it appropriate to use contribution margin pricing?
(See page 146.)

Additional questions

11.1 The Souvenir Co Ltd manufactures a range of commemorative and souvenir items. It intends to launch, in the next year, a stainless steel souvenir mug. This product has a variable cost of £8 per unit to produce and production capacity is available to produce up to 3,000 units per annum.

Market research shows that the product is price sensitive and the following price–demand relationship applies:

Selling price per unit £	Annual demand (units)
10	3,500
15	3,000
20	2,400
25	2,100
30	1,600
35	900

You are asked to determine the launch price which will maximise the net benefit to the company.

The company has heard a rumour that a competitor is due to launch a competing product priced at £22. How will this affect the optimum price for The Souvenir Co Ltd to charge for this product?

11.2 A company which produces motor cars has a reputation for producing high quality, stylish and technically advanced cars. It has developed a new model which is expected to demonstrate all these qualities and to compete successfully in the executive car market. The company's dealership network is excellent and servicing and spare parts operations enhance the perceived value of its vehicles. However its record of delivery of vehicles to meet the demand for them is poor, and a waiting list often develops which means that the company considers that orders are lost because of the poor availability of its products. When its last vehicle was launched demand was so great initially in relation to supply that for a period of time the value of a second-hand vehicle exceeded its price when new. The company's costing systems are excellent and provide a firm basis for its pricing decisions.

The board of directors is meeting to decide upon the pricing strategy for the vehicle and has asked you to advise on the options available to them and a possible course of action to follow.

11.3 Dash Chemicals Ltd produces two products in a single process and using the same direct labour. Standard costs and margins for these products are as follows:

	Product X £	Product Y £
Selling price	50	30
Cost of sales:		
Direct materials	7	5
Direct labour	16	8
Variable overheads	16	8
	39	21
Contribution	11	9

Fixed overheads are £50,000 and this amount is recovered on a direct labour basis using the standard capacity of 10,000 hours. Labour is charged at a rate of £8 per hour.

Capacity constraints mean that production of product Y is limited to 4,000 units and demand is expected to exceed this quantity. All of product X which can be manufactured can be sold and there is no capacity constraint.

Calculate the product mix which will maximise the profits of the company, given the capacity constraints.

11.4 Hitech Products Ltd have developed a new high-technology consumer durable product which it intends to launch onto the market immediately. A price of £149 has been set for the product which market research shows should be attractive to customers at this price.

Costs of £6 million have been incurred in developing this product. Variable costs of production are estimated to be £45 per unit and fixed costs (excluding development costs) are expected to be £250,000 in the first year. Estimated production and sales for the first year have been projected at 25,000 units.

The product has an expected production life of five years, and development costs can be expected to be recovered over this period.

(a) Calculate the unit profitability of this product based upon this information.

The managing director has read in the trade press that the public are concerned about the high level of profitability made by companies manufacturing this type of high-technology product and so the government is considering introducing a special tax. It is expected that this tax would equate to £30 per unit for this particular product.

The board of directors has considered raising prices to take account of this tax but research has shown that a price rise would affect demand for the product as follows:

price increased by full £30 – expected annual sales 5,000 units

price increased by £10 – expected annual sales 12,000 units.

(b) The board has asked you to evaluate the effects on profitability of any price rise and to recommend a price which would maximise the profit of the company from this product if the tax is imposed at the expected level.

12 The relevant costs for operational decisions

Objectives

After studying this chapter you should be able to:

- categorise costs as either relevant or irrelevant to any particular decision
- outline the factors which need to be taken into account in making decisions
- describe the principles of decision relevance
- discuss the problems associated with decision relevant costing.

Jones Ltd – a building contractor

Jones Ltd, a building contractor, proposes to tender for a contract to build a small office block. It is expected that any tender exceeding £250,000 will not be accepted. One of the company's surveyors has worked 50 hours overtime in preparing the following tender:

	£	£
Materials:		
Direct materials from stock	80,000	
Special materials	20,000	100,000
Labour:		
Direct labour –		
skilled 10,000 hours @ £10 per hour	100,000	
apprentices 2,000 hours @ £6 per hour	12,000	
Supervisory staff	20,000	132,000
Overheads:		
Production overheads	25,000	
Depreciation on equipment	10,000	
Administration overheads @ 5%	13,350	48,350
Other:		
Preparation of tender – 50 hours @ £20 per hour		1,000
Total cost		281,350

The following notes have been provided with the draft tender:

- **Materials** – direct materials from stock have been valued at original purchase price. Replacement cost would be £95,000. Special materials will be purchased as needed and are valued at cost.
- **Labour** – direct skilled labour is paid at the rate of £6 per hour with overheads being added at the rate of £4 per hour. Of the overheads, 50 per cent can be considered to be fixed and the remainder variable. All skilled labour will be recruited for this contract. Apprentices are paid at the rate of £4 per hour with £2 being added for overheads. Again 50 per cent of the overheads are considered to be a fixed cost. Apprentices are employed by the company and no additional recruitment is envisaged. Supervision will be from existing resources but it is expected that £5,000 will be incurred in extra overtime costs.
- **Overheads** – production overhead is 60 per cent fixed and 40 per cent variable. Depreciation is for existing equipment but includes £1,000 for the hire of special equipment. Administrative overhead is a fixed cost and has been charged in accordance with normal practice.
- **Preparation of tender** – this work has already been completed but incurred 50 hours of overtime in its completion.

The MD particularly wishes to make a successful tender for this contract and has asked Sarah King, the management accountant, to prepare a report and advise whether it is possible to submit a tender of less than £250,000.

Introduction

The managers of a business are regularly faced with making decisions which will affect the operations of that business. In the next chapter we will examine a selection of the types of decisions made by managers and how accounting information can be used to aid these decisions. The approach taken to making these decisions is based upon the relevance of any particular accounting information in the context of decision relevant costing. First therefore we need to identify the meaning of decision relevant costing and to examine the factors which determine relevance in any particular context.

All managers are required to make operating decisions and the need to make such decisions means that they are faced with a choice of alternative courses of action. The steps in the decision-making process therefore require the identification of the alternatives available and an evaluation of the effect of those alternatives prior to deciding upon the course of action to follow. Management accounting can assist the manager in the evaluation of alternatives but the decision made needs to be based upon the objectives of the business. This decision-making process can be modelled as shown in Figure 12.1.

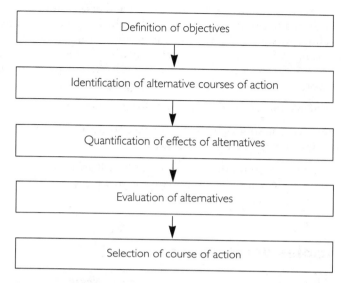

Figure 12.1 The decision-making process

In quantifying the effects of the alternative courses of action available to the business a decision relevant approach is used. This requires the classification of the costs and benefits associated with the decision into two categories:

- relevant costs and benefits
- irrelevant costs and benefits.

This classification depends upon the decision to be made and we shall see later (in Chapter 18) that it is possible for any particular cost or benefit to be relevant for one decision and irrelevant for another. In general therefore *relevance* can be defined as follows:

> Relevant costs and benefits used in the quantification of the effects of decisions are those which are determined by the selection of that particular decision. These are also known as incremental costs.

All other costs and benefits are irrelevant.

In the previous chapter we considered the classification of costs into fixed costs and variable costs, although previously (in Chapter 3) we recognised the existence of semi-fixed and semi-variable costs which contain an element of both fixed and variable costs. Decision relevant costing requires the classification of costs into fixed and variable. In this context however it is important to remember that this classification depends upon the time horizon chosen. Thus in the very long term all costs can be considered to be variable as even land and buildings can be sold or acquired and the associated costs varied. Conversely, in the very short term all costs must be regarded as fixed. Thus even direct labour, for example, is fixed in the short term as the costs of labour cannot be dispensed with without giving the people involved appropriate notice, however short that may be.

The time horizon is thus important for the classification of costs into fixed and variable and the time scale of a decision horizon is crucial to the identification of relevant costs and benefits. This time scale will vary from one decision to another and indeed the relevant costs associated with a decision will vary according to the time scale chosen. We shall see in the next chapter how a company might make one decision based upon a short time horizon but a different decision if a longer time horizon is chosen.

The general principle for setting time horizons for decision making is as follows:

> A decision relevant approach adopts whatever time horizon the decision maker considers appropriate for a given situation.

In other words, a manager must decide for him or herself an appropriate time scale for any decision to be made and so it is important that the principles of decision relevant costing are fully understood.

The principles of relevance

In seeking to identify the costs and benefits which are relevant to any particular decision the following principles should be adhered to in classifying costs and benefits as either relevant or irrelevant.

Only future costs and benefits are relevant

Any decision to be made is based in the present and will affect the future of the business. The past has already happened and cannot be affected by any decision made now. Any costs incurred in the past cannot therefore be determined by the decision to be made and so these past costs are therefore irrelevant to the current decision.

Only costs and benefits which differ between alternatives are relevant

Relevant costs and benefits are incremental costs and benefits associated with alternative courses of action. If the costs will be incurred or the benefits accrued, whatever the decision made or course of action followed, then they are not affected by the decision. Thus they are irrelevant for evaluating the alternatives available.

Only cash flows are relevant

The effects of a decision will be measured in terms of cash flows incurred or generated, rather than any notional costs. Thus overhead apportionments are not costs incurred but merely a method of allocating costs incurred elsewhere. Similarly, depreciation is not a cash flow but merely an allocation of a cost previously incurred with the purchase of the asset. Although these costs are affected by the decision made, this is only in terms of how these costs are allocated and the overall costs incurred by the business are not affected, merely internal allocations. It is for this reason that these costs are not relevant and it is only changes to cash flows which are relevant to any particular decision.

We will look at examples of decisions which illustrate these principles in the next chapter. From these principles however we can see that the costs obtained for product costing and control purposes (see Chapters 3 to 8) are not necessarily appropriate for decision making. We can see also that marginal costing provides a suitable basis for decision making but that even this costing method needs to be adapted to each particular decision in order to use decision relevant principles.

The classification of costs

Decision relevant costing requires the classification of costs into relevant and irrelevant costs, and we have seen that these can vary according to the decision to be made. Moreover it is not always readily apparent, as we shall see, which costs are relevant to a decision and which are not. It is however possible to classify costs in a variety of different ways and in order to identify relevant costs the following possible classifications are helpful:

- *Historical or replacement cost* In making a decision, future cash flows are relevant and so this would imply that replacement rather than historical cost is relevant for decision making.
- *Controllable and uncontrollable costs* If a future cost is not controllable by the business then it cannot be affected by the decision to be made. Thus only controllable costs are relevant. In this context it is important to recognise that once a course of action is initiated then the costs become committed (see below) and may cease to be controllable costs.
- *Avoidable and unavoidable costs* Some future costs are unavoidable by a business whatever decision is made while others can be avoided depending upon the course of action selected. Thus avoidable costs are relevant while unavoidable costs are irrelevant.
- *Committed and discretionary costs* If future costs have already been committed as a result of past decisions then they must be regarded as unavoidable and hence irrelevant. Future costs which have not been committed are known as *discretionary costs* and these can be either relevant or irrelevant depending upon whether or not they are affected by the current decision.
- *Differential cost* This is also known as *incremental cost* and is the change in total cost resulting from a change in activity level or a decision made. Thus the total change in relevant costs resulting from a decision is the differential cost of that decision.
- *Sunk cost* This is a cost which has already been incurred as a result of a past decision or a future cost which has been committed because of that past decision. All sunk costs are irrelevant.
- *Opportunity cost* These costs arise because of the scarcity of resources and the competing opportunities for the use of these resources. An *opportunity cost* can be defined as the benefit forgone as a result of pursuing one course of action rather than the next best alternative course of action. Opportunity costs are relevant to a decision.

Identifying decision relevant costs

In order to identify decision relevant costs let us look at the tender prepared for Jones Ltd and the figures contained in that tender.

Materials: direct materials

Direct materials have been valued at historical cost but their replacement cost is higher. It has been assumed that these materials have alternative uses in the business. Replacement cost is therefore the relevant cost. If they had no alternative use then the relevant cost to this decision would be that of the only alternative use for them, i.e. their scrap value.

Relevant cost for direct materials = £95,000

Materials: special materials

Special materials will be purchased as needed. Hence they are a discretionary cost and avoidable if the contract is not won. They are thus a relevant cost.

Relevant cost for special materials = £20,000

Labour: direct skilled labour

This will be recruited for the contract and the cost is therefore discretionary and avoidable. However the labour costs attract overheads and this can be divided into variable cost – which is avoidable if the labour is not employed – and fixed cost – which is committed and will be incurred by the company whether this labour is employed or not. The relevant costs therefore are the direct costs of the skilled labour and the associated variable overheads.

Relevant cost for direct skilled labour = £80,000

Labour: apprentices

Apprentices are already employed by Jones Ltd and hence are a committed cost; in this context they can be regarded as a fixed cost. Associated with the apprentices' costs however is a variable overhead resulting from their employment on this contract, which is therefore a discretionary cost. Thus this variable overhead is a relevant cost while the remainder is irrelevant.

Relevant cost for apprentices = £2,000

Labour: supervisory staff

The costs of these staff can be regarded as a committed fixed cost. However, additional overtime will be worked on this contract and the cost of this is a controllable cost and therefore a relevant cost.

Relevant cost for supervisory staff = £5,000

Overheads: production overheads

These can be divided into fixed and variable overheads. Again the fixed overheads are not a cash flow but merely a reallocation of other costs; they are thus irrelevant. The variable overheads however are avoidable costs and hence are relevant to this decision.

Relevant cost for overheads = £10,000

Overheads: depreciation

Depreciation on equipment is not a cash flow and hence is not relevant to the decision. Within this figure however is an amount for the hire of special equipment and this is an avoidable cost which is therefore relevant.

Relevant cost for equipment hire = £1,000

Overheads: administrative overheads

These are merely a reapportionment of costs incurred elsewhere rather than a cash flow and hence irrelevant to the decision.

Relevant cost for administration overheads = nil

Overheads: preparation of tender

Although the cost of preparation of the tender includes overtime, which is a variable cost, this cost has already been incurred. This is therefore a sunk cost and so irrelevant.

Relevant costs for tender preparation = nil

By considering individually the decision relevance of all the costs contained in the tender, Sarah King will be able to revise the tender. She suggests that the following represents the relevant costs for inclusion in the tender:

Revised tender

	£	£
Materials:		
Direct materials from stock	95,000	
Special materials	20,000	115,000
Labour:		
Direct labour		
skilled – variable cost only	80,000	
apprentices – variable cost only	2,000	
Supervisory staff – overtime only	5,000	87,000
Overheads:		
Production overheads – variable only	10,000	
Hire of equipment	1,000	1,000
Total cost		213,000

This shows therefore that the managing director of Jones Ltd would be able to submit a tender below the maximum acceptable price of £250,000 and still cover all the relevant costs. These relevant costs however assume that no alternative use exists for any of the resources to be utilised and hence there is no opportunity cost of undertaking the work. We will look at the effect of opportunity cost in the next chapter.

Factors affecting decision relevance

Although accounting information enables the quantification of the effects of the alternative decisions which can be made, this will obviously not be the sole basis for making the decision. Other factors which need to be taken into account in the decision-making process are as follows.

The value of information

The more complete and accurate the information available on which to base the decision the better will be the evaluation of the alternatives, and hence the decision made. Thus information is valuable and it is worth devoting effort to obtaining accurate and relevant information before any decision is made. It must be remembered however that there is a cost associated with obtaining information and so it is necessary to balance up the value of the information with the cost of obtaining it, and not to incur costs in excess of the value of the information obtained.

Constraints

In any situation there may well be constraints which affect the decision, or constrain the alternatives available. Examples of constraints to the decision include:

- the objectives of the business
- differences in short- and long-term evaluations
- capacity restrictions
- the economic climate.

Cost of capital

Some operating decisions involve capital expenditure, and capital is scarce in most organisations. Capital expenditure decision therefore involve the allocation of scarce resources and so the opportunity cost of capital becomes a relevant cost for the decision. We will consider capital expenditure decisions in detail in Chapter 14.

Uncertainty

Making operating decisions involves the evaluation of the future consequences of these decisions and so there is an element of uncertainty surrounding these decisions. This needs to be taken into account in the evaluation of the alternatives and an assessment of the level of risk attached to each alternative made. It is also necessary to undertake sensitivity analysis in order to assess the reliability of the quantifications obtained. We will consider the effects of uncertainty in detail in Chapter 15.

Qualitative factors

Accounting information allows the quantitative evaluation of the effects of alternative decisions but it is essential that the qualitative effects of any decision are also recognised and taken into account, even if it is not possible to evaluate these factors in accounting terms. Indeed qualitative factors may be more important in some circumstances than quantitative factors. Possible qualitative factors affecting operating decisions include:

- the effect of decisions upon staff morale
- the effect of decisions upon customers and their perceptions of the business
- the dependence of the business upon a restricted number of suppliers or customers
- future impact upon sales, particularly if repeat sales are an essential part of the business
- the impact upon capacity and constraints in operations
- customer goodwill
- staff recruitment.

Problems with decision relevant costing

Although decision relevant costing is the approach which is needed for individual operating decisions there are problems which are associated with using this approach. These can be categorised as follows.

Generalising decision making

Each individual decision is made using a decision relevant approach and identifying relevant costs. Each decision is therefore treated as a one-off, but if a succession of such decisions is made there is a danger that costs of the business, which are irrelevant to each individual decision, are ignored altogether. Thus, for example, if Jones Ltd tenders for contracts using a decision relevant approach on each occasion then some of the costs of the business, such as administrative overheads and supervisory staff costs, will never be considered as relevant, even though these costs are essential to the continuance of the business.

For long-term success all the costs of the business need to be considered and the sum of all contributions needs to cover all costs. This problem was considered in detail in Chapter 9 in the context of marginal costing. Thus decision relevant costing is appropriate for individual decisions but the long-term impact upon the business needs to be considered, particularly if a succession of one-off decisions is being made.

Availability of resources

We have mentioned the need for capital expenditure for certain decisions but we can broaden this out to consider the availability of resources generally. Although certain decision can be made which treat costs, such as labour costs, as variable, in the long term it is not generally possible to recruit labour as needed and dispense with it when not needed. In other words, the resources of the business cannot easily be increased and reduced continually to meet the fluctuating needs of the business. However, this may often be possible in the short term by using sub-contractors and employing staff on temporary contracts, and this seems increasingly to be a feature of modern business operations. The costs of the business cannot be considered to be infinitely variable in the long term, and these methods of recruiting labour are not always available, particularly if training is involved before such recruits can be useful to the business.

There is a need therefore for individual decisions to be made within the context of a longer-term plan, and those decisions need to be constrained by the longer-term objectives of the business (see Chapter 13).

Managerial acceptance

Decision relevant costing conflicts with traditional costing methods and problems of identifying relevant costs and appropriate time horizons can make this approach appear to be very subjective. This can lead to resistance from managers for accepting this approach to decision making. The problem of sunk costs also arises because if the business has invested resources in a particular course of action and especially if managers have invested their time and effort in such a course then there is a sense of ownership of that particular course of action. The decision to abandon this course, on the basis of the evaluation using decision relevant costing, can therefore meet with considerable resistance. This in turn can have an impact upon managerial performance in the future. It is important that a business manager in such a situation is aware of the politics of the situation, and the way in which any particular decision may be received by other managers involved in the decision-making process.

Conclusion

We have examined a decision relevant approach to making operating decisions and have seen that it can affect the decision made by managers. We have also seen that there can be problems with this approach and that relevant costs and benefits are determined not just by the nature of the decision to be made; they are also determined by the choice of time horizon selected by managers as appropriate to the decision. Thus choice can affect the decision which is actually made and changing the time horizon can change the decision concerning the optimum course of action to be taken.

In the next chapter we will examine a decision relevant approach to a variety of operating decisions and explore the effect upon decision making.

Summary

- Decision relevant costing is a method of assisting managers to make decision by taking into account appropriate costs and benefits. It requires that these costs and benefits be categorised as:
  - relevant
  - irrelevant.
- Decision relevant costing is only appropriate for individual decisions and not for ongoing ones.
- The time horizon chosen for evaluating the decision is crucial to that decision. Any time horizon can be chosen but should be appropriate.
- The principles of decision relevance are:
  - only future costs and benefits are relevant
  - only costs and benefits which differ between the alternatives are relevant
  - only cash flows are relevant.
- Relevant cost classifications are:
  - replacement cost
  - avoidable cost
  - discretionary cost
  - controllable cost
  - differential cost
  - opportunity cost.
- Irrelevant cost classifications are:
  - historical cost
  - uncontrollable cost
  - unavoidable cost
  - committed cost
  - sunk cost.
- Factors which need to be taken into account in the decision-making process are:
  - the value of information
  - constraints affecting the decision
  - the cost of capital
  - risk and uncertainty
  - qualitative factors.
- Problems associated with decision relevant costing are:
  - generalising the one-off nature of the decisions
  - availability of resources to meet changing needs
  - managerial acceptance and decision ownership.

Bibliography and further reading

Drury C, *Management and Cost Accounting*, 3rd edition, Chapman & Hall 1992, (Chapter 10)

Emmanuel C, Otley D and Merchant K, *Accounting for Management Control*, 2nd edition, Chapman & Hall 1990, (Chapter 6)

Lucey T, *Management Accounting*, 3rd edition, DP Publications 1992, (Chapter 13)

Sizer J, *An Insight into Management Accounting*, 3rd edition, Penguin 1989, (Chapter 4)

Self-review questions

1 Identify the appropriate time horizon to be used for decision making.
   (See page 154.)

2 Define and distinguish between relevant and irrelevant costs and benefits.
   (See page 153.)

3 Explain the three principles of decisions relevance.
   (See page 154.)

4 (a) Distinguish between committed and discretionary costs.
   (b) Explain why one type of cost is relevant and the other is irrelevant.
   (See page 155.)

5 Explain the meaning of:
   (a) sunk cost
   (b) opportunity cost
   (c) differential cost.
   (See page 155.)

6 (a) Explain why qualitative factors are important to decision making.

   (b) Suggest four types of qualitative factor which should be taken into account in the decision-making process.
   (See page 159.)

7 Explain why decision relevant costing is only appropriate for individual decisions.
   (See page 159.)

8 Explain the problems of managerial acceptance of the decision relevant costing approach.
   (See page 160.)

Additional questions

12.1 Alpha Manufacturing Co Ltd make consumer electrical goods as well as some of the components which go into their manufacture. The board is considering production levels for the next year and is particularly concerned with the production of two components, numbers 32 and 34, and two finished goods, numbers V23 and V46. Budgeted unit costs, selling prices and production levels are as follows:

Unit product costs (£)	Component 32	Component 34	Product V23	Product V46
Direct material	16	24	14	30
Direct labour	8	5	14	27
Variable overheads	6	3	8	11
Fixed overheads	18	10	16	28
Total cost	58	42	52	96
Unit selling price (£)			45	90
Production level (units)	6,000	8,000	6,000	4,000

It is possible for the company to buy in the components at the following prices:
Component 32   £50
Component 34   £30

These components are not used in the two finished products under consideration but are used in other products manufactured by the company.

The board considers that it is unprofitable to manufacture the two finished products and the manufacture of these should be discontinued. It also considers that manufacture of the two components should be discontinued and that they should be bought in.

You are asked to comment on this proposed course of action.

12.2 The Acme Refinery Co has on hand 30,000 litres of fuel oil. This oil may be sold in its present state or refined further to produce petrol. This refining takes place in the refining department which is currently operating at 80 per cent of capacity. Fuel oil currently sells for £1 per litre while petrol sells for £2 per litre

Yields from the refining process are as follows;

Petrol   75%
Residual fuel oil   10%
Loss   15%

The refinery has a capacity of 150,000 litre per period and processing costs are as follows:

80% capacity   £40,000
100% capacity   £45,000

Should the company sells the fuel oil in its present state or refine it further to produce petrol?

12.3 Amber Sports Ltd is considering introducing a new product, the Dandie, into the sporting goods market. Market research has indicated that the company could expect to sell 10,000 units of the Dandie at a price of £35 per unit.

The company accountant has however prepared a statement which indicates that it will not be profitable to introduce this product. This statement is as follows:

	£	£
Income (10,000 units @ £35)		350,000
Expenditure:		
Wages	135,000	
Salaries	12,000	
Materials	70,000	
Variable overheads	60,000	
Rent	32,000	
Head office costs	50,000	359,000
Loss		(9,000)

These figures have been prepared on the following basis:

- *Wages* This figure represents three hours per unit at a rate of £4.50 per hour. There is no surplus labour available and this need for labour will be provided by transfer of labour from another product which currently makes a contribution per labour hour of £1.

- *Salaries* This figure is made up of the salaries of two people who are currently employed by the company at a salary of £6,000 each. If the Dandie is not produce one of these people will remain employed but the other will only work part-time at a salary of £2,000 per annum.

- *Materials* This cost represents 10,000 kilograms of material X which was purchased by the company three years ago at a cost of £7 per kilogram. This material has no other use but has a scrap value of £2 per kilogram.

- *Variable overheads* This represents a cost of £6 per unit and is entirely incremental.

- *Rent* This figure represents an allocated cost of £20,000 for a part of the existing premises of the company plus an additional cost of £12,000 for additional premises required for the manufacture of this product.

- *Head office costs* Total head office costs would increase by £10,000 if the company decides to proceed with this product. The balance of the cost represents a share of total head office costs.

Should the company proceed with the manufacture of the Dandie?

13 Making operational decisions

Objectives

After studying this chapter you should be able to:

- explain the principles of decision relevance
- identify relevant costs and a time horizon for any particular decision
- calculate decision relevant costs for decision making.

Introduction

We have previously considered marginal costing (Chapter 9) and the concept of contribution towards fixed costs and profit, and have seen how this can be used in decision making to help a business manager to make different decisions to those which would be made using conventional costing methods. Decisions made on this basis can help the business in the short term. We have also extended this to consider decision relevant costing and seen that the classification of costs into relevant and irrelevant costs can help the decision-making process. The identification of relevant costs however depends upon the particular decision being made and the time horizon chosen for the decision.

In this chapter therefore we will explore such decision making in greater detail by considering a variety of different operating decisions which business managers are concerned with making. The decisions which we will consider are:

- acceptance or rejection of a special order
- making or buying in components
- deciding upon whether or not to replace existing equipment
- altering the product mix
- evaluating regional performance.

Acceptance or rejection of a special order

Alpha Company

Alpha Company produces machine components. It has a budgeted output for the next quarter of 100,000 units and orders for 80,000 units at a selling price of £27 per unit. Its estimated costs of production are:

	£000s
Direct labour	900
Direct materials	300
Variable overheads	300
Fixed overheads	600
Total cost	2,100

The company currently has no orders for the additional 20,000 units which it plans to produce but has the option to fulfil a special order for these units at a price of £18. Should the company accept the order?

Alpha Company has the possibility of selling its excess production at a special price of £18 per unit but in the short term it also has the options of producing these units for stock or producing less output and operating with spare capacity. Rejection of the special order therefore means that one of these alternatives must be selected and the decision must be made by carefully considering the alternatives.

Using absorption costing the cost of production of each unit is:

£2,100,000/100,000 = £21

This would imply rejecting the order as the cost of production exceeds the selling price.

Using this method of costing Alpha Company would not accept the special order as its costs are not covered by the selling price. Using decision relevant costing however the analysis would be different, and we can consider both a short-term analysis and a long-term one.

Short-term analysis

In the short term the capacity of the company must be regarded as fixed and so its fixed overheads cannot be influenced by the decision. These costs are therefore irrelevant.

The following assumptions are also made:

- No alternative orders exist or are expected for the excess production at a higher price.
- Accepting this order will not affect the normal selling price. Thus there are no implications as far as demand for the product is concerned from other customers. This is an important factor as the short-term decision must not impact upon the long-term operating of the company; otherwise a long-term analysis is needed.
- The special order is a once only order and will not be repeated. If the order is

expected to be repeated then a long-term analysis is needed. This special order can be viewed as a special promotional offer which could potentially lead to further orders in the future at the normal selling price.

- Direct labour is assumed to be variable and labour can be employed to produce only the number of units actually manufactured.

In considering the acceptance of this type of order it is important to determine when a company should accept it. The assumptions above discuss the possible effect on other sales and on the future of the business, and in these circumstances a longer-term analysis is appropriate. The capacity of the company is also an important consideration and we have considered capacity in Chapter 3. However, it is also important to consider the efficiency of the company in producing at different levels of capacity. Many modern production environments (see Chapter 7) require the company to operate its machinery at a certain minimum level of capacity in order to gain the economies of scale which are needed to be able to sell the products at a competitive price. In such circumstances, a company may need to produce at a level above those for which it has received orders and this will affect its decision regarding the acceptance of a special order.

The analysis therefore is as follows.

Short-term analysis

Variable cost of production

	£000s
Direct labour	900
Direct materials	300
Variable overheads	300
Total variable cost	1,500

Therefore:

Cost of producing 20,000 units is

£1,500,000/100,000 × 20,000 = £300,000

and revenue from the order would be

20,000 × £18 = £360,000

Thus the contribution to fixed overheads from fulfilling this order would be:
Revenue – variable cost

i.e.   £360,000 – £300,000 = £60,000

The company would benefit from accepting the order under this analysis.

Alternative short-term analysis

Under an alternative short-term analysis labour would be regarded as a fixed cost because it would be impossible to reduce the amount of labour employed within the factory in the short term. Direct labour would thus become a irrelevant cost.

The analysis would therefore be as follows.

Longer-term analysis

Variable cost of production

	£000s
Direct materials	300
Variable overheads	300
Total variable cost	600

Therefore:

Cost of producing 20,000 units is

£600,000/100,000 × 20,000 = £120,000

and revenue from the order would be

20,000 × £18 = £360,000

Thus the contribution to fixed overheads from fulfilling this order would be:

Revenue – Variable cost

i.e.   £360,000 – £120,000 = £240,000

The company would also benefit from accepting the order under this analysis.

Long-term analysis

In the longer term, capacity need not be regarded as fixed and it would be possible to reduce the capacity of the company and thereby reduce the fixed overheads. On this time scale therefore the fixed overheads become a controllable cost and are thus relevant.

The analysis therefore is as follows.

Long-term analysis

Revenue from the order:

20,000 x £18 = £360,000

Cost of fulfilling the order

£21 per unit x 20,000 units = £420,000

(fixed overheads have been assumed to be proportional to production)

Contribution:

£360,000 – £420,000 = (£60,000)

The order is not profitable under this analysis and would therefore be rejected.

This example illustrates the need to consider factors outside the immediate decision, such as the long-term effects of the decisions. It shows that a decision which might be beneficial in the short term would not necessarily be so in the longer term when more costs become variable. It is important therefore to recognise that decision relevant costing should only be applied to special one-off decisions and not to repeated ones.

The different effect of time scales applies equally to all the other examples in this chapter but the analysis is restricted to the short term. It should be recognised however that a business manager faced with any of these decisions would need to consider the longer-term implications of these decisions. It would also be necessary to consider non-financial issues (e.g. customer goodwill) in arriving at the decision and such a decision would not be made on the basis of accounting analysis alone.

Making or buying in components

Beta Company

Beta Company manufacture components which it uses in its manufacture of a final product. The unit cost of producing this component is:

	£
Direct labour	120
Direct materials	470
Variable overheads	60
Fixed overheads	250
Total cost	900

An outside company has provided a quote for supplying this components to the company and has quoted a price of £600 per unit. Should the company accept this quote and purchase from the outside supplier?

In this example, it is assumed that Beta Company produced a variety of components and finished products and that the particular component in question is produced in a production schedule along with other products. In this case therefore the direct labour is assumed to make this component and other products, and that the elimination of this component from the production schedule would not reduce the direct labour costs of the company but would merely spread the cost over the remaining products. In the short term therefore direct labour can be regarded as a committed fixed cost and so is not relevant to the decision.

The analysis would therefore be as follows.

In the short term fixed costs will remain unchanged and are not relevant to the decision. Additionally, in the short term direct labour costs can be treated as fixed because the company will be unable to avoid incurring these labour costs. The relevant costs for this decision therefore are:

	£
Direct materials	470
Variable overheads	60
	530

We can see therefore that Beta Company should not purchase the component from the outside supplier but should continue to manufacture it.

If however it was possible to alter the production schedule so that the excess direct labour need not be employed if this component is not produced then the direct labour would become a discretionary cost and so relevant to the decision.

In this case the analysis would be as follows.

In the short term, fixed costs will remain unchanged and are not relevant to the decision. Additionally, in the short term, direct labour costs can be treated as fixed because the company will be unable to avoid incurring them. The relevant costs for this decision are thus:

	£
Direct labour	120
Direct materials	470
Variable overheads	60
	650

Beta Company should therefore purchase from the outside supplier.

This example illustrates the importance of the correct identification of relevant costs.

If the company was operating at full capacity and was not in a position to recruit any more direct labour but could schedule production so that it either produced this component with the direct labour or more of a different product, then there would be an opportunity cost involved in using the labour for this component rather than the alternative product. If, for example, the direct labour used in the manufacture of one unit of this component could be switched to the manufacture of another product which yielded a contribution of £100 for the same number of direct labour hours, then the opportunity cost of producing one of this component would be the £100 forgone by not producing the other product. This opportunity cost is a relevant cost and needs to be included in the analysis.

In this case therefore the analysis would be as follows.

In the short term, fixed costs will remain unchanged and are not relevant to the decision. Additionally, in the short term, direct labour costs can be treated as fixed because the company will be unable to avoid incurring them. The relevant costs for this decision therefore are:

	£
Direct labour	120
Direct materials	470
Variable overheads	60
Opportunity cost of lost production	100
	750

Beta Company should therefore purchase from the outside supplier and switching direct labour to the production of the alternative product.

In making this type of decision however a company would not base its decision solely upon an analysis of relevant costs . Other factors would need to be considered. These include:

- The need to ensure *quality* is maintained if outside suppliers are used – the quality issue may be critical to the company and outweigh any financial considerations.
- The problems associated with treating *labour as a variable cost*, particularly if training is involved, were considered in Chapter 12. These considerations may affect the decision made and may mean that labour is treated as a fixed cost, even in the longer term, because of the need to retain trained staff.
- *Outsourcing* is a feature of the modern business environment and the ability to establish a long-term relationship with a supplier may be attractive.
- A *guarantee of supply* is important to a business and this may be a reason why it would wish to continue producing components itself.

Replacing old equipment

Beta Company is considering replacing some old equipment with a new machine. The costs involved are:

Cost of new machine	£12,000
(expected life of three years with zero scrap value)	
Savings in production costs from new machine	£3,000 p.a.
Disposal value of old machine	£4,000
Book value of old machine	£15,000
(expected remaining life is three years with zero scrap value)	

Should the company purchase a new machine to replace its existing one?

We have seen in our consideration of decision relevant costing that only cash flows are relevant to the decision and that depreciation is therefore not a relevant cost. In this example however we are faced with the book value of the existing machine. The book value equals the original cost less the depreciation charged to date. If this machine is kept in use then it will be depreciated over the remaining three years of its life and the depreciation charge will be £5,000 in each of the three years. If the machine is disposed of however there will be a one-off charge to the accounts of the total book value of £15,000. This will however be partly offset by the current disposal value of the machine which, if sold now, will realise £4,000. This disposal value will be a cash inflow and so relevant to the decision whereas the book value is a sunk cost and so irrelevant.

The analysis for this decision therefore is as follows.

Analysis of cash flows from the purchase of the new machine:

	£
Reduced production costs (three years)	9,000
Sale proceeds of existing machine	4,000
Purchase cost of new machine	(12,000)
Cash flow	1,000

The company will benefit from the purchase of the new machine.

Note: The book value of the existing machine will be recorded as an immediate expense if the machine is sold now but will be recorded as an expense over the next three years if the machine is kept. This cost is therefore not relevant to the decision.

Capital investment decisions will be considered in detail in Chapter 14. There is also an element of risk associated with this kind of decision and this is considered in detail in Chapter 15.

Product mix decisions

Gamma Company

Gamma Company make three products. Production requirements for each product are as follows:

	Product A	Product B	Product C
Contribution per unit (£)	15	10	12
Machine hours per unit	5	2	2
Estimated demand (units)	400	400	300

The company has a limited machine capacity of 1,500 hours and wishes to utilise this capacity to best effect. What is the most appropriate product mix?

In this example Gamma Company has a capacity constraint. In order to meet the estimated demand for all the products the following number of machine hours would be needed.

Calculation of machine hours needed to meet estimated demand:

Product	Machine hours per unit	Demand	Total machine hours
A	5	400	2,000
B	2	400	800
C	2	300	600
			3,400

Output is therefore limited by the machine capacity available and so machine hours is the limiting factor for this company (see Chapter 19). The production of each of the three products has an opportunity cost involved and that is the cost of not producing one or other of the alternative products.

When a *limiting factor* exists then a company can maximise its performance not by a consideration of the contribution per unit of each of the products but instead by concentrating upon the limiting factor and maximising the contribution per unit of the limiting factor (see Chapter 7).

In this case, the relevant benefit for the decision is the contribution per machine hour of each product, which can be calculated as follows.

Analysis of contribution per limiting factor:

	Product A	Product B	Product C
Contribution per unit (£)	15	10	12
Machine hours per unit	5	2	2
Contribution per machine hour (£)	3	5	6
Ranking of production	3	2	1
Estimated demand (units)	400	400	300

The optimum product mix therefore is that which, based upon the estimated demand for each product, maximises the contribution from the limiting factor; in this case machine capacity. Thus the highest ranked product will be produce first, up to its estimated demand, followed by the second highest ranked product. The remaining machine hours will be used to make the lowest ranked product.

This therefore can be calculated as follows.

Optimum product mix:

Product	No. of units produced	Machine hours used	Cumulative machine hours	Contribution £
C	300	600	600	3,600
B	400	800	1,400	4,000
A	20	100	20	300
	1500	1,500		7,900

Note that this analysis produces a different product mix from one based upon maximising contribution per unit, which would be as follows.

Analysis based on maximising contribution per unit:

	Product A	Product B	Product C
Contribution per unit (£)	15	10	12
Ranking of production	1	2	3
Estimated demand (units)	400	400	300

Product mix:

	No. of units produced	Machine hours used	Contribution £
Product A	300	1,500	4,500
Product B	–	–	–
Product C	–	–	–
		1,500	4,500

It can be seen therefore that the limiting factor is important in a decision and that maximising contribution per limiting factor will maximise company performance.

Evaluating regional performance

Delta Company

Delta Company operates on a regional basis and is organised into three regions. Analysis of sales and costs for each region is as follows:

	England £000s	Scotland £000s	Wales £000s
Sales	1,200	1,000	800
Variable costs	450	470	500
Fixed costs	350	300	350
Profit	400	230	(50)

The company is considering pulling out of Wales because it operate at a loss. Analysis of fixed costs however shows that some costs for each region are common to the company. The analysis of these fixed costs reveals:

	England £000s	Scotland £000s	Wales £000s
Specific fixed costs	200	150	200
General fixed costs	150	150	150
Total	350	300	350

Should the company pull out of the unprofitable Welsh region?

We will consider the evaluation of divisional performance in detail in Chapter 22, but this example is designed to illustrate the identification of relevant costs for deciding whether to pull out of a region or not. In this example, therefore, a first analysis shows that the Welsh region is operating at a loss and Delta Company is considering pulling out of it. A decision relevant costing approach, at first glance, would suggest that fixed costs are irrelevant to the decision, but further analysis of these fixed costs shows that they can be divided into those which are incurred specifically for this region, and therefore are relevant, and those which are general to the company, and therefore irrelevant to this decision.

A correct analysis therefore is as follows.

Analysis of regional profitability:

	England £000s	Scotland £000s	Wales £000s
Sales	1,200	1,000	800
Variable costs	450	470	500
Contribution to fixed costs	750	530	300
Specific fixed costs	200	150	200
Contribution to general fixed costs	550	380	100

This shows that the company would perform worse if the Welsh Region was closed and so the decision should be made to retain it. This again illustrates the need for correct identification of relevant costs and benefits in any analysis.

This example is concerned with market segmentation. *Segmentation* occurs when a market can be separated into discrete parts whichcan be kept separate from each other. This segmentation can be on the basis of geographical area, customer type, product type, or even time bands (e.g. rail off peak and peak travel). This analysis can be applied to any segmentation decision and can be used for decisions concerning adding a segment as well as for eliminating a segment.

Conclusion

All business managers are faced with making operating decisions of the kind illustrated in the above examples, and Chapter 12 covers the factors to be considered in using decision-relevant costing for these decisions and the possible problems involved. This chapter however illustrates the following key principles:

- decision relevant costing is only appropriate for short-term, one-off decisions and not to ongoing business decisions
- short-term decisions need to be considered in the context of their longer-term impact on the performance of the business
- the time horizon considered is crucial to the evaluation of the effect of any decision and can influence the decision made
- identification of relevant costs and benefits is not a simple process but correct identification is crucial to an analysis of the effects of any decision.

Summary

- Decision relevant costing is a method of assisting managers to make decision by taking into account appropriate costs and benefits. It requires that these costs and benefits be categorised as:
  - relevant
  - irrelevant.
- Decision relevant costing is only appropriate for individual decisions and not for ongoing ones.
- The time horizon chosen for evaluating the decision is crucial to that decision. Any time horizon can be chosen but should be appropriate.
- The principles of decision relevance are:
  - only future costs and benefits are relevant
  - only costs and benefits which differ between the alternatives are relevant
  - only cash flows are relevant.

Bibliography and further reading

Drury C, *Management and Cost Accounting*, 3rd edition, Chapman & Hall 1992, (Chapter 10)

Emmanuel C, Otley D and Merchant K, *Accounting for Management Control*, 2nd edition, Chapman & Hall 1990, (Chapter 6)

Lucey T, *Management Accounting*, 3rd edition, DP Publications 1992, (Chapter 13)

Sizer J, *An Insight into Management Accounting*, 3rd edition, Penguin 1989, (Chapter 4)

Self-review questions

1 Explain the difference which can result from adopting different time horizons for decision making.
(See page 167.)

2 Explain the relevance of opportunity cost for decision making.
(See page 171.)

3 Explain why book value is an irrelevant cost.
(See page 172.)

4 Explain the importance of limiting factors for decision making.
(See page 174.)

5 What is segmentation and why is it important to decision making?
(See page 176.)

6 Explain why decision relevant costing is only appropriate for individual decisions.
(See page 177.)

Additional questions

13.1 Midlands Manufacturing Ltd produces a variety of industrial engineering products, including the Corecast. The management accounts of the company show that this product was produced at a loss last year and the company is considering dropping the product from its range.

Costing data is as follows:

	£	£
Sales revenue		450,000
Cost of goods sold:		
Raw materials	100,000	
Direct labour	230,000	
Factory overhead	62,000	392,000
Gross margin		58,000
Selling expenses	41,000	
Administration expenses	40,000	81,000
Loss		23,000

Factory overhead is made up as follows:

	£
Indirect labour (fixed)	18,000
Royalties (1% of sales)	4,500
Depreciation	8,400
Other fixed cost	3,200
Other variable cost	27,900
	62,000

Selling and administration expenses comprise the following:

	Fixed cost £	Variable cost £
Selling expenses	26,000	15,000
Administration expenses	40,000	–

If this product is discontinued, fixed costs will remain unchanged apart from a reduction of £4,000 in the costs of indirect labour.

Advise the company on whether this product should be discontinued.

13.2 Direct Printing Ltd is considering replacing one of its printing presses. This press has been in use for a number of years and currently has a book value of £6,000. It has a remaining expected life of three years and will be depreciated over that period at the rate of £2,000 per year. Estimated scrap value of the machine is at present £2,000 but after another three years this scrap will have an estimated value of £300.

A new machine will cost £17,000 and will have an estimated life of five years with a disposal value at the end of this period of £2,000.

Purchasing this new machine will save production costs of £2,500 per annum.

Should the company purchase this new machine?

13.3 Betta Products Ltd manufactures one product which its sells at £45. It is currently manufacturing 120,000 of this product and its estimated costs of production are:

	£
Raw materials	2,200,000
Direct labour	1,500,000
Variable overheads	375,000
Fixed costs	650,000
	4,725,000

The company currently has spare capacity which would enable it to produce an extra 30,000 units without affecting its fixed costs.

A retailing organisation has approached the company and asked it to supply 20,000 units but is only willing to pay a price of £36 per unit.

(a) Should Betta Products Ltd accept this order?
(b) What factors need to be taken into account in making this decision?

14 Making capital expenditure decisions

Objectives

After studying this chapter you should be able to:

- outline the differences between capital expenditure decision and short-term decisions
- describe the main methods of evaluating investment proposals
- evaluate capital investment proposals using any of these methods
- describe the other factors needed to be considered in any evaluation
- outline the features of life cycle costing
- describe the main ways of allocating resources.

Flatpack Furniture Ltd – the manufacturer of self-assembly furniture

Flatpack Furniture Ltd is a subsidiary of a major multinational. The subsidiary company manufactures and sells self-assembly furniture. The board is considering investing in new equipment which will increase the production capability of the company. This new equipment has a capital cost of £1,000,000 and an expected life of five years. At the end of this period the equipment will have a nil residual value.

If the new equipment is purchased, it is expected that additional sales revenue of £700,000 per annum will be generated from the increased production. Variable costs of production account for 65 per cent of total sales revenue and this will be unchanged if the new equipment is purchased.

Flatpack Furniture Ltd has been set a target return on capital employed of 20 per cent by its parent company (see later). This target is based upon the net book value of the assets employed at the beginning of each year. The company has a cost of capital of 15 per cent.

The board is undecided whether or not to invest in this new equipment and has asked David Leigh, the company's management accountant, to advise them on the implications of the decision.

Introduction

In the previous chapters we have considered how accounting can help the business manager in making operating decisions. These decisions are essentially short-term in nature. We now turn to an examination of making capital investment decisions, and these decision are long-term in nature. The expenditure incurred in making capital investment may be incurred over a short period of time, such as in Flatpack Furniture Ltd's consideration of new equipment, or may be incurred over a longer period of time, such as if a new factory is to be built. The distinguishing feature of capital investment decisions however is the time scale over which the benefits can be expected to accrue, and this takes place over an extended period running into years.

The new equipment being considered by Flatpack Furniture Ltd will accrue benefits over the next five years until the life of the equipment is exhausted. A new factory however can be expected to last for a much longer period and give benefits throughout that period. Thus capital investment decisions involve incurring costs in the present and immediate future, in the expectation of accruing benefits in the future. Analysing such decisions therefore requires not just a calculation of the costs and benefits arising from the decision but also an evaluation based upon time scales and taking into account when costs will be incurred and benefits can be expected to accrue.

An example of a particularly long-term investment is the decision to build the Channel Tunnel. Evaluating this proposal involved calculating the costs of the investment, which were spread over several years, and then calculating the revenue, which was expected to arise over an even longer period. With such a long time scale to consider there is obviously an element of risk attached to investing in this project, and we will consider risk in Chapter 15. In this chapter, however, we consider methods of evaluating such an investment proposal. These methods remain the same whatever the size of the investment and whatever the expected time scale involved.

Another factor which influences business decisions regarding capital investment is the effect of tax regulations upon the decision. These regulation can affect such decisions because the extent to which capital allowances are given and the timing of the tax payments on costs incurred can make a significant difference to a business in deciding when and how to undertake capital investment. The effect of taxation on such decisions is a complex subject which is outside the scope of this book. We shall therefore ignore taxation effects in our consideration of capital investment decisions.

Capital budgeting

All businesses need to incur capital expenditure at some time, whether it is a small plumber buying a new van, Flatpack Furniture Ltd buying new equipment, or a retailer building a new hypermarket. Capital investment in a business is essential both to replace existing assets as they become worn out (and fully depreciated) and to provide additional assets in order to improve the performance of the business. This improved performance can be in terms of reduced costs of production, increased quality, increased output, or changes in the product mix. It is important therefore that capital expenditure proposals are considered in the context of the objectives of the organisation and its long-term plan, in order to ensure that any proposed expenditure helps the business to achieve its objectives.

Whatever the size of a business, capital investment will represent significant activity by the business and will involve committing a significant proportion of the resources of the business to the investment. It is also likely that the investment, once committed to, will be irreversible, or at least the costs of changing the decision will be substantial. As each investment decision is so important to the business in terms of the resources involved, making capital investment decisions are very important to the business and a detailed analysis of costs and benefits is needed before a decision is made. Although each such decision is an individual one, and made on its own merits, its consequences can impact upon the business in other areas.

We have seen previously that a business operates in an environment of scarce resources and that there are competing uses for those resources. This is equally true of the resources available for capital investment and a business is likely to have a variety of proposals for capital expenditure, all of which will improve its performance. The available resources however are unlikely to be sufficient to undertake all possible investments which will improve performance, and so some form of selection is needed in order to decide which to undertake and which to defer or cancel. One effect of a capital expenditure decision therefore is that it excludes the possibility of undertaking alternative investments.

Capital investment naturally involves expenditure and this needs to be incorporated into the budgeting process (see Chapters 2 and 19) in order to be able to calculate the effects of the expenditure on the cash flow of the business. This expenditure also needs to be financed through cash inflows and these can be either through raising finance externally (i.e. borrowings or share issues), or internally through using the profits generated from the company's trading activities or cash generated from the sale of other assets. In practice, a combination of externally raised funds and internally generated funds may well be used but budgeting for the capital expenditure is necessary in order to plan for the extent of the commitment involved and for its timing.

Life cycle costing

All capital investment decisions involve expenditure in the acquisition of the asset but they also involve a commitment to future expenditure in using the asset. In order to plan capital investment effectively it is important to recognise this and to incorporate both acquisition and operating costs into the evaluation. Thus, for example, an asset which has a high acquisition cost but low operating costs may be more effective for a business than one which has a low acquisition cost but high operating costs. An evaluation of capital investment based solely on acquisition costs will not take this into account and the most effective decision may not be made.

Evaluating capital investment decisions in this manner is known as *life cycle costing, or terotechnology*. It is defined by the Chartered Institute of Management Accountants as:

> The practice of obtaining over their life-times, the best use of physical assets at the lowest cost to the entity. This is achieved through a combination of management, financial, engineering and other disciplines.

The costs incurred over the full life cycle of an asset are the following:

- acquisition costs (e.g. research and development, purchase price, installation and testing)
- operating costs (e.g. maintenance, energy, spares, training)
- ongoing capital costs (e.g. equipment upgrades, modifications)
- disposal costs (e.g. demolition, salvage, site reclamation).

Life cycle costing takes into account all of the costs associated with an asset in the evaluating of capital expenditure proposals.

Allocating scarce resources between capital investment proposals

Given that a company will have insufficient resources to undertake all the capital investment options available to it, there is a need to identify those which are the most important for it to undertake. This involves an evaluation of the costs and benefits of each option in order to determine its attractiveness, and there are a variety of techniques for doing this which we will examine later. First however we need to recognise that there are constraints on capital investment which might exist for a company, and which provide a mechanism for an initial screening of capital investment proposals. These are as follows.

Capital rationing

Capital rationing exists when there is an absolute limit to the amount of capital expenditure which can be undertaken by a business in any particular period of time. This limit may be imposed through outside constraints, such as the inability to raise funds through the financial markets: this is known as *hard capital rationing*. Alternatively, this limit may be imposed internally within the company: this is known as *soft capital rationing*. This limit may be determined by the finite borrowing limit available to the business. Alternatively, this limit may be externally imposed.

Thus the parent company of Flatpack Furniture Ltd may determine a limit to the amount of capital expenditure which Flatpack Furniture Ltd can undertake in any one period. Externally imposed limits are currently a feature of British local government whereby maximum levels of capital expenditure are set by central government. The existence of a limited supply of capital for investment means that a business must select between the alternatives available to it. In doing so, it will select those alternatives which give the best returns. This therefore implies that a ranking of alternatives is needed in order to determine priorities to arrive at the most effective investments for the business to undertake with the limited supply of capital available.

Target returns

An alternative method used by businesses to initially screen investment proposals is to set a target return which the proposal must achieve in order for it to be considered. This can be set internally within the business or imposed from elsewhere. Thus for Flatpack Furniture Ltd the parent company has imposed a target on it which has been set as 20 per cent of *return on capital employed (ROCE)* (see Chapter 22). Such a target provides a criterion for the initial evaluation of capital investment proposals and any proposal which fails to project such a return will be rejected by the company as it will not help it to meet its target ROCE. Such a rejection process provides a means of initially screening investment proposals. Those which meet the target will either be accepted if the resources available to the business are sufficient to meet all the proposals, or will be subject to further evaluation to decide between alternatives if the total resources are insufficient for all proposals.

In the case of Flatpack Furniture Ltd a target has been set in term of ROCE but it is possible to set a target in terms of any of the evaluation methods available to a business.

Methods of depreciation

When a capital investment has been undertaken it is included as an asset in the balance sheet of the business. Because it has a finite life however it will be depreciated over the expected life of that asset. Thus the equipment being considered for purchase by Flatpack Furniture Ltd has an expected life of five years and will be depreciated over that period. There are two main methods of depreciating an asset which we will consider here, although other methods exist. These two methods are:

● straight line depreciation
● annuity depreciation.

Straight line depreciation

The *straight line method of depreciation* is based on depreciating the capital cost of the investment in equal instalments throughout its life.

> For Flatpack Furniture Ltd the depreciation charge for the new equipment would be:
>
> | | |
> |---|---|
> | Capital cost of equipment | £1,000,000 |
> | Life of asset | 5 years |
> | Annual depreciation charge | £1,000,000/5 = £200,000 |

Annuity depreciation

The *annuity method of depreciation* takes into account both the capital cost of the investment and the cost of capital associated with that investment. Its aim is to equalise the total cost of the investment, in terms of principal sum and interest, throughout the life of the investment. The annual depreciation charge will thus vary from year to year. This charge is calculated based upon the use of an *annuity factor,* which can be found from the table given in Appendix A.

For Flatpack Furniture Ltd the calculation would be as follows:

Capital cost of equipment   £1,000,000
Life of equipment   5 years
Cost of capital   15%

The annuity factor is   3.352

Thus the depreciation charge can be calculated as follows:

Annual payment = Capital cost ÷ Annuity factor
                = £1,000,000 ÷ 3.352
                = £298,300

The calculation is as follows:

Year	Annual payment	Interest charge	Capital payment	Capital outstanding at end of year
	£	£	£	£
1	298,300	150,000	148,300	851,700
2	298,300	127,755	170,545	681,155
3	298,300	102,173	196,127	485,028
4	298,300	72,754	225,546	259,482
5	298,300	38,918	259,482	—

Where:

Interest charge = Capital outstanding at end of previous year x
                    Cost of capital (15%)

Capital payment = Annual payment – Interest charge

Note: capital payment equals the annual depreciation charge.

The annuity method of depreciation seeks to take into account the time value of money. The two methods of depreciation have quite different effects as far as evaluating capital investment proposals is concerned. We will go on to consider these effects.

Evaluating capital investment proposals

All capital investment proposals need to be evaluated in order to assess the net benefit to the business of undertaking the investment. A variety of methods of evaluation are available to the business. These are:

- payback
- return on investment
- accounting rate of return
- residual income
- net present value
- internal rate of return.

Payback

The *payback method* is the simplest method of evaluating a capital investment proposal. Research has shown that it is the most frequently used method in the UK for capital investment appraisal. *Payback* is expressed in term of time and is simply the length of time required for the stream of cash benefits from an investment to recover the initial cash outlay.

Thus for Flatpack Furniture Ltd this would be calculated as follows:

Capital cost of equipment   £1,000,000
Annual increase in revenue   £700,000
Annual net increase in cash flow
  = Increase in revenue – Increase in costs
  = £700,000 – (£700,000 x 65%)
  = £245,000

Payback period = $\dfrac{\text{Total capital cost}}{\text{Annual net cash flow}}$

  = £1,000,000/£245,000
  = 4 years and 1 month

This method of evaluation would indicate that the investment should be made if a target payback period of greater than four years one month is used but not if a lesser period is used.

It should be noted that the longer the payback period which is forecast by the analysis the greater is the level of risk involved in the investment. The question of risk will be considered in detail in Chapter 15.

Return on investment

Return on investment (ROI) is calculated as the total cash benefits from the investment expressed as a percentage of the cost of the investment. It is measured on a year by year basis.

Thus for Flatpack Furniture Ltd, ROI would be calculated as follows.

Using the straight line method of depreciation:

Year	Capital outstanding at start of year £	Net cash flow £	ROI %
1	1,000,000	245,000	24.5
2	800,000	245,000	30.6
3	600,000	245,000	40.8
4	400,000	245,000	61.2
5	200,000	245,000	122.5

Using the annuity method of depreciation:

Year	Capital outstanding at start of year £	Net cash flow £	ROI %
1	1,000,000	245,000	24.5
2	851,700	245,000	29.8
3	681,155	245,000	36.0
4	485,028	245,000	50.5
5	259,482	245,000	94.4

With a target ROCE of 20 per cent set for the company this evaluation indicates that the investment should be made.

We can see from the above that the annuity method differs in its calculation of ROI in that it tends to average out the ROI year by year. Nevertheless, there is a tendency for the ROI to increase year by year as the book value of the asset diminishes.

Accounting rate of return

ROI has the problem of the rate of return varying from one year to the next and this makes it difficult to compare alternative projects with differing rates of return through-out the life of the investments. For example, in the case of Flatpack Furniture Ltd this return varies between 24.5 per cent and 122.5 per cent. Because of this problem this technique is normally used in its modified form – *accounting rate of return (ARR)*. This is calculated as follows:

$$\text{ARR} = \frac{\text{Average net cash inflow}}{\text{Average net investment}}$$

where these averages are taken as the average over the expected life of the project.

Thus:

$$\text{Average net cash flow} = \frac{\text{(Incremental cash flow/Incremental costs)}}{\text{Expected life of the project}}$$

and

Average net investment

$$= \frac{\text{(Total cost of investment} - \text{Residual value at end of life)}}{\text{Expected life of the project}}$$

Thus for Flatpack Furniture Ltd this would be calculated as follows.

Using the straight line method of depreciation:

Average net cash flow
= (Incremental cash flow/Incremental costs)

      Expected life of the project

= £245,000

Average net investment
= (Total cost of investment − Residual value at end of life)

      Expected life of the project

= (£1,000,000 + £800,000 + £600,000 + £400,000 + £200,000 − 0)

                 5

= £600,000

ARR = Average net cash inflow

       Average net investment

   = £245,000

     £600,000

  = 40.8%

Using the annuity method of depreciation:

Average net cash flow = (Incremental cash flow/Incremental costs)

                    Expected life of the project

          = £245,000

Average net investment
= (Total cost of investment − Residual value at end of life)

      Expected life of the project

= (£1,000,000 + £851,700 + £681,155 + £485,028 + £259,482 − 0)

                 5

= £655,473

$$ARR = \frac{\text{Average net cash inflow}}{\text{Average net investment}}$$

$$= \frac{£245,000}{£655,473}$$

$$= 37.4\%$$

With a target ROCE of 20 per cent set for the company this evaluation indicates that the investment should be made.

Both ROI and ARR have the disadvantage that they ignore the time value of money. The *time value of money* means that expenditure incurred at the present time costs more than expenditure incurred in the future, and the further into the future the expenditure is incurred the less is the cost. Equally, the closer to the present that income is received the greater is its value. This is because a company has alternative uses for all of its funds and so incurring expenditure in the present prevents an alternative use of these funds. In practice, the alternative use of any cash is considered to be the return which could be achieved from investing the cash and the time value of money can be equated to the opportunity cost of that money. Using these methods of evaluation therefore mean that projects with the same average inflow would be evaluated as the same, even if the inflows for one project occurred mostly early in the life of the project while for the other they occurred mostly in the later life of the project.

Residual income

We will consider residual income (RI) as a means of evaluating divisional performance in detail in Chapter 22. In this context however *residual income* is the net cash flow from a project less a charge for cost of capital. Thus:

Residual income = Net cash flow from project − cost of capital employed

Residual income can be used to evaluate capital investment proposals by calculating the residual income from the proposal for each year and then summing to find the total net residual income. If the calculation shows a net positive residual income then the investment proposal adds value to the company.

Thus for Flatpack Furniture Ltd residual income is calculated as follows.

Using straight line method of depreciation:

Year	Capital outstanding at start of year £	Net cash flow £	Cost of capital (@ 15%) £	Residual income £
1	1,000,000	245,000	150,000	95,000
2	800,000	245,000	120,000	125,000
3	600,000	245,000	90,000	155,000
4	400,000	245,000	60,000	185,000
5	200,000	245,000	30,000	215,000

Using the annuity method of depreciation:

Year	Capital outstanding at start of year £	Net cash flow £	Cost of capital (@ 15%) £	Residual income £
1	1,000,000	245,000	150,000	95,000
2	851,700	245,000	127,755	117,245
3	681,155	245,000	102,173	142,827
4	485,028	245,000	72,754	172,246
5	259,482	245,000	38,922	206,078

Any positive residual income indicates that the investment adds value for the company and should therefore be undertaken.

Although residual income takes into account the cost of capital it does not take into account the time value of money. One problem with most investments is that the expenditure is incurred at the start of the project while the benefits accrue at a later date. This can mean that the residual income of a project in its early period may well be negative, even though the overall residual income is positive. When targets are set in terms of residual income then a project with a negative residual income in its early years may well be rejected as failing to meet the target even though it is ultimately beneficial to the business.

Net present value

In order to take into account the time value of money it is necessary to undertake an evaluation which recognises that the further in the future a cash inflow occurs the less value it has to the business. Such techniques are based upon the *discounted cash flow technique*. This is a technique which attempts to calculate the present value of a future cash flow. It requires the use of a *discounting rate* to calculate the present value. This discounting rate equates to the rate of return which can be expected from an investment, and thus it is normal to use the cost of capital as a discounting rate.

For Flatpack Furniture Ltd a discounting rate of 15 per cent would be used.

The present value of a future cash flow can be calculated from the following formula:

$$pv = \frac{fv_n}{(1 + k)^n}$$

where:

pv = present value
fv_n = future cash flow for the year
n = the number of periods in the future
k = discounting rate (in decimal form)

Present values can be calculated using this formula but can also be calculated using the discounting factor tables (see Appendix A).

The *net present value (NPV)* of an investment is arrived at by discounting all future cash inflows and outflows to arrive at present values and then summing to give the net present value.

For Flatpack Furniture Ltd this would be calculated as follows:

Net cash outflow: Year 0 = £1,000,000

Net cash inflow:

Year	Net cash flow £	Discount factor (@ 15%)	Net present value £
1	245,000	0.870	213,150
2	245,000	0.756	185,220
3	245,000	0.658	161,210
4	245,000	0.572	141,140
5	245,000	0.497	121,765
	1,225,000		822,485

NPV =   Discounted net cash inflow – discounted net cash outflow

  =   £822,485 – £1,000,000
  =   (£178,515)

When the cash flows are discounted this demonstrates that the proposed purchase does not result in a benefit for the company, using the current cost of capital. This indicates that the investment should not be undertaken.

While NPV is a method of investment appraisal which takes into account the time value of money, the value of the calculation is dependent upon the discounting factor selected. Changing this factor can alter the respective NPV's of alternative investments and so lead to a different decision being made. The choice of discount factor by the business is therefore of crucial importance in the evaluation of capital expenditure proposals and needs to reflect the opportunity cost of capital. In practice, a business often uses a calculation known as the *weighted average cost of capital (WACC)* which is a calculation which reflects this opportunity cost and is derived from a calculation of the alternative uses of capital throughout the business.

Internal rate of return

Internal rate of return (IRR) is an alternative techniques which also takes into account the time value of money. IRR represents the true interest earned by an investment over its life. It therefore equates to the discounting rate, causing the NPV of a project to be zero.

IRR can be found by an iterative process – using a number of different discount rates until one is found for which the NPV equals zero.

For Flatpack Furniture Ltd this might be calculated as follows.

Using a discounting rate of 6 per cent:

  Net cash outflow: Year 0 = £1,000,000

Net cash inflow:

Year	Net cash flow £	Discount factor	Net present value £
1	245,000	0.943	231,035
2	245,000	0.890	218,050
3	245,000	0.840	205,800
4	245,000	0.792	194,040
5	245,000	0.747	183,015
	1,225,000		1,031,930

NPV = Discounted net cash inflow – Discounted net cash outflow
    = £1,031,930 – £1,000,000
    = £31,930

Using a discounting rate of 10 per cent:

Net cash outflow: Year 0 = £1,000,000

Net cash inflow:

Year	Net cash flow £	Discount factor	Net present value £
1	245,000	0.909	222,705
2	245,000	0.826	202,370
3	245,000	0.751	183,995
4	245,000	0.683	167,335
5	245,000	0.621	152,145
	1,225,000		928,550

NPV = Discounted net cash inflow – Discounted net cash outflow
    = £928,550 – £1,000,000
    = (£71,450)

Interpolating the two values:

£31,930 + £71,450 = £105,380

Therefore:

IRR = 5 + (£31,390/£105,380 x 5)
    = 7.2%

Note: further iterations would be used to obtain a more accurate approximation.

However, because the cash flows in this case are equal for each year we can calculate the IRR by using the table in Appendix A in conjunction with the following formula:

$$\text{Discounting factor} = \frac{\text{Investment cost}}{\text{Annual cash flow}}$$

For Flatpack Furniture Ltd this would be calculated as follows:

$$\text{Discounting factor} = \frac{\text{Investment cost}}{\text{Annual cash flow}}$$
$$= \frac{£1,000,000}{£245,000}$$
$$= 4.082$$

From the tables (see Appendix A) this shows a rate of return of slightly in excess of 7 per cent.

Therefore IRR = 7%

With a cost of capital of 15 per cent then a rate of return of 7 per cent from this investment indicates that the investment should not be undertaken.

Calculating the internal rate of return can be a tedious process but fortunately the use of computers, or even programmable calculators, makes such a calculation a realistic possibility for investment appraisal, even for large and complex proposals.

The IRR also has a technical problem associated with it. Most projects have a net cash outflow at the start of the project and this is followed by a stream of net cash inflows. However, if circumstances are difference and some of the future years also have net cash outflows then the calculation will produce more than one value for the IRR. Care must be taken in interpreting results in such a situation. Techniques have been developed to overcome this problem; these are outside the scope of this book. You should however be aware of this technical problem.

Conclusion

We have looked at a variety of methods of evaluating capital investment proposals, each of which has advantages and disadvantages. In practice, each of these methods is used by business managers to evaluate proposals, although the payback method is the most commonly used in the UK. We can see from the calculations for Flatpack Furniture Ltd that some methods of evaluation indicate that the proposed investment is attractive and should be undertaken, while other methods indicate that the investment is unattractive and should not be undertaken. One of the problems of capital investment appraisal therefore is in determining the method of evaluation to be used and the appropriate assumptions to make. This can lead to quite different conclusions being drawn concerning the benefit to be derived from any investment opportunity. It is perhaps for this reason that many companies opt for payback, as the simplest method.

It is important to recognise that, although capital investment will not normally be undertaken without an evaluation using one or other of these methods, this will not be the sole basis for appraising capital investment proposals and the decision between alternatives will not be made solely on the basis of this evaluation. Other factors which need to be considered are:

- the objectives of the business
- availability of finance in terms of quantity and timing
- cash flow effects and their incorporation into the overall cash budget
- qualitative factors and non-quantifiable costs and benefits.

Not all factors can be described completely in financial terms and these non-quantifiable factors may be of significant importance to the value of the investment. Possible non-quantifiable benefits can be classed as:

- *social benefits* – for example, the provision of a new canteen for workers or the provision of a visitors centre
- *ethical benefits* – for example, the provision of new safety facilities in the production environment or investment to reduce pollution.

These types of investment will have financial aspects which can be incorporated into the analysis. They may also have future benefits in terms of sales or customer relations. There will remain however a non-quantifiable element and this may outweigh the financial factors in the decision-making process.

We can see that accounting can help the business manager to make capital investment decisions but that accounting alone does not lead to an appropriate method of optimising decision making.

Summary

- Capital investment decisions are long-term decisions and involve incurring costs in the present for expected future benefits.
- Capital expenditure involves significant use of resources and these needs must be calculated and incorporated into the budgeting process. It is also necessary to consider the financing of capital expenditure.
- Life cycle costing (terotechnology) provides a means of evaluating proposals taking into account not just the initial cost but also the ongoing costs of any investment.
- Resources for capital investment are scarce and ways of allocating resources are:
  - capital rationing
  - setting target returns.
- The two methods of depreciating assets are:
  - straight line depreciation
  - annuity depreciation.
- The methods of evaluating proposals are:
  - time based method: payback
  - return based methods: return on investment; accounting rate of return; residual income
  - time value of money methods: net present value; internal rate of return.
- The most commonly used method in the UK is the payback method. Each method has strengths and drawbacks and can give different evaluations, depending upon the assumptions made.
- Any evaluation of a capital investment proposal needs to take into account other factors as well as an accounting based evaluation of costs and benefits.

Bibliography and further reading

Drury C, *Management and Cost Accounting*, 3rd edition, Chapman & Hall 1992, (Chapters 14 and 15)

Emmanuel C, Otley D and Merchant K, *Accounting for Management Control*, 2nd edition, Chapman & Hall 1990, (Chapter 12)

Lucey T, *Management Accounting*, 3rd edition, DP Publications 1992, (Chapters 17 and 18)

Sizer J, *An Insight into Management Accounting*, 3rd edition, Penguin 1989, (Chapter 8)

Self-review questions

1 Explain the effects of capital investment on the budgeting process.
(See page 182.)

2 What is terotechnology and why is it significant for the evaluation of capital investment proposals? What are the main types of costs incurred during the life of an asset?
(See page 182.)

3 Explain the meaning and significance of capital rationing in the allocation of resources.
(See page 183.)

4 Describe the alternative methods of asset depreciation.
(See page 184.)

5 What is the most commonly used method of evaluating capital expenditure proposals?
(See page 186.)

6 Explain why the time value of money is significant in considering capital expenditure.
(See page 189.)

7 Contrast the respective merits and disadvantages of the following methods of evaluation:
(a) residual income
(b) accounting rate of return
(c) internal rate of return.
(See page 187 onwards.)

Additional questions

14.1 Rubber Fabrications Ltd is planning to introduce a new product which would require the acquisition of new machinery. This new machinery will cost £300,000 and will have a life of five years. At the end of this period there will be no scrap value for the machinery. It is company policy to depreciate machinery using a straight line basis.

The new machinery will be installed in an existing building on the site which is currently used for the storage of raw materials. This would mean that additional storage space would need to be acquired and suitable storage can be leased at a cost of £20,000 per annum payable in arrears. Rental costs on the building to be used for the new machinery is currently £15,000 per annum.

The new product would generate sales of £750,000 per annum for a production cost of £575,000. In addition the company would incur selling costs of £25,000 per annum.

You are required to evaluate this investment using:
(a) payback period
(b) accounting rate of return
(c) internal rate of return.

14.2 The engineering department of Byrne Baron Ltd wishes to introduce new operating methods into the production process. This would involve capital expenditure of £350,000 on new equipment but would reduce annual production costs from £825,000 to £775,000.

The equipment would have an estimated useful life of ten years with no scrap value at the end of the period. This equipment would be depreciated on a straight line basis.

The company will approve the purchase of the new equipment if it produces a rate of return on investment exceeding 20 per cent and a payback period of less than six years.

Should the proposal be accepted?

14.3 Machin Distribution Ltd is considering undertaking an investment in new warehouse handling equipment. This equipment will cost £200,000 and have an expected life of ten years. The equipment would be depreciated, in accordance with company policy, using a straight line basis and would have no salvage value at the end of its life. Materials handling cost would be reduced by using this new equipment from £275,000 per annum to £255,000. The company uses a weighted average cost of capital of 15 per cent in evaluating its investments.

You are asked to calculate the following for the proposal:
(a) residual income
(b) net present value
(c) accounting rate of return.

14.4 The Luxury Tailoring Co Ltd sell high quality men's clothing. The company is considering making some capital investment in its warehouse stock control systems. The board has details of two alternative projects which seem to be attractive, and has asked you to advise which one is the most suitable for the company, based upon its normal evaluation techniques of payback and ARR.

Details of the projects are as follows:

	Option 1 **£000s**	**Option 2** **£000s**
Initial cost	80	60
Reduced annual running costs:		
Year 1	20	25
Year 2	25	15

	Option 1 £000s	Option 2 £000s
Year 3	25	15
Year 4	30	15
Estimated residual value	nil	nil

Reduced cost has been calculated after deduction of depreciation, using a straight line basis, over the four year life expectancy of the investment.

The board has also asked you to advise it as to the best way of evaluating these alternative investments.

15 The effects of risk and uncertainty

Objectives

After studying this chapter you should be able to:

- explain the meaning of risk and uncertainty
- construct a probability distribution and calculate expected values
- perform sensitivity analysis
- describe people's differing attitudes to risk
- outline alternative decision-making criteria
- describe the role of portfolio theory in risk reduction.

The Anytown Dance Group – planning a dinner dance

The Anytown Dance Group, a registered charity, is celebrating its 25th anniversary this year. For each of its previous year's existence it has held an annual dinner dance with the primary purpose of raising funds. The committee wishes to hold a dinner dance again this year but there is concern that the economic climate is such that it may adversely affect both the number of tickets which the group is able to sell and the selling of advertising space in the programme.

The Treasurer has reported that the costs and revenues for this year, if the dinner dance were to be held, are likely to be as follows:

	£
Costs:	
Dinner dance:	
Hire of town hall	2,000
Hire of band	3,000
Food @ £15 per person	
(based on a guaranteed minimum of 450 people)	
Prizes for raffle and competitions	1,100
Hire of photographer	250
Programme production:	
Fixed cost of £2,500 plus £20 per page of content	

	£
Revenues:	
Dinner dance:	
Ticket price (per person)	28
Average raffle sales per person	6
Average photography sales per person	3
Programme:	
Advertising revenue per page	100

These figures are based upon past experience updated for current prices.

The Treasurer has also reported that the past attendance at the dinner dance has been:

Number of tickets sold	Number of occasions
300–399	5
400–499	7
500–599	9
600–699	3
	24

The number of programme advertising pages sold has been, in the past:

Number of pages sold	Number of occasions
28	6
32	5
36	4
40	7
44	2
	24

The committee have had an offer of some market research to estimate the likely attendance at this year's event and the likely amount of advertising revenue which could be expected. This market research would cost £1,000.

The committee need to make a decision at its next meeting as to whether or not to take advantage of this market research. They would also like an indication of the revenue they could expect if they decided to go ahead with the dinner dance this year.

Introduction

We have seen that managerial decision making involves deciding between alternative courses of action. Managers do this by forecasting the outcomes from each of the alternatives available to them and then deciding upon the appropriate course of action to follow. Thus decision making involves forecasting the future effects of a present decision and there is therefore an element of uncertainty involved in the forecast, and a level of risk attached to any decision made. A manager's job is to reduce the level of risk and uncertainty involved in decision making in order that the forecasting of outcomes provides as reliable a basis as possible for making the decisions.

The theoretical distinction is normally made between risk and uncertainty, and the two are defined as follows.

Risk

This term is used to apply to a situation where there are several possible outcomes but past experience, or research, provides statistical evidence which enables the prediction of possible outcomes.

Uncertainty

This term is used to apply to a situation where there is no evidence to enable the possible outcomes to be predicted.

> For the Anytown Dance Group we can see that past experience provides evidence to project possible outcomes from the decision to hold a dinner dance, and so there is risk attached to the decision. There is however also some uncertainty attached to the decision because of the changed economic climate, which means that any prediction based upon past experience may not be reliable. In practice, an element of both risk and uncertainty will apply to most decisions.

In decision making it is desirable to reduce uncertainty surrounding the decision and thus enable the forecasting of outcomes to be more reliable. This suggests that the more information that is available the more likely is the uncertainty surrounding a decision to be reduced. Information therefore has a value, as we have seen previously. There is also a cost involved in obtaining that information, and to be of benefit the value of the information obtained must exceed the costs of obtaining it. Later in this chapter we will look at ways of quantifying this value of information in order to decide whether or not it is beneficial to obtain additional information.

Reducing uncertainty however can be achieved not just through the acquiring of additional information; it can also be achieved through the quantification of existing information, and the converting of it into expected outcomes. This is effected through the use of statistical techniques based upon probability theory.

Probability and expected values

The likelihood of an event occurring is known as its *probability*, and this is expressed in decimal form with a value ranging between 0 and 1. A value of 0 indicates that an event will not occur while a value of 1 indicates a certainty that the event will occur. Probabilities range between these two absolutes and thus a probability of 0.2 indicates that an event is expected to occur on 2 occasions out of 10. When a range of possible outcomes exists and a probability can be assigned to each of them then the sum of the probabilities for all possible outcomes must equal 1. This is because one of the possible outcomes *must* occur.

When a range of possible outcomes exists for an event it is possible to construct a probability distribution showing the range of outcomes with their associated probabilities. When making managerial decisions therefore this is one way of reducing uncertainty, through evaluating the likelihood of each outcome occurring and constructing a probability distribution. For business decisions it must be recognised that this is a subjective process based upon a manager's past experience, his or her expert knowledge of the subject area, and his or her assessment of the current and future situation. Probabilities assigned in this way are unlikely to be absolutely correct and different managers may well assign different probabilities to the same event. This means that any predictions based upon these subjective probabilities are prone to error. Nevertheless this provides a basis for managers to forecast future outcomes which are likely to be more accurate than using intuition alone.

In the case of the Anytown Dance Group we can see that it is possible to construct a probability distribution for the number of tickets likely to be sold based upon the information reported by the Treasurer. This probability distribution would be as follows:

Number of tickets sold	Number of occasions	Probability
300–399	5	0.208
400–499	7	0.292
500–599	9	0.375
600–699	3	0.125
	24	1.000

For advertising pages sold a probability distribution could also be constructed, as follows:

Number of pages sold	Number of occasions	Probability
28	6	0.250
32	5	0.208
36	4	0.167
40	7	0.292
44	2	0.083
	24	1.000

Probability distributions enable the calculation of the expected outcome of an event. This outcome is known as the expected value of the decision. Thus:

Expected value = Sum of the weighted possible outcomes arrived at by means of the probability distribution

The expected value of ticket sales for the Anytown Dance Group is arrived at by calculating the possible revenue for each range of ticket sales and multiplying by the probability. The sum of the individual calculations is the expected value of ticket sales.

This would be calculated as follows:

Ticket sales	Income £	Food £	Fixed costs £	Profit £	Prob- ability £	Expected value £
350	12,950	6,750	6,350	(150)	0.208	(31)
450	16,650	6,750	6,350	3,550	0.292	1,037
550	20,350	8,250	6,350	5,750	0.275	2,156
650	24,050	9,750	6,350	7,950	0.125	994
						4,156

Notes:
Ticket sales: the mid-point of the range is used.
Income per ticket = Price of ticket + Raffle sales + Photographs
= 28 + 6 + 3 = 37
Food: cost is £15 per person but for a minimum of 450 people
i.e. minimum cost is £15 × 450 = £6750.
Fixed cost = Hire of town hall + Hire of band + Raffle prizes +
Hire of photographer
= £2,000 + £3,000 + £1,100 + £250 = £6,350
Profit = Income – Food cost – Fixed cost
Expected value = Profit × Probability

Similarly, the expected value of advertising revenue can be calculated as follows:

Pages sold	Income £	Cost £	Profit £	Probability	Expected value £
28	2,800	3,060	(260)	0.250	(65)
32	3,200	3,140	60	0.208	12
36	3,600	3,220	380	0.167	63
40	4,000	3,300	700	0.292	204
44	4,400	3,380	1,020	0.083	85
					299

Notes:

> Income = £100 per page sold
> Cost = Fixed cost of £2,500 + Variable cost of £320 per page
> Profit = Income – Cost
> Expected value = Profit x Probability

Calculating the expected value of a decision provides a means of reducing uncertainty through the quantification of the possible outcomes, so this can help in the decision-making process. Using expected values however has the problem of ignoring the range of alternatives and of ignoring any skewness in the probability distribution. It assumes that the representation of the outcomes as a single figure is sufficient for decision making. The range of the probability distribution obviously affects the reliability of the expected value and a widely ranged distribution is likely to make the expected value less reliable than for a narrowly ranged distribution. In order to take this effect into account it is often helpful to undertake some kind of sensitivity analysis. It is also useful to look at the best case and the worst case positions in relation to the break-even position in order to use managerial judgement in assessing likely levels of risk. Thus decision will tend to be made not just upon the accounting analysis but also using the expertise gained from actually operating in a managerial position.

Sensitivity analysis is an attempt to measure how wrong the expected value calculated can be before an alternative decision would be preferable.

In the case of the Anytown Dance Group, for ticket sales the sensitivity analysis calculation would be as follows.

Expected number of tickets sold:

Number of tickets	Probability	Expected number
350	0.208	73
350	0.292	131
350	0.375	206
350	0.125	81
		491

Expected value of sales = 491 x £37 = £18,167

Variable cost = 491 x £15 = £7,365

Therefore:

Contribution = £10,802

Fixed costs = £6,350

Sensitivity analysis:

Sensitivity = Contribution

Fixed costs

= £10,802

£6,350

= 1.70, i.e. 70%

This shows that an error of 70 per cent can be made in the estimate of ticket sales, but that if the actual sales were less than 351 rather than the 491 predicted the group would be better off financially by not holding the dinner dance.

The value of information

Having calculated expected values for the sales of tickets and advertising revenue it is now possible to calculate the expected outcome from holding the dinner dance, based upon the information available.

The calculation is therefore:

Expected outcome = Expected value of ticket sales + Expected value of advertising revenue

= £4,156 + £299

= £4,455

From this we can see that the group can expect to make a profit from holding the dinner dance. We know however that this expectation is somewhat unreliable and that there is a possibility of making a greater profit than this, but also the possibility of making a loss. More information would therefore be helpful to the committee in deciding whether or not to proceed.

More information could indeed be made available to the committee if it chooses to undertake some market research. This information however has a cost associated with it. It is therefore important to know whether or not this additional information is worth the cost of acquiring it.

The way to assess the value of information is to start by calculating the value of perfect information. Perfect information would predict the outcome of the decision exactly. The value of that information therefore is the difference between this outcome and the expected value calculated.

Thus:

> Value of perfect information
> = Outcome from perfect information − Expected value calculated

In no circumstance would it be worth acquiring additional information when the cost of acquiring it exceeds the difference in benefit which could result from possession of the information. This therefore establishes the maximum value of information and in practice that information would be worth acquiring if the cost of acquisition was less than the additional benefit from its possession. The difference would be the added value of the possession of that information.

In practice, perfect information is never obtainable and there is a need to estimate the extent to which accuracy of forecasting is increased from the possession of additional information, in order to determine if that information is worth acquiring. This requires managerial judgement.

For the Anytown Dance Group additional information is only of value if it prevents the group from making a loss. This will only happen if ticket sales of 350 or less occur. Thus, for the group, the information is only worth the expected loss from selling this number of tickets. This can be calculated as follows:

Loss from sales of 350 tickets £	Profit from advertising £	Total loss £	Joint probability	Expected value £
150	(65)	215	0.208 × 0.250	(11)
150	12	138	0.208 × 0.208	(6)
150	63	87	0.208 × 0.167	(3)
150	204	(54)	0.208 × 0.292	3
150	85	65	0.208 × 0.083	(1)
				(18)

The value of information is therefore £18.

Notes:
Loss from sales of 350 tickets previously calculated.
Profit from advertising: shown as for each possible number of pages sold.
Joint probability = Probability of selling 350 pages × Probability of selling each number of advertising pages.

Value of information: £18
Cost of information: £1,000

The cost of the information outweighs its value and is therefore not worth acquiring.

Attitudes to risk

In practice, statistical techniques for evaluating alternatives can help to reduce uncertainty but they cannot eliminate the risk associated with any particular decision. The decision is therefore ultimately dependent upon managerial judgement, and people make decisions based upon their attitudes to risk. In terms of their attitudes to risk, people can be classified into three types:

- *Risk seeking* A risk seeker is a person who will value a positive outcome more highly than a negative outcome. When faced with two equal possibilities of a profit or a loss arising from a particular decision, a risk seeking person will choose to proceed because of the possibility of profit.
- *Risk averse* A risk averter would value the negative outcome more highly than the positive and in the same situation would choose not to proceed because of the possibility of a loss.
- *Risk neutral* A risk neutral person would value both outcomes equally and would be indifferent about whether to proceed or not in this situation.

Different people have different attitudes to risk and this influences their decision making and how they value possible outcomes. Research has shown however that for important business decisions, such as capital expenditure appraisal, managers tend to be risk averse in their decision making. They therefore tend to choose decisions which might have lower expected values than other decisions but which have less risk associated with them. Managers of a business have responsibilities to the owners of that business (i.e. the shareholders) and one of these responsibilities is to act as stewards of that business and to maintain the value of the business and its future viability. This duty will tend to lead managers towards less risky decisions, which they are making on behalf of the owners of the business, than they may perhaps make on their own behalf.

Alternative decision-making criteria

In some situations it is not possible to assign meaningful estimates of probability to the possible outcomes of a decision. In such a situation a manager can make decisions, not by evaluating the possible outcomes of the decision, but by comparing the alternatives and selecting one by comparison with the others. There are three methods of achieving this.

Maximin technique

This technique is based upon maximising the minimum loss which can occur. Thus the manager will select the option which gives the minimum loss in comparison with the alternative decisions (i.e. risk aversion).

Maximax technique

This technique is based upon maximising the possibility of maximum gain from a decision and so the manager will select the alternative which gives maximum expected profit (i.e. risk seeking).

Minimax regret technique

This technique is based upon measuring the opportunity loss resulting from any particular decision. This is done by comparing the expected outcomes of the alternatives. Thus a manager would compare the possible outcomes of the alternatives and calculate the maximum opportunity loss from making each decision. He or she would then select the option which would minimise the possible opportunity loss.

Portfolio theory

Given that all decisions involve an element of risk, and that this cannot be accurately quantified, one way to optimise the performance of a business is through portfolio analysis. This is based upon the premise that decisions are not made in isolation but that a manager has a continuing stream of decision to make. Risk averse decision making will tend to lead to a lower level of performance than might otherwise be obtained through accepting a higher level of risk. Portfolio theory assumes that the best outcome will be obtained on some occasions while the worst will be obtained on others, but with a spread of outcomes between these two extremes on most occasions. Optimum performance can therefore be achieved through managing the level of risk accepted by the business. Thus risk averse decisions will be made on some occasions but risk seeking decision on others.

Portfolio theory states that spreading risk in this manner and making a mixture of risky and less risky decisions will lead to better overall performance than always seeking risk averse decisions.

Portfolio theory is obviously not appropriate for the Anytown Dance Group which has only one decision to be made. It is however a technique which can be used in most business situations where there is a need to evaluate risk for a continuing stream of decisions, and to balance up the risk between decisions.

Conclusion

Risk and uncertainty are inevitable elements of managerial decision making, and we have looked at a variety of ways of reducing this level of risk and uncertainty in the decision-making process. It is inevitable however that this risk and uncertainty cannot be completely eliminated and that managers will, to some extent, need to make decisions using their judgement, and basing decisions upon their skill and experience. This means that generally some wrong decisions will be made by a manager – at least they will prove to have been wrong with the hindsight of the future results of the decision becoming apparent. The techniques which we have considered in this chapter, when combined with other accounting techniques in this book, will help a business manager in this decision making and will lead to better performance than might otherwise be attained.

It must be recognised however that all decisions are based upon the analysis of the information available to the person making that decision. The better the quality of that information the better will be the analysis leading to the decision making. There consequently needs to be an emphasis in all organisations upon the quality of data collection procedures, and this is one of the functions of accounting systems. Good data collection is an essential prerequisite of any analysis, as any techniques used for that analysis are limited by the quality of the information being analyzed.

Summary

- Decision making involves elements of risk and uncertainty. A manager attempts to reduce these through analysis.
- Constructing probability distributions enables expected values to be calculated.
- Sensitivity analysis is used to measure how sensitive the decision made is to the assumptions used.
- Although additional information is valuable in the decision-making process, the cost of acquiring that information should not outweigh the value of that information.
- In terms of their attitudes to risk people can be classified as:
  - risk seeking
  - risk averse
  - risk neutral.
- Alternative decision-making criteria based upon the comparison of alternative are:
  - maximin technique
  - maximax technique
  - minimax regret technique.
- Portfolio theory states that optimum performance can be achieved by risk management between decisions rather than treating each decision in isolation.

Bibliography and further reading

Drury C, *Management and Cost Accounting*, 3rd edition, Chapman & Hall 1992, (Chapter 13)

Gregory G, *Decision Analysis*, Pitman 1988, (Chapters 4, 13 and 14)

Lucey T, *Management Accounting*, 3rd edition, DP Publications 1992, (Chapter 13)

Sizer J, *An Insight into Management Accounting*, 3rd edition, Penguin 1989, (Chapter 8)

Self-review questions

1 Explain the difference between risk and uncertainty.
   (See page 201.)

2 What methods exists to reduce the level of uncertainty?
   (See page 201.)

3 What is a probability distribution? How does it enable expected values to be calculated?
(See page 202.)

4 What is the purpose of sensitivity analysis?
(See page 204.)

5 What determines whether additional information is worth acquiring?
(See page 206.)

6 Describe the differing attitudes to risk, and normal risk attitudes in managerial decision making.
(See page 207.)

7 Describe the alternative decision-making criteria based upon a comparison of alternatives.
(See page 207.)

8 Explain the value of portfolio theory to decision making.
(See page 208.)

Additional questions

15.1 Carrol Cosmetics Ltd is proposing to launch a new brand of cosmetic which has a variable cost of production of £3.50 per unit. The company is considering the price at which to launch the product and the sales manager has estimated demand at various price levels as follows:

	Selling price (£ per unit)			
Sales volume (units)	**5.00**	**6.00**	**7.00**	**8.00**
20,000		20%	60%	80%
30,000	10%	30%	30%	20%
40,000	40%	25%	10%	
50,000	30%	20%		
60,000	20%	5%		

Construct a probability distribution of expected income at each price level and determine which price will maximise profitability.

15.2 Trevor's Tyres Ltd supplies replacement tyres for motor vehicles. The expected demand for one particular type of radial tyre is as follows:

Demand	Probability
60	0.3
70	0.5
80	0.2

Gross margin on a tyre is £12 but because of storage costs the company must absorb a cost of £4 on each tyre which is not sold during the month. The company acquires stock on a monthly basis based upon expected demand.

(a) Calculate the optimal number of tyres for the company to order at the beginning of each month in order to maximise gross margin.
(b) Calculate the expected value of perfect information.

15.3 Market Trading Ltd sells a perishable product among its range. It purchases this product at a cost of £1.00 per unit and sells it for £1.50 per unit. Over the last 60 trading days sales have been as follows:

Daily sales (units)	100	150	200
Number of days	7	30	23

Calculate:

(a) the expected value of daily sales of Market Trading Ltd
(b) the expected profit per day if the company is able to return for full credit all unsold units at the end of each day
(c) the number of units the company should stock in order to maximise profits if all unsold units need to be scrapped
(d) how much the company should be prepared to pay for perfect information regarding daily sales.

16 Internal supply in divisionalised companies

Objectives

After studying this chapter you should be able to:
- outline the objectives of a transfer pricing system
- describe the various methods used to set transfer prices
- calculate transfer prices using each of these methods
- discuss the problems associated with transfer pricing in practice.

HQP Ltd – a divisionalised company manufacturing generating machinery

HQP Ltd is a company manufacturing generating machinery. It is organised into two divisions – the Components Division which manufactures three components A23, B24 and C35, and the Machinery Division which manufactures finished products named micro, mini and power generators. Component A23 is used to make the micro-generator, component B24 the mini-generator and component C35 the power generator. The Components Division sells its components to the Machinery Division as well as to other specialist producers at the same price.

The Components Division has a maximum monthly capacity of 50,000 units but processing constraints mean that it must produce at least 10,000 of each component in order to maintain this capacity. The additional capacity can be used for any mix of components. Price and cost data for the division is as follows:

	Product		
	A23	B24	C35
	£	£	£
Selling price per unit	30	30	45
Variable cost per unit	10	18	15
Fixed costs (total)	60,000	120,000	100,000

The Machinery Division has recently been forced to work below capacity because of difficulties in obtaining supplies of the components manufactured by the Components Division. Consequently, the board of HQP Ltd has instructed the managers of the Components Division to sell all its production to the Machinery Division. Price and cost data for the Machinery Division is as follows:

| | **Product** | | |
	Micro £	Mini £	Power £
Selling price per unit	85	90	90
Variable cost per unit:			
Components purchased	30	30	45
Processing	15	15	25
Fixed costs	120,000	150,000	250,000

The Machinery Division is currently producing 10,000 of each generator but has the capacity to produce up to 20,000 more units, in any mix, if the components are available. The board's instruction will make these components available. The division is able to sell all it can produce of any of its products at the selling price.

The board's instruction has led to conflict between the divisions concerning the product mix produced by the Components Division. The board therefore has asked Don Davis, the management accountant, to investigate and advise on the best product mix to maximise the profits of HQP Ltd.

The problems of internal supply

When goods or services are supplied by one division of a divisionalised company to another division then the normal market condition of supply and demand being brought into equilibrium by the price mechanism do not apply. This is because the company is in effect supplying these goods or services to itself. The nature of a divisionalised company however is that each division operates to a large extent autonomously and its performance is measured and evaluated according to targets set by central management (see Chapter 22). Although the supply of goods or services from one division to another is a transaction which is internal to the company, a mechanism needs to be in place to effect this transfer in the books of the company. This mechanism also needs to reflect the relative performance of the two divisions in making this supply. This mechanism is known as *transfer pricing*.

Transfer pricing is the process which determines the price at which goods are transferred from one division to another within the company. The goods or services transferred are often raw materials or components produced by one division which are used by the other division in its production. Such internal trading therefore tends to be common in companies which are vertically integrated. A *vertically integrated* company is one in which various divisions involved in different stages in the production process are owned by one company. Thus HQP Ltd is vertically integrated because the Components Division and the Machinery Division are both involved in the same production process but in different stages, i.e. producing components and manufacturing final products using these components. Transfer prices are necessary in such circumstances in order to determine the separate performance of each division involved in the transfer of the product. Such pricing needs therefore to be set on a basis which is equitable to both the selling and buying divisions, and which helps to ensure that the overall objectives of the company are met. At the same time the pricing mechanism must provide motivation to the management of both divisions to maximise the performance of their individual divisions.

Transfer pricing is an internal bookkeeping exercise which does not affect the overall profit of the company but merely the respective performance of the divisions involved in the transfer. Because transfer pricing affects the performance of individual divisions however it can affect the operating decisions of the management of a division. This can in its turn impact upon the overall company profitability and one of the main aspects of transfer pricing is to encourage behaviour within the divisions which ensures that overall company profitability is maximised.

The setting of transfer prices therefore is crucial in this respect. In some circumstances the central management may require that the output of one division is transferred to another division for use in its production processes. This is particularly the case when the division receiving the transferred product is experiencing supply problems. It can also be the case when the sale of such product to other companies facilitates their competition against a division of the company. In such cases, internal supply is in the best interests of the overall company and the transfer mechanism may consist of not just a pricing mechanism but also of rules governing what production must be supplied by one division to another.

This is the case for HQP Ltd where the supply problems of the Machinery Division have led to the central management requiring that all the output of the Components Division be transferred to the Machinery Division rather than being sold to other specialist producers. These other producers can be regarded as being in competition with the Machinery Division and it is naturally in the best interests of the company to help its own division rather than competitors. The transfer mechanism can therefore be seen to be designed to achieve overall benefit to the company through the internal transfer of products from one division to another. This internal transfer can however have consequences which lead to behaviour which is not in the best interests of the company. We shall see later how this might happen and the possible consequences of such behaviour.

The objectives of transfer pricing

The setting of transfer prices should be designed to maximise company performance. Specifically therefore the transfer pricing mechanism should meet the following objectives.

Encourage goal congruence

The transfer prices set should be such that the desire of divisional management to maximise divisional performance is consistent with the overall company objectives and does not encourage sub-optimal decision making by the divisional management. Thus the divisional management should not be motivated to fulfil divisional goals at the expense of corporate goals.

Ensure divisional autonomy

One of the main benefits of divisionalisation is that such a structure gives autonomy to divisional management and so leads to better overall performance by the company (see Chapter 22). When internal transfers take place however this autonomy may be diluted and care needs to be taken in setting transfer prices so that central control of the pricing mechanism does not eliminate divisional autonomy, and hence the motivational aspects of divisionalisation. Equally, internal supply necessitates the interdependence of the divisions involved and care must be taken to manage this interdependence so that the performance of one division is not dependent upon the actions taken, and performance of, another division.

Facilitate performance evaluation

The transfer prices set should enable the measurement and evaluation of performance of each division to be undertaken, independently of the performance of the other division involved in the transfer. This evaluation should also be able to assess the value of each division as an economic unit within the company independently of the assessment of other divisions.

Promote internal competition

The setting of transfer prices should provide each division with targets against which their performance can be measured. One of the features of these targets is that they will motivate each division to improve performance and measure their performance against those of the other divisions. This is of particular relevance for a company with several divisions which may be in competition with each other due to the similar nature of their capabilities and of the products which they produce. The motivational aspects of this are discussed in Chapters 18 and 22. It is important however that this promotion of internal competition should not be at the expense of overall company objectives. Equally the competition should not be based solely upon financial targets with the possibility that the quality objectives of the company are sacrificed (see Chapter 7).

In practice, these objectives are in conflict with each other and the desire to ensure the maximisation of overall company performance can only be met by central management involvement in the transfer pricing mechanism. This central control inevitably reduces divisional autonomy and hence the motivational aspect of divisionalisation, which is one of the main benefits of this kind of structure. Complete autonomy for the division however can lead to sub-optimal performance for the company as a whole, as each division seeks to maximise its performance without regard for the effect of the decisions made on other divisions and the company as a whole. This poses something of a dilemma for companies organised on a divisional basis and there is no simple solution. Research studies however suggest that companies are generally prepared to accept a certain level of sub-optimality in performance in order to allow autonomy to divisional management because of their belief that this is more than compensated for by the improved performance resulting from a divisionalised structure.

The dichotomy between company objectives and divisional performance exists in HQP Ltd and is a source of conflict between the divisions. We will investigate what effects the transfer pricing mechanism can have on the performance of the divisions and of the company in some detail later. First however we must consider the different transfer pricing methods which might be used.

Methods of setting transfer prices

A variety of methods exist by which companies can arrive at the transfer prices to be used for internal transfer of goods or services. These methods can be classified into three types depending upon whether the transfer price is determined by:

- market conditions
- production costs
- negotiation.

We will look at each class of methods in turn.

Market based transfer pricing

If a market for the product involved in the transfer exists outside the company then it is possible to set a transfer price which reflects the market price for the product. Such conditions would lead to optimal decision making by both divisions involved in the transfer because it would not matter to them whether the product was bought and sold internally or in the market outside the company. Frequently however this is not the case because the specialist nature of the product concerned, or its terms of supply, means that no precisely identical product exists against which the prices set can be compared. Also supply problems can mean that the open market price is unduly affected by whether or not the division enters the market. Thus internal supply can limit open market supply for competitors and thus cause a market price to exist which would be different to that prevailing if the two divisions of the company enter the market to sell and buy the product.

There may be significant costs involved in buying or selling in the open market and the internal transfer of the product would eliminate these costs, resulting in an overall cost saving to the company which would benefit at least one of the divisions involved. In such circumstances, market based transfer prices may be modified to a price different from the market price to reflect the buying and/or selling costs saved by the company.

Cost based transfer pricing

Cost based transfer pricing systems are frequently used because of the absence of an established market to determine prices. Such pricing mechanisms are relatively simple to use in calculating prices, using the traditional cost accounting in use within the organisation. Cost based transfer pricing is therefore simple to use but has a number of disadvantages. The main one is that such a method provides no incentive for the supplying division to operate efficiently and seek ways of cost reduction and more efficient operations, in order to minimise costs and be able to price competitively for market conditions. Instead, all costs which are incurred can be passed on to the buying division because of the existence of a guaranteed market for the product. This can then cause problems for the buying division which may need to sell its product outside the company.

The buying division may well therefore appear to be performing poorly because of the unnecessarily high transfer price paid by it for its supply from the other division. This problem is particularly severe when the supplying division has spare capacity but is able to recover the costs, including all the fixed costs, of that spare capacity by increasing its overhead absorption rate and reflecting this in its transfer price. The division in such a case has no incentive to seek alternatives for its spare capacity or to take alternative action. Cost based transfer pricing therefore is likely to lead to sub-optimal decision making within the divisions and can also affect performance evaluation unfairly between the divisions. This in turn can affect the motivation of divisional management who feels unfairly treated.

Nevertheless, cost based transfer pricing is widely used and a number of methods exist.

Full cost transfer pricing

The *full cost* of the product is the basis of pricing. Thus the total fixed costs are absorbed into the product cost and passed on to the buying division, including the fixed costs of under-employed plant.

Full cost plus transfer pricing

The *full cost plus a mark-up for profit* is passed on to the buying division, thereby giving the selling division a guaranteed level of profit and performance against its target. The selling division however has no incentive to reduce costs. Indeed reducing production costs through improved performance will reduce the level of profit achieved by the division and the incentive therefore exists to keep costs high.

Variable cost transfer pricing

Only the *variable cost of production* is passed on to the buying division. Although variable cost approximates to economic marginal cost (see Chapter 9) and hence leads to decisions which are in the interest of the company as a whole, the problem with this method of transfer pricing is that the supplying division will always operate at a loss. Performance evaluation therefore becomes meaningless for this division and the motivational effect of divisional autonomy is negated.

Variable cost plus transfer pricing

The *variable cost plus a percentage mark-up* is passed on to the buying division. This has the advantage of providing the selling division with a means to recover its fixed costs, and also an incentive to minimise those costs. It is therefore a means of evaluating the performance of the selling division but only to a limited extent.

Dual transfer pricing

One possible way of solving the problem of variable cost transfer pricing is that the transfer takes place at *variable cost* but that the *ultimate profit of the buying division is shared between the two divisions*, thereby giving them both a stake in the overall profit made. This provides motivation for both divisions but the arbitrary allocation of profit between them makes performance evaluation less meaningful and makes the performance of each division dependent upon the performance of the other. Divisional autonomy is thereby reduced.

The relative merits of these various methods are summarised in Table 16.1.

Table 16.1 The advantages and disadvantages of the various cost plus transfer pricing methods

Method	Advantages	Disadvantages
Full cost	Basis of pricing decision	No incentive to reduce costs
Full cost plus	Profit motivation for division	No incentive to reduce costs
Variable cost	Leads to decisions which are in the company's interest	No motivation for division
Variable cost plus	Motivation for division	Limited performance evaluation possibilities
Dual pricing	Motivation for both divisions involved	Separate performance evaluation difficult

Negotiated transfer pricing

An alternative to transfer prices set according to rules or formulae is for the price to be negotiated between the divisions. This would be appropriate if a price acceptable to both divisions could be arrived at. The range of prices which might be considered acceptable is likely to be one which is above the full cost of production of the supplying division but still enables the buying division to sell at a profit. In other words, an acceptable range would enable both divisions to make a profit and therefore have some motivation for improving performance. In practice, the bargaining power of the two divisions is unlikely to be equal and the central management would be required to arbitrate when disagreement existed.

Negotiation is time consuming and likely to involve managerial time from both of the divisions and from the central management. This time could probably be better employed in managing operational activities. Additionally, negotiations could lead to resentment by one or both divisional managements, particularly if a centrally imposed price is required, and this would reduce divisional autonomy and motivation. Negotiated transfer pricing is therefore rarely used in practice.

The provision of central services

In our discussion so far we have focused upon the transfer of goods or services from one operational division to another and there is a tendency to think that transfer pricing is only appropriate to such internal transfers. The principles apply equally however to centrally supplied services, the costs of which are passed on to the users of those services. A particularly common example of such central services is the provision of central computer services and the passing on of the cost of such services to the end users. The question of setting transfer prices based upon market prices or on costs frequently arises in this connection. The most common solution of passing on the actual costs can be regarded as full cost transfer pricing. The motivational and performance considerations of transfer pricing are equally relevant to the provision of such central services. This type of problem tends to exist in all organisations, whether they are organised on a divisional basis or not.

The question of how to charge for centrally supplied services is a complex subject which is outside the scope of this book. At this point it is sufficient to appreciate that the methods of transfer pricing, and the issues involved, are equally appropriate to this subject matter.

The operational consequences of transfer pricing

We have seen that the transfer pricing system can lead to sub-optimal decision-making behaviour in a divisionalised organisation. We will now look at the operational consequences of such a transfer pricing system by considering its operation as far as HQP Ltd is concerned.

The company has set a transfer price which is based on market conditions, because the Components Division is able to sell its products on the open market to other specialist producers. The company has however decided that all this output must be internally transferred to the Machinery Division because of its supply difficulties. The management of the Components Division must however make operational decisions about its product mix and in seeking to maximise its profits it will produce the following output and profit:

Optimum product mix for Components Division

	Product		
	A23	**B24**	**C35**
	£	£	£
Selling price per unit	30	30	45
Variable cost per unit	10	18	15
Contribution per unit	20	12	30
(selling price less variable cost)			
Optimum product mix (units)	10,000	10,000	30,000

Divisional profit

£

Total contribution of product:	
A23	200,000 (10,000 × 20)
B24	120,000 (10,000 × 12)
C35	900,000 (30,000 × 30)
	1,220,000
Less fixed costs	
(60,000 + 120,000 + 100,000)	280,000
Divisional profit	940,000

The product mix for the Machinery Division is determined by the availability of components and so is dependent upon the performance of the Components Division. The Machinery Division's performance based upon the decisions of the Components Division will therefore be as follows:

Product mix for Machinery Division

	Product		
	Micro	**Mini**	**Power**
Product mix (units)	10,000	10,000	30,000
(determined by the output from the Components Division)			

Contribution per unit of production

	£	£	£
Selling price per unit	85	90	90
Variable cost per unit	15	15	25
Transfer price of components	30	30	45
Contribution per unit	40	45	20
(selling price less variable cost and transfer price of components)			

Divisional profit

	£
Total contribution of product:	
Micro	400,000 (10,000 × 40)
Mini	450,000 (1,000 × 450)
Power	600,000 (30,000 × 20)
	1,450,000
Less fixed costs (120,000 + 150,000 + 250,000)	520,000
Divisional profit	930,000

The company profit from this product mix will be as follows:

Company profit

	£
Components Division	940,000
Machinery Division	930,000
Total	1,870,000 .

We can see however that the optimum product mix for the Machinery Division, and the resulting profit for the division and for the company, would be as follows:

Optimum product mix for Machinery Division

	Product		
	Micro	**Mini**	**Power**
Contribution per unit (£)	40	45	20
(selling price less variable cost and transfer price of components)			
Product mix (units)	10,000	30,000	10,000

Divisional profit

	£
Total contribution of product:	
Micro	400,000
Mini	1,350,000
Power	200,000
	1,950,000
Less fixed costs (120,000 + 150,000 + 250,000)	520,000
Divisional profit	1,430,000

Product mix for Components Division
(determined by requirements of Machinery Division)

| | Product | | |
	A23	B24	C35
Product mix (units)	10,000	30,000	10,000
Contribution per unit (£) (selling price less variable cost)	20	12	30

Divisional profit

	£
Total contribution of product:	
A23	200,000
B24	360,000
C35	300,000
	860,000
Less fixed costs (60,000 + 120,000 + 100,000)	280,000
Divisional profit	580,000

Company profit

	£
Components Division	580,000
Machinery Division	1,430,000
Total	2,010,000

This would however require that the product mix for the Components Division can be determined by the needs of the Machinery Division rather than by its own performance maximising needs. This would have the effect of reducing the profits of the Components Division although the company profit would be increased by these decisions. This is better for the company but the divisional management of the Components Division would be reluctant to make decisions that would reduce the performance of its division. This then is a source of conflict within the company between the divisions.

The objective of the company however is to maximise its overall performance and hence its profitability, rather than the performance of either division. The product mix which would do this, and the resultant profit, is as follows:

Optimum product mix for HQP Ltd

Components Division	A23	B24	C35
Contribution per unit (£)	20	12	30
Machinery Division	**Micro**	**Mini**	**Power**
Contribution per unit (£)	40	45	20
Company contribution	60	57	50

(Combination of contribution from component and from final product)

Product mix (units)	30,000	10,000	10,000

Company profit

	£
Total contribution of product:	
Micro	1,800,000
Mini	570,000
Power	500,000
	2,870,000
Less fixed costs (280,000 + 520,000)	800,000
Company profit	2,070,000

Summary of company profitability according to product mix

	£
Product mix determined by Components Division	1,870,000
Product mix determined by Machinery Division	2,010,000
Product mix determined by company	2,070,000

From the HQP example, we can see that the product mix which would maximise company performance is one which would be chosen by neither of the divisions. This illustrates the conflict inherent in a divisionalised company between the goals of the divisions and the overall corporate goals, and hence a problem with the transfer pricing system. The only way to achieve corporate objectives is to impose rules in the transfer pricing system and this means that some divisional autonomy must be sacrificed. One such rule has been introduced by HQP Ltd in requiring all the output of the Components Division to be transferred to the Machinery Division. This has had the effect that the performance of one division is dependent upon the performance of the other. This has led to a situation whereby the performance of each division is difficult to assess independently as they cannot operate independently of each other. It has also introduced conflict between the divisions and is likely to lead to a loss of motivation from the management of one of the divisions whose product mix decisions are constrained by the requirements of the other division.

The internal transfer rule has been introduced by HQP Ltd because of the supply difficulties being experienced by the Machinery Division. The Components Division has been able to sell its excess production to other producers. These other producers are likely to be in competition with the Machinery Division and it is not in the best interests of the company to help its competitors at the expense of its own performance. If however it was possible for the Machinery Division to obtain the necessary supplies of components from other sources then this internal transfer rule could be removed and each division could operate optimally.

The resulting decisions, product mix and profitability would therefore be as follows:

Optimum product mix for HQP Ltd
(without supply problems and an internal transfer rule)

Components Division	A23	B24	C35
Contribution per unit (£)	20	12	30
Optimum product mix	10,000	10,000	30,000

Divisional profit (previously calculated) £940,000

Machinery Division	Micro	Mini	Power
Contribution per unit (£)	40	45	20
Optimum product mix	10,000	30,000	10,000

Divisional profit (previously calculated) £1,430,000

Company profit

	£
Components Division	940,000
Machinery Division	1,430,000
Total	2,370,000

In order to achieve this optimum the Components Division would need to sell 20,000 units of product C35 to outside producers and the Machinery Division would need to purchase 20,000 units of component B24 from other suppliers.

The difference between this profit and the profit made from maximising profit with an internal supply policy is the *opportunity cost* of the internal transfer policy.

Opportunity cost   = £2,370,000 – £2,070,000
                   = £300,000

This illustrates the point made earlier that market based transfer pricing will lead to optimal decision making by the divisions. It also illustrates the need for central management intervention to ensure that corporate objectives are achieved if supply problems exist.

The problem of internal supply

Although internal supply between divisions of a company can provide benefit to the company as a whole this depends upon the transfer pricing mechanism. Such a mechanism is necessary to enable the evaluation of the performance of each division independently. In practice, however, there is a conflict between the need to give autonomy to divisional management and the desire to achieve corporate objectives. Internal supply also makes it more difficult for divisions to operate independently of each other and make performance maximising decisions. This in turn makes the evaluation of performance of each division independently more difficult and less meaningful.

Although these problems are recognised by company managers no satisfactory solution to them has been discovered. As mentioned earlier however research suggests that company managers consider that the performance improvements achieved by giving autonomy to divisional managers outweighs the loss in performance due to sub-optimal decisions. The actual approach taken by each company operating in a divisionalised structure will depend upon its own needs and perception of the situation affecting its own company. No universal approach is found in dealing with these problems.

It is important therefore for a business manager to understand the principles of transfer pricing and the consequences arising from any decision taken in setting up and operating a transfer pricing system.

Summary

- A business divided into divisions needs a mechanism to evaluate the performance of these divisions when the output of one division is transferred to another division as an internal supply. This mechanism is the transfer pricing system.
- The objective of transfer pricing is to encourage decision making within the divisions which maximises company performance through meeting the following objectives:
  - encouraging goal congruence
  - ensuring divisional autonomy
  - facilitating divisional performance evaluation
  - promoting internal competition.
- In practice, the objectives of maximising company performance and ensuring divisional autonomy are in conflict with each other. Research shows that companies are generally prepared to accept sub-optimal performance which is compensated for by the performance improvements reaped from allowing divisional autonomy.
- Methods used to set transfer prices are the following:
  - market based transfer pricing

- production cost based transfer pricing, including full cost transfer pricing
- full cost plus transfer pricing
- variable cost transfer pricing
- variable cost plus transfer pricing
- dual transfer pricing.
- Internal transfer creates an interdependence between divisions which can affect the separate evaluation of each division's performance. This interdependence can also affect divisional management motivation and be a cause of conflict between the divisions.
- The transfer pricing mechanism, and associated problems, apply equally to the provision of services centrally.

Bibliography and further reading

Drury C, *Management and Cost Accounting*, 3rd edition, Chapman & Hall 1992, (Chapters 25 and 26)

Emmanuel C, Otley D and Merchant K, *Accounting for Management Control*, 2nd edition, Chapman & Hall 1990, (Chapter 11)

Lucey T, *Management Accounting*, 3rd edition, DP Publications 1992, (Chapter 20)

Sizer J, *An Insight into Management Accounting*, 3rd edition, Penguin 1989, (Chapter 10)

Self-review questions

1 (a) What is the problem when internal transfers of production between divisions takes place?
(b) What mechanism is used to deal with this problem?
(See page 213.)

2 What are the main objectives of a transfer pricing mechanism?
(See page 214.)

3 Explain how market based transfer prices lead to optimal decisions by divisional managers.
(See page 216.)

4 How do buying or selling costs affect the transfer price set when based upon market prices?
(See page 216.)

5 Explain the difference between full cost and variable cost transfer prices.
(See page 217.)

6 Why does full cost transfer pricing discourage the supplying division from making productivity improvements?

(See page 217.)

7 Why does variable cost transfer pricing fail to motivate the management of the supplying division?

(See page 217.)

8 Explain what is meant by negotiated transfer pricing and the problems associated with it.

(See page 218.)

Additional questions

16.1 Amalgamated Ceramics plc is organised into a number of divisions. Division A is operating at full capacity and makes two components, X and Y, using the same labour for both products. Production capacity for the division is limited by the labour force and 10,000 production hours are available. Budgeted capacity involves producing 4,000 units of Y, for which company orders have been received, and the remainder of capacity is to be used to produce X.

Direct costs of manufacture are:

	X £ per unit	Y £ per unit
Materials	20	14
Labour	20	15

Direct labour is paid at the rate of £20 per production hour.

Overheads for the company are absorbed on the basis of direct wages and the overhead cost for Division A is estimated to be £170,000, with 60 per cent being fixed and the remainder variable. The division prices at full cost plus 50 per cent.

Division B of the company wishes to purchase from Division A 2,500 units of component X which it proposes to incorporate into its final product. This final product will be sold at a price of £200 per unit. Division B's cost of processing is £35 per unit.

Recommend a price range at which the component should be sold to Division B.

16.2 Outline the main features of a cost based system for setting transfer prices between divisions within a company, and the main types of cost based transfer pricing. What are the problems with cost based methods of pricing and what alternatives exist?

16.3 Willenden Co has two divisions. Division A manufactures a unique component which it sells to Division B. This component is not sold outside the company and cannot be obtained elsewhere. Division B incorporates one unit of this component into its final product.

The costs of Division A are as follows:

Fixed costs   £500,000
Variable costs   £100 per unit

The manager of Division A aims to maximise the performance of his division and has set a transfer price of £500 per unit. The division has a maximum production capacity of 5,000 units, but will produce only the number of units demanded by Division B.

The costs of Division B, in addition to the cost of this unit are:

Fixed costs   £1,000,000
Variable costs   £200 per unit

Sales of the final product are dependent upon price and market research has revealed the following demand at different price levels:

Price (£ per unit)	Demand (units)
1,400	2,000
1,250	3,000
1,100	4,000
950	5,000
800	6,000

If Division B produces at a level which just satisfies the demand at any particular price, calculate the price level which will maximise the profits of the division and the resulting profit for the company.

16.4 Motor Vendors Ltd is a company which buys and sells motor vehicles. It is organised into three divisions:

New vehicles – manager Sunil Metah
Second-hand vehicles – manager Alison Burton
Repair workshop – manager John Lewis

When Sunil Metah sells a new vehicle to a customer he is often expected to take a second-hand vehicle in part exchange and in such cases the vehicle is passed to Alison Burton for resale.

The Repair workshop does work for the other departments of the company as well as for outside customers. John Lewis charges such customers for materials used and for labour at the rate of £20 per hour. This labour charge is made up as follows:

	£
Direct labour cost	8.00
Other variable costs	3.00
Fixed costs	4.00
Profit	5.00
	20.00

The managing director of the company wishes to be able to reward his managers on the basis of their results and has asked you to advise him of an appropriate basis. He has suggested that the following transaction is typical:

A new vehicle is sold for £20,000 – cost to Motor Vendors Ltd is £15,000. A second-hand vehicle is taken is part exchange at an allowance of £6,000. This vehicle needs repairs prior to resale – this involves a materials cost of £80 and 60 hours of labour time. After repair the vehicle can be sold for £5,500. A similar vehicle, without any repairs needed, could be purchased from another dealer for £4,500.

How would you advise the managing director?

Part 4
CONTROLLING BUSINESS PERFORMANCE

17 The control of stock

Objectives

After studying this chapter you should be able to:
- identify and explain the reason why a company will need to hold stock
- explain the different types of stock held
- describe the typical features of a stock control system
- calculate the value of stock held and issued using different stores issue pricing.

Office Furniture Ltd – manufacturer of a range of office furniture

David Merchant is the managing director of Office Furniture Ltd, a company which manufactures a range of office furniture. He is concerned about the materials control procedures operating in the factory, particularly in relation to the manufacture of its major product, a standard sized office desk. It appears to him that an excess amount of raw materials is being used in the manufacture of these desks, and this is affecting company profitability. He has contacted Sarah Kitson, the management accountant of the company, and asked her to investigate the procedures in operation.

Sarah has arranged for a physical stock take to take place at the beginning and end of the month of May for raw materials, work in progress and finished desks. The results of these stock takes are as follows:

	Stock at 1st May	Stock at 31st May
Finished desks	800	1,025
Work in progress	360 desks	150 desks
Degree of completion:		
Timber	66.7%	80.0%
Varnish	35.0%	40.0%
Raw materials		
Timber	45,000 sq ft	50,000 sq ft
Varnish	1,000 litres	950 litres

Paul Brown, the sales manager has confirmed that sales during the period amounted to 4,850 desks.

John Atkinson, the works manager, has provided Sarah with an estimate of materials used in the production of a desk, allowing for normal wastage. His figures are as follows:

Timber   30 sq ft
Varnish   0.5 litre

Peter Ackroyd, the stores manager, has provided Sarah with information regarding the purchase and issue of materials for the production of the standard desk during May. His figures are as follows:

Purchase of materials:
4 May   120,000 sq ft of timber   @ £1.50 per sq ft
6 May   400 litres of varnish   @ £1.15 per litre
12 May   1,800 litres of varnish   @ £1.30 per litre
18 May   75,000 sq ft of timber   @ £1.75 per sq ft

Materials issued:
12 May timber valued   @ £123,000
17 May varnish valued @ £2,752
20 May timber valued   @ £172,500

He has also confirmed that the stock in hand at 1 May was priced as follows:

Timber   £1.40 per sq ft
Varnish   £1.20 per litre

Materials are issued from stock on a first in, first out (FIFO) basis (see later).

Sarah Kitson knows that she needs to calculate the quantities of stock issued during May and the consequent book value of the stock remaining at the end of May. She also knows that she needs to calculate the amount of raw materials which should have been used in production, based upon John Atkinson's estimate, and to investigate any differences which are revealed. She then needs to report her findings to the managing director.

Types of stock

A company holds stock both as an essential part of its production process and as an essential part of its sales and distribution process. These stocks are however basically different in nature. The first type is held for the company's internal purposes in order to operate efficiently in a production environment; the second type is held for external purposes to met demand from customers efficiently. It is therefore possible to categorise the stock which a company holds into the following types.

Raw materials

These are purchased by a company from its suppliers and are used in the manufacture of the products which the company produces.

In the case of Office Furniture Ltd raw materials will consist primarily of wood and varnish which are the main components of the office furniture produced, but will also include such items as screws, glue, handles etc. The materials are all used in the manufacture of the products of the company and are held as stocks of raw materials until needed in the manufacturing process.

Work in progress

A product often goes through several processes in its manufacture. In between processes the product is in a part manufactured state and no longer consists of raw materials but is not yet a finished product. In terms of value the raw materials have had value added from the processes undertaken but do not yet have the value of a finished product. These items are known as *work in progress* which signifies that they need further processing in order to become a finished product. Work in progress is classified and valued separately from raw materials and the value attached is an attempt to estimate the value added from the production processes undertaken. Where a product undergoes several processes it can be expected that work in progress will consist of a variety of items at different stages of production.

In the case of Office Furniture Ltd the work in progress has been estimated in terms of the percentage of production processes which have been completed.

Finished goods

Once production has been completed the product is finished and is known as *finished goods*. These are then available for sale to customers. Finished goods are therefore held after completion until they can be sold.

Reason for holding stock

The different types of stock held by a company are varied in nature and are held for a variety purposes. The reasons for holding stock are as follows.

Raw materials

To ensure continuity in the production processes
This is particularly important if the production process needs to operate at a particular level in order to operate efficiently. Thus some processes (e.g. in a chemical processing plant) need to operate continuously in order to be effective so raw materials must be on hand to enable this process to continue and to prevent its disruption.

Seasonal availability
Some raw materials are only available on a seasonal basis (especially natural products) and there is a need to obtain sufficient stocks to last from one season to the next.

Bulk purchasing discounts

For some materials it is possible to obtain substantial discounts from purchasing in bulk and this makes it attractive to the company. This discount must be considered against the costs of holding stock (discussed below) in order to decide whether or not it is advantageous to the company to take advantage of bulk purchasing discounts.

Work in progress

This type of stock is held because of the different nature and speed of the various production processes and acts as a buffer between the different processes in order to ensure their efficient operation.

For example, with Office Furniture Ltd the varnishing process is time consuming because of the need to allow for drying between coats. At this point in the production process therefore there is likely to be a considerable amount of work in progress stock.

Finished goods

To ensure sufficient goods to meet demand

Most businesses do not manufacture goods to order but instead supply from stock so that they can supply within an acceptable time frame. For this type of business therefore it is essential to keep a supply of finished goods in stock in order to meet demand.

Seasonal fluctuations

The demand for some goods is seasonal with demand occurring mainly at a particular time of year. In order to maintain production processes however the company will manufacture goods continuously throughout the year and the stock of finished goods will build up during the year and be sold in the appropriate season. An example of this is toy manufacturing where the majority of goods are sold during the pre-Christmas season.

Obsolete stock

There is a danger when finished goods are held in stock until demanded by customers that this stock becomes obsolete and hence unsaleable. Although this is not a reason for holding stock, it is nevertheless one reason why stock may be held and a danger to be recognised in considering the extent of stockholding. In valuing stock therefore it is essential to bear this in mind and value stock at its sale value (if less than cost), revaluing when necessary. This will be considered further in the discussion of control procedures (see later).

The cost of raw materials

While the purchase cost of raw materials is the main cost of the stock held by a company, this is not the only cost involved with stock. In addition, the following must be taken into account:

- costs of obtaining stock
- costs of holding stock.

Additionally, there are costs involved in not having materials to hand when needed and these are known as *stockout costs*.

The factors involved in these costs are as follows.

Costs of obtaining stock

Administration
Administrative effort is involved in obtaining stock and ensuring its delivery. This effort involves the ordering procedure, the checking procedure on its arrival and the payment procedure for the goods received. These procedures involve different people. For example, a stores clerk will order stocks, a storekeeper will physically check the goods on arrival, a stores clerk will certify bills for the stock for payment and an accounts clerk will arrange for the payment to be made. This segregation of duties is a normal feature of audit and control in a large business.

Transport
It is often necessary to arrange and pay separately for the transport of stock. This involves not just the delivery of raw materials from suppliers to the company but also its transport around the manufacturing site. Raw materials are transported from where they are held in stock to the relevant production process and also work in progress is transported from one process to the next.

Costs of holding stock

Storage costs
Goods held in stock need to be stored and therefore adequate storage space needs to be provided. The provision of storage space is a cost which the business must bear. Given that these materials are valuable, storage space must be secure enough to safeguard the stock. The storage space also needs to be appropriate to the type of stock held. Thus for Office Furniture Ltd the stocks of timber will need to be stored in an environment which will prevent deterioration from adverse weather conditions and so will need to be protected from wet weather and extremes of temperature. Generally speaking, the more valuable the stock and the more prone to deterioration then the greater is the need for special storage facilities. This in turn adds to the cost of the stock.

Handling costs
The stores in which raw materials are kept need to be secure and records need to be kept of items received into stock and issued from stock. Thus there are handling costs of stock which involve not just physically moving stock but also the keeping of records. Depending upon the size of stock kept this could involve one or more people being fully involved in storekeeping, thereby increasing the cost of stock. If stock is prone to deterioration then there is a need to ensure that the oldest stock is issued first and so the physical management of the stores becomes more time consuming and costly. The principle of issuing the oldest stock first and ensuring that this cycle is maintained is known as *stock rotation*.

Insurance
As stock is valuable it must be insured against loss and damage in the same way as other components of the company will be insured.

Loss and deterioration

Although precautions will be taken by the company to prevent the loss or deterioration of stock through the provision of adequate storage facilities there is nevertheless this possibility. Deterioration is of particular significance for the types of materials which deteriorate through ageing and care must be taken to ensure that the oldest items of a particular type are always issued before newer items. There is also the possibility that changes in the production process or range of goods manufactured could lead to particular items of stock becoming obsolete. The stock control procedures will need to identify stock which is no longer used and arrangements made for its disposal.

Interest on capital invested

The amount of stock held by a company represents capital invested in the company. This is part of the *working capital* of the company. Such capital has a cost and one of the costs of stock therefore is the *interest on capital invested in stock*.

Stockout costs

We can see therefore that there are costs involved in holding stock in addition to the purchase cost of the stock itself but also that there are reasons for holding stock which are integral to the business' operations. This might lead us to suppose that the company should minimise its stockholding and this is indeed one of its objectives. It needs to be recognised however that there are also *stockout costs* – that is costs incurred by the company because it does not have stock available to satisfy its production requirements. These costs can be identified as follows.

Loss of production

If a company runs out of a particular item of stock this will halt the production process not just for the particular process for which this item is needed but also for all the processes in the manufacture of that particular product. For a company such as Office Furniture Ltd, which makes a range of products, this can disrupt the whole production schedule for all products. Any such disruption to production can be costly and time consuming to recover from. This is especially true in a continuous production environment where lack of an item of stock can lead to the close down of the entire process, which can then take weeks to restart. This kind of process is relevant in oil refining, chemical production and ceramics, and has been considered in detail in Chapter 6.

Loss of future sales

Disruption to the production schedule from lack of stock will cause delays in production and this can lead to delays in the supply of goods to customers. It can however have a greater impact than this because it is possible that these delays can lead to a loss of goodwill from customers which will cause them to purchase goods from other suppliers in the future. Thus a stockout situation can cause not just an immediate problem but also a future one. Orders which would have been received are lost to competitors because of the perceived unreliability of the company amongst its customers.

Cost of urgent reorders

One way to recover from a stockout situation is to urgently reorder a quantity of the item concerned. Doing this however involves cost not just because the cost of purchase of a small quantity urgently will be at a higher price but also in the ordering and handling costs of the stock ordered in this way.

Optimising stock levels

The control of stock therefore is an issue of some importance to a company and the procedures used are known as *stock control* or *inventory control*. The objective of such control is to minimise the cost of stock while at the same time maximising its availability. Stock control therefore involves planning the need for particular items of stock, assessing their availability and ensuring that stock is available when required. It also involves, at the same time, ensuring that the level of stock is no higher than necessary. Controlling the cost of stock requires systems to ensure that the costs of obtaining and holding stock are minimised and systems for ensuring that the level of stock held is the minimum necessary for the efficient functioning of the business.

Various techniques have evolved for the controlling of stock levels and the following are of particular significance.

Economic Order Quantity (EOQ)

In addition to calculating when to order an item of stock it is also necessary to calculate how much to order at any one time. In general, the larger the size of any particular order the greater the discount which can be obtained. This needs to be offset however against the costs of holding stock described below. The company will therefore need to calculate both of these and arrive at a calculation, by means of mathematical techniques, which will show the size of order which should be made to the company's best financial advantage. The size and timing of such an order is known as the *economic order quantity (EOQ)*.

This technique involves calculating the level of stock for each item which needs to be held, calculating the size of order which needs to be placed for that item and the timing of the order. This can be calculated by the following formula:

$$EOQ = \sqrt{\frac{2DS}{I}}$$

where
D = demand per period for the stock item
S = the cost of placing an order
I = the cost of holding one unit of stock for one period.

This calculation leads to ordering appropriate amounts at appropriate times to achieve maximum benefit to the company. Thus the costs of holding stock must be offset against the discounts which can be obtained from making large orders and the costs which the company must bear if the stock of any items runs out. To do this it is necessary to calculate the rate of usage of the stock item and to know the time delay between ordering more of the item and its being delivered into stock.

In theory, it is then possible to reorder at a point in time which will ensure that new stock is delivered at the time when existing stock has just been completely used. In practice, a safety margin is also needed to allow for irregularities in usage and delivery times, and to ensure that the production schedule is not disrupted by a stockout situation. This can be illustrated in Figure 17.1.

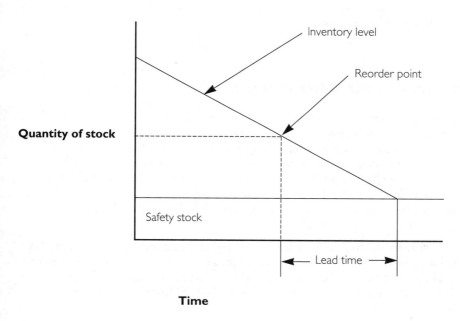

Figure 17.1 Calculation of reorder point for stock

Techniques such as material requirements planning (see Chapter 8) are used to arrive at a knowledge of future requirements of each item of stock, which will depend upon the scheduling of production for the future.

Just in time (JIT)

This technique is one which has gained increasing importance in recent years and has been adopted by companies who have copied the techniques of Japanese manufacturing companies, where JIT originated. The aim of the technique is to eliminate the need for the holding of stock altogether by ensuring that raw materials are delivered regularly in small quantities as they are needed in the manufacturing process. The raw materials are therefore not delivered into stock but instead are delivered directly to the production department in which they are needed on a time scale which ensures that the production schedule can be met.

Techniques such as MRP are used to determine the requirements for raw materials and these techniques must accurately predict needs. The ordering process also needs to be efficient but more importantly delivery of raw materials from suppliers needs to be regular and on a time scale demanded by the company because buffer stocks do not exist to prevent disruption to production. These requirements of JIT tend to mean that companies have used the technique to reduce stock levels but have not gone as far as eliminating stores and the holding of stocks altogether.

The British practice of stockholding can be contrasted with the Japanese practice insofar as the average Japanese stockholding is three days while the average British stockholding is two weeks' usage quantity.

Inventory control procedures

We have seen the importance of control procedures, not just in ensuring that stock is ordered and held to meet requirements, but also as far as cost control is concerned. An essential part of cost control is the recording of materials as they are received into stock and issued from stock to the production processes. These control procedures form part of the cost accounts of the company and enable such information as product costing to be calculated, but they also form the control of the stock itself and the stock levels recorded can be checked by means of a physical stock check such as Sarah Kitson has arranged for Office Furniture Ltd.

Raw materials are received into stock and recorded at the price at which they have been charged to the company and this can result in the same type of item being held in stock at several different prices. This then leads to the question of what price is appropriate to record issues from stock. Several different methods of stores issue pricing are used, as follows.

First in, first out (FIFO)

This method assumes that the oldest items of stock will be issued first at the price at which they were received into stock, followed by the next oldest (at the appropriate price) etc. FIFO is the most commonly used method in industry. It is a method recommended by SSAP 9 (see Chapter 5) and is acceptable to the Inland Revenue.

Last in, first out (LIFO)

This method is the opposite of FIFO as it assumes that the newest items will be issued first at the price at which they were received into stock. Although this method is not recommended by SSAP 9 and is not acceptable to the Inland Revenue it has the advantage that, in inflationary times, the costs charged to production more nearly reflect replacement costs. It is nevertheless little used in practice because of it unacceptability for financial reporting.

Average cost

This method involves the calculation of the average cost of all the items of a particular type of stock, and using this price for issues from stock. This method is recommended by SSAP 9 and is acceptable to the Inland Revenue. The problem with it is that the average needs to be recalculated every time more items are received into stock and this can be time consuming. However, the use of computers now makes the calculation relatively simple to perform.

Standard cost

This is an adaptation of average cost pricing which sets an average (i.e. standard) to be used throughout a time period. This method will be considered further in Chapter 20.

Office Furniture Ltd uses the FIFO method of stores issue pricing and so its stores ledger accounts for timber and varnish will be as follows:

Stores ledger account (timber)

	£		£
Opening balance 45,000 @ £1.40	63,000	12 May 45,000 units @ £1.40	63,000
4 May 120,000 units @ £1.50	180,000	40,000 units @ £1.50	60,000
18 May 70,000 units @ £1.75	122,500	20 May 80,000 units @ £1.50	120,000
		30,000 units @ £1.75	52,500
		Closing balance 40,000 @ £1.75	70,000
	365,500		365,500

Stores ledger account (varnish)

	£		£
Opening balance 1,000 @ £1.20	1,200	17 May 1,000 litres @ £1.20	1,200
6 May 400 litres @ £1.15	460	400 litres @ £1.15	460
12 May 1,800 units @ £1.30	2,340	840 litres @ £1.30	1,092
		Closing balance 960 @ £1.30	1,248
	4,000		4,000

If Office Furniture Ltd was to use the LIFO method then the timber account would be as follows:

Stores ledger account (timber)

	£		£
Opening balance 45,000 @ £1.40	63,000	12 May 85,000 units @ £1.50	127,500
4 May 120,000 units @ £1.50	180,000	20 May 70,000 units @ £1.75	122,500
18 May 70,000 units @ £1.75	122,500	35,000 units @ £1.50	52,500
		5,000 units @ £1.40	7,000
		Closing balance 40,000 @ £1.40	56,000
	365,500		365,500

If Office Furniture Ltd was to use the average cost method then the timber account would be as follows:

Stores ledger account (timber)

	£		£
Opening balance 45,000 @ £1.40	63,000	12 May 85,000 units @ £1.47	124,950
4 May 120,000 units @ £1.50	180,000	20 May 110,000 units @ £1.60	176,000
18 May 70,000 units @ £1.75	122,500		
		Closing balance 40,000 @ £1.60	64,050
	365,500		365,500

Average cost calculations:

4 May

$(63,000 + 180,000)/(45,000 + 120,000) = £1.47$

18 May

$(63,000 + 180,000 - 124,950 + 122,500)/(45000 + 120,000 - 85000 + 70000) = £1.60$

Physical stock taking

The book records of stock show the amount of stock which the accounts record as being in existence. A business will confirm, or otherwise, that this stock physically exists by means of a physical count of stock on a regular basis.

The records for Office Furniture Ltd and the results of the physical stock take are as follows:

Comparison of book and physical stocks

	Book stock	Physical stock	Difference
Timber (units)	40,000	50,000	10,000
Varnish (litres)	960	950	10

When discrepancies exist investigation is necessary in order to see what the reasons are for them. This will be part of Sarah Kitson's task; one which she will need to do in order to produce her report to the managing director. As a result of the stock take there is also a need to adjust the stock account so that the quantities shown reflect the actual physical quantities held in stock. As the physical stock for both these accounts exceeds the book quantities this will result in an abnormal gain on each of these accounts which needs to be credited to the profit and loss account. Equally, if the physical quantities had been less than the book quantities this would have resulted in a debit to the profit and loss account. These debits or credits arise because the amounts charged to production are different from the quantities actually used.

Stock control procedures

In order to investigate the stock control procedures of Office Furniture Ltd, Sarah needs to calculate the number of standard desks which have been completed during May. This calculation is as follows:

Number of standard desks completed during May

Quantity sold	4,850
Closing stock	1,025
	5,875
Less opening stock	800
Completed desks	5,075

Using the information supplied by John Atkinson, Sarah is able to calculate the amount of material which should have been consumed by the production of desks achieved during May and compare this with the amount of material actually consumed. Her calculation is as follows:

Comparison of materials that should have been consumed with material actually consumed

	Timber		Varnish	
Desks completed	5,075		5,075	
Less opening WIP equivalent	240	$(360 \times 2/3)$	126	(360×0.35)
	4,835		4,949	
Add closing WIP equivalent	120	(150×0.8)	60	(150×0.4)
Equivalent production	4,945		5,009	
Consumption per desk	30.0		0.5	
Total estimated consumption	148,350.0		2,504.5	
Actual consumption	195,000.0		2,240.0	
Excess usage	46,650.0		(264.5)	

The discrepancies revealed from Sarah's calculations will lead her to investigate the control procedures operating in the factory. Possible reasons for the discrepancies are as follows:

- timber
  - inaccurate recording of goods received and issued
  - inaccurate record keeping in production
  - inaccurate usage estimates
  - excess wastage
  - pilfering in the factory
  - inaccurate estimate of degree of completion of WIP
  - inaccurate record of stock of finished goods
- varnish
  - inaccurate recording of goods received and issued
  - pilfering in the stores
  - inaccurate record keeping in production
  - inaccurate usage estimates
  - excess wastage
  - inaccurate estimate of degree of completion of WIP
  - inaccurate record of stock of finished goods.

These differences and their possible reasons suggest that there are inadequate controls in record keeping and in the physical control of stock. Also that there are inadequate estimates of usage or problems in the production process which lead to excess wastage of materials. This is of obvious concern to the managing director of the company as this will affect the profitability of the products. Each of these possible factors will require further investigation in order to ensure that procedures are operating satisfactorily.

This illustrates the interaction between accounting and the various facets of production. It demonstrates how accounting can help the business manager in the control of the production process. Accounting can reveal problems in the control of stock which are essential to solve as they affect the profitability of the business.

Summary

- The three different types of stock which a company holds are:
  - raw materials
  - work in progress
  - finished goods.
- Stock is held for a variety of purposes.
- Costs involved with stock are:
  - costs of obtaining stock
  - costs of holding stock.
- There are costs associated with lack of stock (stockout costs).
- Stock control aims to minimise stock costs while maximising availability.
- Techniques for optimising stock levels include:

- EOQ
- JIT.
- Stores issue pricing methods are:
  - FIFO
  - LIFO
  - average cost
  - standard cost.

Bibliography and further reading

Drury C, *Management and Cost Accounting*, 3rd edition, Chapman & Hall 1992, (Chapters 3 and 4)

Lucey T, *Management Accounting*, 3rd edition, DP Publications 1992, (Chapters 8 and 12)

Sizer J, *An Insight Into Management Accounting*, 3rd edition, Penguin 1989, (Chapter 2)

Storey R, *Introduction to Cost and Management Accounting*, Macmillan 1995, (Chapter 3)

Self-review questions

1 Identify three different types of stock held by a company and one reason for holding each type of stock.
(See page 232.)

2 Describe five different costs associated with stock.
(See page 234.)

3 Explain the meaning of stockout and identify the associated costs.
(See page 235.)

4 Name the most common bases for calculating stock issue pricing.
(See page 238.)

5 What is the purpose of stock control?
(See page 240.)

6 Explain the benefits of stock control to a business manager.
(See page 242.)

Additional questions

17.1 On 1st January Bill Winter set up in business buying and selling components for automobiles. On the same day he purchased 1,000 items of stock costing £1.00

each. On 12th January he purchased a further 1,000 items costing £1.20 each, and on 25th January a further 1,000 items costing £1.30 each.

Sales during January were as follows:

5th January	100 items
13th January	600 items
23rd January	500 items
27th January	900 items

The selling price of all items sold was £2.50.

Calculate the value of stock remaining at the end of January using FIFO, LIFO and average cost methods.

17.2 The following information relates to one of the raw materials of the Component Manufacturing Co Ltd:

Usage	200 units per week
Ordering cost	£30 per order placed
Stockholding cost	£0.10 per unit per week
Safety stock	50 units
Lead time of order	2 weeks

Usage of this raw material is fairly uniform over time and so the average stock holding can be assumed to be one half of the order quantity.

Calculate the economic order quantity for this raw material and determine the reorder point.

17.3 The stores account of the Garment Manufacturing Co Ltd for the month of May is as follows:

Opening balance	2,000 units @ £9
Purchases	1,600 units @ £10
Issues	1,500 units

During the month, 1,200 finished garments were produced and the following costs were incurred:

Direct labour	£25,000
Overheads allocated	£12,000

Of the garments produced, 1,000 were sold during the month and the remainder were left in stock. There was no opening stock of finished goods.

If the selling price of the finished garments was £65 each calculate the difference in profit made during the month based upon stores issued using FIFO and LIFO bases.

18   Setting targets

Objectives

After studying this chapter you should be able to:

- describe the purposes of an operational control system
- explain the impact of the budgeting process on managerial behaviour
- discuss managerial behaviour in terms of motivation theories.

Broughton Economies Ltd – a large chemical engineering company

Broughton Economies Ltd is a large, centrally controlled chemical engineering company. It has a number of departmental managers who are each responsible for the performance of the department which they manage. Targets are set centrally by the board in consultation with the accounts department and each manager is allocated a budget to control the activities of his or her department and a target level of activity, and is required to assume responsibility for deviations from the budget. Managers are thus accountable for achieving the budget targets, which include all departmental costs, whether controllable or not.

Recently, the board has become concerned about the performance of the company and the fact that most managers are regularly failing to meet the targets set. This is impacting on the overall productivity and profitability of the company. Both the managers concerned and the accounts department have failed to provide reasons for this problem. The board has therefore employed an outside consultant, Elizabeth Turner, with extensive experience in organisational performance and behaviour consulting to advise them about the reasons for, and suggest solutions to, this problem. The board has asked her to prepare a report outlining possible reasons and recommendations for a course of action to improve the situation.

The function of management accounting

We have seen that management accounting can be used by the managers of a business in order to help them plan and control the operating of that business. Accounting can be seen to be the language of business, and using the language of accounting it is possible to translate operational problems and decisions into plans which are precise in nature. It is also possible to monitor those plans as they are put into effect and to control the business. Accounting can be used to measure not just the performance of the business but also the performance of individual departments, activities and even managers. The precise nature of the quantitative information given by accounting makes the evaluation of performance a relatively straightforward exercise. We have also seen that the communication of the plans for the business, and the subsequent performance of the business in terms of meeting the plans, is helped by the use of accounting.

One of the main purposes of accounting information therefore is to aid communication throughout the organisation, as well as enabling the planning and control of the operations involved in the activity of the business. Another purpose of accounting information, which is achieved through the budgeting and reporting system, is to encourage goal congruence amongst the managers of the organisation (see Chapter 22). The techniques which we have investigated can be seen to be helpful to a business manager in understanding these functions of management.

Management accounting is an important tool for business management and we have seen examples of how it can be used:

● achieve operational control of the business
● influence managerial behaviour and facilitate goal congruence
● provide motivation to managers
● measure and evaluate performance
● plan the future of the business
● facilitate decision making.

We have also considered how the way in which accounting information, particularly management accounting information, is used can have an effect upon the performance of the business and upon the behaviour of individual managers within it. Additionally, we have seen that some of the techniques of management accounting have problems associated with them and need to be understood within the context in which they are being used in order to be effective tools for managers. One of the contexts is that of the people themselves involved in the management process, as all organisation operate through people. We now need therefore to look in detail at the effect which the use of accounting for control and performance measurement purposes might have upon the people involved in the management and operation of a business.

Operational control of a business

We have looked at the need for operational control of a business and seen how management accounting forms a part of the control system of a business. For control systems to be effective they need to have a reporting mechanism built into them so that current performance can be evaluated and corrective action taken, if necessary, to prevent deviations from the plan. Thus an important part of the control mechanism is feedback. This can be shown as in Figure 18.1.

Figure 18.1 The control system

Feedback is necessary so that individual managers can be informed of how the business is performing in relation to the planned level of performance and in order to indicate what corrective action needs to be taken to correct deviations from the plan. Thus individual managers need feedback on the performance of that part of the business for which they are responsible. Accounting information from the accounting control system, in the form of reports on current performance, is an important part of that feedback. Feedback needs to be frequent and regular but also needs to timely so that it is received as soon after the action as possible. This is important in order to ensure that the feedback can be related to the actual decisions made and so that any corrective action can be speedily taken. Detailed feedback given long after the event is of little value in the operations of a business.

We have previously considered how accounting information can be used to help managers control that part of the business for which they are responsible. It is not sufficient however for each individual manager to ensure the optimum performance of his or her area of responsibility because this will not in itself necessarily lead to the optimisation of overall company performance. We have seen examples of this in Chapters 16 and will also consider this aspect in detail in Chapter 22. This feature of performance measurement is true for the managers of all parts of a business, whether it is organised divisionally or not.

For optimum performance for the company, managers need to be aware of what the company's objectives are and how their own performance in the particular area for which they are responsible fits into the overall company plan. Equally, the feedback on current performance needs to detail not just the performance of their own particular area but also of the company as a whole. This will help managerial performance by enabling managers to assess their performance individually in terms of the overall company performance, and also help them to feel more involved in company performance. It also facilitates synergy as managers can see how a certain action which they might take can influence company performance even if it does not necessarily improve their individual performance. Thus a team approach to management leads to better performance than does an individualistic approach.

Behavioural theories

The control of the performance of a business needs to be considered in terms of the people who are involved in that business and behavioural scientists have investigated in detail the factors that lead to improved performance in people. McGregor (1960) in his book, *The Human Side of Enterprise*, stated:

> Every managerial decision has behavioural consequences. Successful management depends – not alone, but significantly – upon the ability to predict and control human behaviour.

McGregor argued that managers' behaviour towards others was influenced by their assumptions regarding human nature. He separated these assumptions into two categories and called them Theory X and Theory Y. *Theory X* is based upon the assumption that people dislike work and will avoid it if at all possible, and that they have little ambition, want to avoid responsibility and be directed. Theory X therefore assumes that people need to be controlled and directed in order to get them to put effort into the achievement of organisational objectives. This theory therefore requires strict control systems which report upon performance, particularly deviations from planned performance, not just to the person him or herself but also to his or her supervisor for corrective action.

Theory Y, on the other hand, assumes that people are conscientious and committed and capable of self-direction to meet the objectives of the company if committed to them. This theory leads to a greater co-operation in working and is based upon gaining commitment through an understanding of corporate goals.

Emery and Thorsrud (1963) identify six criteria which a job needs to have in order to maintain the interest of an employee. Such a job must:

- be reasonably demanding in terms other than sheer endurance, yet provide a certain amount of variety
- allow the person to learn as he or she works
- give the person an area of decision making or responsibility which can be considered to be his or her own
- increase the person's respect for the task he or she is undertaking
- have a meaningful relationship with outside life
- hold out some sort of desirable future, and not just in terms of promotion, because not everyone can be promoted.

The management of a business therefore needs to take into account the needs of the people working in that business, and this must be reflected in the control system of that business. Specifically, this needs to be reflected in:

- the setting of targets
- the recognition of achievements
- the reward structure for the level of performance achieved.

Setting targets

The targets set for managers need to be achievable but research has shown that targets which are difficult to achieve and which stretch managers have a higher motivational effect than those which are relatively easy to achieve. On the other hand, targets which are too difficult to achieve are felt to be unreasonable and therefore lead to a loss of motivation. Targets are set in the budgeting process, which we will consider later, but it is important to recognise here that research has also shown that people tend to set harder targets for themselves than those which are set for them by others. This suggests the need for managerial involvement in the budgeting process.

Recognising achievements

Recognition of achievements has a powerful motivational effect not only for the person recognised but also for others who are aware of the recognition given. It is for this reason that companies have tended to introduce achievement recognition systems, such as the award of merit certificates, distinctions, 'manager of the month' schemes, and prizes for the best performance.

Rewarding performance

The reward structure for managers needs to be related to their performance in such a way that a manager can relate his or her rewards directly to performance. This performance however needs to be measured in such a way that individual managerial performance can be directly translated into company performance. Rewards systems normally operate in the form of bonuses and the payment of a bonus can be related either to the individual manager meeting or exceeding his or her target level of performance, or to the performance of the company as a whole. The first method aims to maximise individual performance while the second one aims to maximise company performance and stresses the fact that each individual is contributing towards company performance.

There is merit in both methods of reward and it is for this reason that managerial rewards and payment tend to be linked to both, with a bonus payable partly for individual performance and partly for company performance.

We will consider in detail in Chapters 20 and 21 the value of setting standards of performance and the problems involved in ensuring that the standards set are reasonable and realistic, and remain so over time. The operational control systems of a business need to recognise this problem and allow for the revision of standards on a regular basis. The systems also need to recognise that business circumstances can change, and that the economic and competitive climate can also change, thereby making theses standards inappropriate. The control systems therefore need to be flexible and to encourage maximum performance rather than merely the achievement of the standards set. This is particularly important in a modern business environment where the emphasis is upon quality and level of service rather than merely the control of the costs identified within the accounting system.

The budget planning process

We will see in Chapter 19 that the budgeting process is essentially a planning process for the operational activities of the company. In terms of individual managers we have also seen that the budgeting process provides a means of communicating to them the plan for the business but also provides a means whereby the plan is translated into individual targets for managers to achieve in running that part of the business for which they are responsible. Research by Ronen and Livingstone (1975) has shown that managerial involvement in the budgeting process, through participation in the development of the budget, leads to higher motivation for managers to achieve the budget targets set. Thus involvement in the setting of targets leads to 'ownership' of those targets by the managers concerned and this in turn leads to a higher motivation towards their achievement. Similarly, research by Rockness (1977) has shown that the setting of a budget which is difficult to achieve will result in better performance than the setting of one which is relatively easy to achieve.

Thus participation in the budgeting process will lead to better performance by managers and hence to better performance by the company itself. In order to achieve this improved performance however managers must also believe that they are in a position to affect the achievement of the budget targets which have been set through the actions which they are able to take. Participation in the budgeting process must therefore be coupled with the responsibility for achieving the targets set and the autonomy to make decisions which will affect the achievement of those targets. Only if all these conditions exist will a manager feel that he or she actually owns the budget for that part of the business for which he or she is responsible, and has the motivation to act accordingly.

Alongside participation in the budgeting process therefore goes the responsibility for achieving the targets set in the process. The measurement of performance of individual managers must reflect this and performance needs to be measured, not in terms of the operations for which the manager is responsible as reflected in the target level of performance set, but rather in terms of the operations which the manager can influence through the decisions made.

In a modern company with highly interdependent processes this can become problematical. In a production environment, for example, the performance of one production process is dependent upon the performance of other processes in the production cycle. If a manager depends upon the receipt of components from another process in the cycle in order to manage the completion of the processing which is his or her responsibility then problems in that component production process can affect the performance of that manager in a way in which he or she cannot influence. Similarly, in a service industry, such as a restaurant, the performance of the restaurant manager, in terms of customer throughput and satisfaction, is dependent upon the performance of the kitchen staff.

Performance measurement systems attempt to recognise these problems through a system of responsibility accounting (see Chapters 19 and 22) but in an integrated business it is not easy to achieve this separation of performance accountability. Nevertheless, the fact that individual performance can be influenced by factors outside the control of a manager can have a demotivational effect. The performance evaluation and reward systems need to recognise this and allow for it as far as possible. Failure to do so can lead to conflict between managers and a consequent waste of managerial effort and reduction in company performance.

Introducing conflict into the operational processes of a company causes managers to attempt to introduce slack into the budget so that the elimination of that slack during the management of operations will help them achieve their targets whatever operational circumstances present themselves.

Research into motivation

Research by Williamson (1964) has emphasised that managers are motivated by the desire to achieve two sets of goals – the goals of the company and their own personal goals. He suggests that personal goals can best be met by the introduction of slack into budgets which will help them achieve the targets by which their own performance will be evaluated. Schiff and Lewin (1970) have found evidence that managers create slack in the budget through both overstating costs and understating revenues. While the existence of slack in the plan for the company may help managers to achieve their personal goals it does not help the company to maximise its performance. This needs to be achieved through the elimination of slack, which needs to motivation of managers to be directed towards the maximisation of company performance through the promotion of goal congruence.

Further budgeting problems

One further problem with budgeting which is brought about by senior managers involving themselves in the budgeting process by means of arbitrating between competing requirements for resources is that managers have a tendency to use the budgeting process as a means of bidding for resources for their own area of responsibility. Thus managers will overstate their requirement for resources in the expectation that senior management will allow less that is stated to be required and reduce the budgets accordingly. This tendency is also brought about by the competitive nature of managers and the fact that, in many companies, the control of a larger budget is perceived to increase the status of a manager relative to his or her fellow managers.

This is a dysfunctional consequence of budgeting which wastes managerial time but more importantly can lead to the allocation of resources being less than optimal. This happens if budgets are scaled down arbitrarily because the true need for resources for each manager's area of responsibility is hidden within his or her over-statement of a need for resources. Thus some managers may be allocated insufficient resources to maximise performance while others may still have slack within their budgets. This problem is brought about by the fact that the resources of the company are scarce and insufficient to meet all needs when coupled with the desire of individual managers to achieve personal goals. Again the promotion of goal congruent behaviour is needed to address this problem.

One approach which has been introduced by companies to address this problem is the use of *zero based budgeting* (see Chapter 19) whereby managers need to justify their need for resources afresh for each budgeting cycle.

The problems of Broughton Economies Ltd ————————

The problems facing Broughton Economies Ltd can be seen to be created by the budgeting process and the way in which managers are not involved in the setting of targets for their own performance. As a consequence of this lack of involvement the managers are not motivated to achieve the targets set. Specific problems which Elizabeth Turner needs to outline in her report are:

- Targets set need to be regarded as achievable by managers. Those set at present are imposed centrally without regard as to whether or not managers view them as achievable.
- Ownership of targets is best achieved through participation in target setting. Targets are set centrally without the involvement of managers.
- Individuals set more difficult target for themselves than those allocated to them, and this could lead to an improvement in company performance as the managers would be motivated to achieve these targets. The managers have no motivation to achieve targets imposed upon them and this is one reason for their achievement failure.
- Allocation of resources is optimised through using the expertise of those involved in operations. This is not the case in this company.
- Managers should only be held responsible for performance which they can influence, i.e. they should only be accountable for their performance with respect to controllable costs (see Chapter 22).
- Central management appears to assume Theory X behaviour by the imposition of targets. Perhaps the assumption of Theory Y would lead to improved performance.
- Feedback needs to be timely to enable corrective action to be taken. There is no indication of what feedback is given and under what time scale.
- Performance measurement needs to promote goal congruence and the feedback and rewards systems need to be allied to this objective. The motivation of managers is dependant on this and this is one reason why targets fail to be met.

Influencing managerial behaviour

One of the most important functions of the accounting control system is to promote goal congruence within the organisation. The effect of goal congruence is that managers of the organisation seek, through their actions, to achieve the goals of the organisation. While it must be accepted that managers have their own personal goals the control system of the organisation should seek to ensure that these personal managerial goals do not conflict with corporate goals. Ideally a manager, in seeking to achieve his or her personal goals, should at the same time be seeking to achieve the goals of the company because these coincide. The budgeting system is an important mechanism for promoting *goal congruence* but the performance measurement system, by which managerial performance is evaluated against the targets derived from the budgeting system, is the most important vehicle for promoting goal congruence.

Goal congruence can be encouraged within a company by the reward structures for managerial performance and by the participatory involvement of managers in the planning stages of budgeting. In order to consider the effectiveness of these methods of encouraging goal congruence it is however necessary to consider motivational theory.

Motivation theories

The *expectancy theory of motivation* was developed by Lawler (1973) and states that a person will be motivated to undertake a task by a combination of his or her expectation that he or she will be able to complete the task and the value which he or she personally attaches to the completion of that task. In other words, the more important the task is to a person the greater the effort which will be put into its completion provided that the person considers that it is possible to complete the task. This theory of motivation therefore suggests that managers should be set targets which are attainable but more importantly they should be involved in the setting of these targets (i.e. they should be involved in the budgeting process) and be given the responsibility for achieving these targets, with their rewards being linked to successful completion.

Herzberg (1966), on the other hand, divides the factors affecting motivation into two groups. He terms these groups hygiene factors and motivational factors. *Hygiene factors* are such things as working conditions, relationships with colleagues and superiors, and salary. His research showed that while dissatisfaction with these factors would demotivate a person at work, improvement in these factors would not provide a motivational force for a person. Motivation is provided by a different set of factors (the *motivational factors*) which include responsibility, recognition and a sense of achievement. Herzberg's theory therefore suggests that involvement in the planning process and responsibility for meeting targets, together with the autonomy to influence the way in which these targets are met, are important motivating forces while the rewards (financial rather than in terms of recognition) are less important, and need only be sufficient to prevent demotivation.

This therefore implies that managers are not motivated primarily by money and the rewards offered to them need to take this into account. Thus while linking reward structures to performance is a part of the process of motivating a manager and encouraging goal congruence, it is actually the challenge set, in terms of responsibility and autonomy, that provides a motivating force when coupled with the recognition of the achievements made. Both of these motivation theories are based upon McGregor's Theory Y behaviour and provide insight into the way an organisation and its accounting information system should be structured in order to provide the maximum incentive for managerial performance.

The importance of feedback and reward

In designing accounting control, budgeting and performance measurement systems it is important to design systems which address the motivational needs of managers as well as encouraging them to seek to achieve corporate objectives. It is necessary however to recognise that people are fallible and can make mistakes and fail to achieve targets. The feedback on performance which is provided is therefore a necessary part of the control system as it can provide information, not just to the individual manager but also to his or her superiors, at an early stage, that a problem exists and targets may not be met. This enables early corrective action to be taken.

If managers are involved in the target setting process and are encouraged to set challenging targets for themselves then it is inevitable that some of those targets will not be achieved. If managers are punished for failure to achieve targets then this will provide a powerful demotivator for managers, who will be reluctant to agree to targets which are difficult to achieve. Overall company performance will thereby be reduced. It is important therefore that managers are rewarded, either financially or through recognition, for success but not penalised for failure, other than by the absence of rewards.

Conclusion

If the accounting control systems of a company are designed and managed properly, with due recognition of the individual needs of managers, as far as motivation and the achievement of personal goals are concerned, then these systems will provide an environment in which managers will be encouraged to maximise not just their individual performance but also corporate performance. Failure to recognise the behavioural implications of accounting control systems will however lead to dysfunctional behaviour, demotivation and conflict. It is imperative therefore that business managers are aware of the behavioural factors involved in accounting and take them into account when making decisions regarding the management of a business.

Summary

- One of the main functions of management accounting is to communicate the plans of the organisation throughout the business. This is to aid operational control.
- A reporting system is necessary to provide feedback on current performance. Feedback enables current performance to be evaluated and corrective action taken when necessary. It enables the individual performance of managers to be evaluated as well as corporate performance. To be useful feedback needs to be given as soon as possible after the event.
- McGregor categorised assumptions regarding human behaviour into Theory X and Theory Y. Control systems are based on Theory X but assumptions about managerial behaviour are based on Theory Y.
- Control systems need to take into account the needs of people, specifically with regard to:
  - setting targets
  - recognising achievements
  - rewarding performance.
- Managerial involvement in the budget planning process increases motivation. This involvement needs to be allied with responsibility for achieving the plan in operation and autonomy to make decisions regarding the implementation of the plan for maximum motivation and performance.
- Managers have personal goals in addition to corporate goals.

- The performance measurement system needs to encourage goal congruence and the reward system should reinforce this.

Bibliography and further reading

Clutterbuck D and Crainer S, *Makers of Management*, Guild Publishing 1990, (Chapter 3)

Drury C, *Management and Cost Accounting*, 3rd edition, Chapman & Hall 1992, (Chapter 20)

Emmanuel C, Otley D and Merchant K, *Accounting for Management Control*, 2nd edition, Chapman & Hall 1990, (Chapters 2 and 3)

Emery F E and Thorsrud E, *Form and Content in Industrial Democracy*, Tavistock 1963

Herzberg F, *Work and the Nature of Man*, Staples Press 1966

Lawler E E, *Motivation in Work Organisations*, Wadsworth 1973

McGregor D, *The Human Side of Enterprise*, McGraw-Hill 1960

Rockness H O, 'Expectancy theory in a budgetary setting: an experimental examination' in The *Accounting Review*, 52 pp.893–903 (1977)

Ronen J and Livingstone J L, 'An expectancy theory approach to the motivational impact of budgets' in The *Accounting Review*, 50 pp.671–685 (1975)

Schiff M and Lewin A Y, 'The impact of people on budgets' in The *Accounting Review*, 45 pp.259–268 (1970)

Williamson O E, *The Economics of Discretionary Behaviour*, Prentice Hall 1964

Self-review questions

1 Why is feedback important:
(a) to the individual manager
(b) to the organisation?
(See page 247.)

2 What goals do managers pursue?
(See page 251.)

3 Explain how involvement in the budgeting process helps to motivate managers.
(See page 250.)

4 How does the setting of targets by individuals differ from those set for them?
(See page 250.)

5 Distinguish between Theory X and Theory Y assumptions of behaviour and explain the significance for accounting control systems.
(See page 248.)

6 What does the expectancy theory of motivation indicate regarding the setting of targets for managers?
(See page 253.)

7 Outline the dysfunctional consequences of budgeting.
(See page 251.)

Additional questions

18.1 Your manager has called you into her office and says to you, 'I have worked out the budgets for next year. This is what you are responsible for:

	£
Direct materials	200,000
Direct labour (12 people)	125,000
Allocated machine costs:	
Operating expenses	80,000
Depreciation	24,000
Allocated production overheads	35,120
Allocated administration expenses	12,346
	476,466

Budgeted production: 125,000 units

She continues:

'It is a tough budget to achieve but I am sure you will do your best.'

You know that your performance will be assessed on how you perform in relation to this budget and that your bonus is dependent upon you achieving it.

Outline the likely problems caused by this approach to budgeting and the essential features of a budgeting system which aims to maximise organisational and individual performance.

18.2 Greenfield Consulting is a management consulting company with offices in several major cities. The managers of the various offices have been complaining continually about the difficulty they have in meeting the targets set for them by the senior management of the company. These targets are set in the budgeting process and include targets for both cost containment and for income generation. The office managers argue that it is difficult to motivate their staff to achieve the targets set, that this causes problems when bonus payments are not received, and is a cause of general demotivation among staff.

The senior management has listened to these complaints and has asked you to prepare a report outlining the cause of the problems and possible solutions.

18.3 Outline the main causes of boredom among factory workers and the steps which a manager can take to motivate his or her staff and provide job satisfaction.

19   Using budgets for planning and control

Objectives

After studying this chapter you should be able to:

- explain the purpose of budgeting
- describe the components of a budget
- calculate the cash implication of a budget
- discuss the purposes of budgetary control
- discuss the implications of budgeting for managerial behaviour.

Industrial Dies plc – industrial chemical manufacturer ————

Industrial Dies plc is a company which manufacture a variety of industrial chemicals using a standardised process which takes one month to complete for each product. Each production batch is begun at the start of a period and transferred to finished goods at the end of the period. The cost structure of production, based upon current selling price, is:

	%	%
Sales price		100
Variable costs:		
Raw materials	35	
Other variable costs	40	
Total variable costs (used for stock valuation)		75
Contribution		25

Activity levels are constant throughout the year and annual sales, which are made entirely on credit, amount to £30 million.

The company is now planning to expand in order to increase sales volume by 50 per cent and unit sales price by 10 per cent. This expansion would not affect the fixed costs of £600,000 per month (which includes £120,000 for depreciation of plant). Variable cost per unit will not be affected by this expansion nor by the price increase planned.

The current end of period working capital position is:

	£000s	£000s
Raw materials	750	
Work in progress	1,600	
Finished goods	1,875	4,275
Debtors		2,500
Cash		800
		7,525
Creditors		875
Net working capital		6,650

In order to facilitate the planned expansion the following operating conditions are expected:

- the average period of credit allowed to customers will be increased from one month to two, effective immediately
- suppliers will continue to be paid on monthly terms
- stocks of raw materials and finished goods will continue to be sufficient for one month's production and sales
- there will be no changes to production periods and other variable costs will continue to be paid in the month of production
- increased production will commence in two months' time, necessitating increased raw materials purchasing the previous month
- the planned price increase will take place in one month's time
- sales volume is expected to increase by 50 per cent in three months' time.

The managing director has asked Angela Jones, the management accountant, to prepare a budget for the planned expansion, detailing the cash flow implications of the plan, the working capital requirements and the expected increase in profit resulting.

The essential nature of budgeting

A budget for a business can simply be described as a plan for the future activity of that business. A budget however is specific in that this plan is quantified in financial terms in order to calculate the financial implications. We can see therefore that budgeting can help the planning process of the business by enabling the evaluation of the financial implications of the proposed activities of that business. We can also see that it can be used to compare alternative proposals for future activity and to evaluate them in terms of their respective financial implications.

A budget takes into account all the activities of the business. This includes not just its normal operations, which we have discussed previously in terms of production levels and product costing, but also possible changes in its operations. These changes can include capital investment (discussed in Chapter 14), changing methods of operation and changing conditions of trading, as is the case for Industrial Dies plc.

Budgeting is concerned with both short- and long-term planning. Short-term planning focuses upon the next period, and is usually on a year by year basis. This plan is normally referred to as the budget, and comprises a detailed plan (in financial terms) of all the activities of the business. This budget is the subject matter of this chapter. Budgets are however produced for long-term planning and these are part of the corporate plan, which we considered in detail in Chapter 2. Long-term budgets are, by their nature, less accurate than the annual budget and hence tend to be completed in less detail. The annual budget can be regarded as one stage in the fulfilment of the corporate plan.

Preparing budgets

A complete budget addresses all the activities of the organisation in detail, and in order to prepare such a budget it is necessary to start by compiling budgets for each activity which is undertaken within the organisation. This will normally be done at a departmental level and so each production department will start by forecasting its planned level of activity (see Chapters 5, 7 and 10) and calculating the financial effect of this planned activity level. Similarly, each service department will produce a budget of the planned costs for its activities. Some costs are incurred centrally, such as rent and rates or telephone costs, and this budget calculation for these expenses will normally be prepared centrally by the accounts department. By combining all these cost budgets of the various departments and activity centres, a budget for the total cost of the organisation can be built up.

The budget does not however consist just of the costs incurred by the business in its operations; it will also be necessary to forecast the revenue expected from its activities. This will consist of sales of the product or service provided by the business. The sales department will therefore also need to prepare a budget based upon the expected sales of the various products or services, based upon expected price levels. Indeed the sales budget is often considered to be the most important part of the budget and hence the first to be completed. The reason for this is that the company will seek to produce the goods which it expects to sell rather than attempting to sell whatever the production budget suggests it can produce. The emphasis therefore is upon the market and the needs of the customer, rather then the needs of the company. Combining this sales budget with the cost budget will enable a budget of all operational activity to be produced. This will, in its turn, be combined with the budget for such items as capital expenditure and research and development (R&D) to enable the overall budget, known as the *master budget*, to be produced.

The components of the master budget is shown in Figure 19.1.

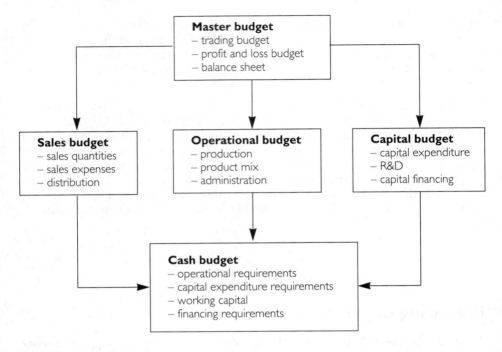

Figure 19.1 The master budget

Co-ordination and responsibility

The final budget needs to be feasible and this requires co-ordination. Thus it is essential that the production budget and the sales budget are related so that the planned level of sales matches the planned level of production, unless changes in stock level are planned. Similarly, planned production, or purchase, of components must match the planned level and mix of final products and the planned activity level in each production department must be co-ordinated to ensure an achievable flow of production through the various departments. The budget therefore needs to be feasible in terms of it being possible to meet the various planned levels of activity but it must also be achievable in that the planned requirements for raw materials, labour and machine time can be met. Equally, the planned level of sales and planned price levels need to meet expectations as far as market conditions are concerned.

Thus *co-ordination* is a requirement in the budgeting process in order to ensure that a feasible and achievable budget is produced. The production of this budget requires communication among all the people concerned in its production as well as co-operation in ensuring that a co-ordinated final budget is produced which is both realistic and feasible. The final version of the budget will only be arrived at after much discussion and revision of individual budgets in order to arrive at a satisfactorily feasible budget. In order to make this process effective it is necessary to have an overall budget co-ordinator (i.e. a nominated senior person) but also to assign *responsibility* for the production of each individual budget. It is normal to give this responsibility for the production of each individual budget to the manager who will be responsible for the achievement of that budget in actual operating conditions. This is known as *responsibility budgeting* and is considered in detail in Chapter 22.

Although negotiation is required in the budgeting process there is also a requirement that the budget be completed. This may mean that a budget is imposed upon certain people and this can have a demotivating effect upon those concerned. An imposed budget is an example of a *top down* method of budgeting while negotiating is an example of a *bottom up* method of budget construction. The implication of these two approaches for the people involved are considered in detail in Chapter 22.

In preparing the budget it is normal to find that one particular factor provides an overriding limit to the activities of the organisation. This factor could be the production capacity of the plant, the availability of labour or raw materials, or the level of demand for the final product or service. This factor constrains the overall planning involved in the budgeting process and is known as the *principal budget factor* or *limiting factor*. It is essential that this factor is identified so that the various budgets can be developed with due regard for this limitation.

It is possible for more than one limiting factor to exist and if this is the case then the budgeting process becomes more complicated and mathematical techniques are often used to plan optimal levels of activity. This is often the case in advance manufacturing technique (AMT) environments where production is constrained by manufacturing limitations, or bottlenecks, in several processes (see Chapter 7). Limiting factors exist at a particular time and can be expected to change or be removed over the longer period. Indeed, one of the functions of the long-term corporate plan is to address such issues as limiting factors and the action to be taken to remove them.

Working capital budgeting

A feasible budget needs to consider not just the production and sales levels to be achieved by the business but also the requirements of the business in terms of the working capital which will be needed to put the plan into effect. These requirements need to be considered not just for the start and end of the budget period but on a continual basis throughout the period. For example, a seasonal goods manufacturer, such as a toy manufacturer, that sells most of its products in the pre– Christmas trading period, may start and finish its budget year with relatively low stock levels, but during the year will have a large build up of stock which is all sold off at one particular time of year, according to its trading cycle. Such a trading pattern has obvious implications as far as working capital budgeting is concerned. The budget process needs to recognise this trading pattern and ensure that a sufficiency of working capital exists throughout the year to finance this stock build up and ensure that the budget remains feasible.

Although working capital includes stock and debtors (less creditors), which must all be budgeted for and managed, the primary concern of working capital budgeting is the cash situation of the organisation. The preparation of a cash budget therefore is an essential part of the budgeting process, and it is important to distinguish between *profit* arising from the activities of the company and cash. Many companies may be operating profitably but suffer from a shortage of cash at particular periods. In fact a shortage of cash is the principal reason for the failure of seemingly profitable companies. The preparation of a *cash budget* is therefore a key part of the budgeting process.

Preparing a cash budget

It is not sufficient for a cash budget to be prepared in terms of the total requirements for the budget period, as what is important is to ensure that sufficient cash is available continuously throughout the year to meet the requirements of the business. Equally, however, at certain times of year a surplus of cash may exist within the business and if the budget makes this apparent it is possible for the business to make productive use of this cash rather than having a surplus sitting in its bank account. Thus a cash budget needs to be prepared month by month (or possibly even more frequently if a critical situation exists) in order to identify the maximum cash needs of the business during the period of the budget and to be able to plan to ensure that this cash is available when required. Businesses which fail are much more likely to fail because of a cash shortage than because they are trading unprofitably, and so cash management is a crucial part of business management. The cash budget therefore has a key role to play in the management of a business.

The cash budget is important for all organisations but is of particular importance if trading is seasonal (e.g as for a toy manufacturer), a major capital investment plan is being undertaken, or there is a major revision to trading conditions. This latter is the case as far as Industrial Dies plc is concerned.

In the case of Industrial Dies plc, the production budget could be produced merely by scaling up the current budget, as the cost structure of its operations remain unchanged. The sales budget can be calculated in a similar manner. The major changes from the planned expansion are in the terms of trade, which will affect working capital requirements, and in the cash flow of the company. Angela Jones therefore needs to recalculate the company's working capital requirements and the cash requirements stemming from these changes. A calculation of the changed working capital requirements would be as follows:

Calculation of working capital requirements:

Monthly sales = £30 million x 1.5/12 = £3,750,000

	£000
Raw materials (one month) (3.75 million x 35%)	1,312
Work in progress (assume 50% increase for sales volume)	2,400
Finished goods (one month) (3.75 million x 70%)	2,812
(i.e. at cost of production)	
Debtors (two months) (3.75 million x 2)	7,500
	14,024
Less creditors (one month's raw materials)	1,312
	12,712
Current working capital	6,650
Increased working capital requirement	6,062

This shows a significant increase in working capital requirements which will need to be financed. The increased cash from sales can be used to finance this increased working capital requirement but the timing of the cash flow changes is also important, as this will have implications as far as the cash requirements of the company are concerned.

A calculation of the cash implications of the expansion plans is therefore needed and a cash budget on a month by month basis will indicate the implications for cash flow of the plan.

A cash budget for the next six months would be as follows:

Cash budget months one to six (in £000s)

Month	1	2	3	4	5	6
Sales	2,500	2,500	2,500	3,750	3,750	3,750
Cash from sales	2,500	–	2,500	2,500	2,500	3,750
Expenditure:						
Raw materials	750	750	1,312	1,312	1,312	1,312
Variable costs	1,000	1,000	1,000	1,500	1,500	1,500
Fixed costs	480	480	480	480	480	480
Total expenditure	2,230	2,230	2,792	3,292	3,292	3,292
Net cash flow	270	(2,230)	(292)	(792)	(792)	458
Opening cash balance	800	1,070	(1,160)	(1,352)	(2,144)	(2,936)
Closing cash balance	1,070	(1,160)	(1,352)	(2,144)	(2,936)	(2,478)

This cash budget shows a net cash outflow during months two to five and even taking into account the cash in hand at the start of the expansion period it can be seen that there is a need for extra cash from month two onwards to finance the expansion of the business. Equally, it can be seen that this need for extra cash is temporary in nature and the increased sales will generate sufficient cash in the longer term. Extrapolating this positive cash flow trend into the future shows that the cash balance will be in surplus from month 11 onwards.

The preparation of a cash budget reveals the need for extra cash therefore in the short term to finance the expansion of the business whereas it can be seen that from the end of month 11 this need has disappeared. Recognising this need for cash in the short term is crucial to the successful implementation of the expansion plans for Industrial Dies plc.

This example illustrates the importance of the cash budget to the planning of operations for a business. Once it has been identified this need for cash will require to be satisfied and arrangements made for the availability of this extra cash. In the case of a large established company such as Industrial Dies plc a short-term need for cash can often be best satisfied by means of a bank overdraft. A newer or less well-established company may find the source of extra cash more problematical, especially if this need is for a longer period. Nevertheless, recognising the need is the first step in the process of seeking such a cash inflow.

Relating cash budgets to profit

Cash budgets detail the expected cash inflows and outflows of a trading period whereas the profit expected during the period will depend upon normal accounting conventions. These include the separation of capital and revenue transactions, taking account of the accruals concept, and including relevant non-cash items such as depreciation. The cash budget and the budgeted profit for a period will never, therefore, coincide.

This can be illustrated by considering the budgeted profit for Industrial Dies plc for the next year, which is calculated as follows:

Operating profit months one to six (£000s)

	Month					
	1	2	3	4	5	6
Sales	2,500	2,500	2,500	3,750	3,750	3,750
Less:						
Variable						
costs (70%)	1,875	1,875	1,875	2,812	2,812	2,812
Fixed costs	600	600	600	600	600	600
Profit	25	25	25	338	338	338

Comparison of operating profit and cash budget is as follows:

Comparison of cash budget with operating profit months one to six (£000s)

	Month					
	1	2	3	4	5	6
Net cash flow	270	(2,230)	(292)	(792)	(792)	458
Profit	25	25	25	338	338	338

Approaches to budgeting

The value of budgeting as a planning tool is very much dependent upon the way in which budgeting is undertaken within the organisation. Obviously, the more accurate is the calculation of costs dependent upon activity levels, the more accurate the budget is likely to be and hence the more useful it will be as a planning tool. This is particularly true if alternative courses of action are to be compared and evaluated. To be effective therefore implies that all the activities of the organisation need to be re-evaluated at the start of the budgeting process, and only planned for inclusion if they can be justified in terms of business needs. This approach is known as *zero based budgeting (ZBB)*. It is defined by the Chartered Institute of Management Accountants as follows:

> A method of budgeting whereby all activities are re-evaluated each time a budget is formulated. Each functional budget starts with the assumption that the function does not exist and is a zero cost. Increments of cost are compared with increments of benefit, culminating in the planning of maximum benefit for a given budgeted cost.

While this is the ideal situation for budgeting it is time-consuming to produce budgets in this manner. Thus ZBB tends not to be used on a continuing basis but is used periodically to ensure that the resources asked for by managers are really required. In other words, managers are expected to justify their need for resources periodically rather than on an ongoing basis in each budget cycle. This approach is used particularly in times of financial constraint, such as during a recession.

In reality, managers will normally prepare budgets by considering current costs and activity levels and adjusting these into the future for known, or expected, variations in costs or levels of activity. This approach is known as *incremental budgeting*. Managers also tend to view the budgeting process as a mechanism for bidding for resources rather than as a planning process for optimising future production activities. They therefore have a tendency to overstate their resource requirements. Thus the budgeting process has other issues than planning incorporated into it and budgeting systems can have dysfunctional consequences for the organisation. These issues are explored in detail in Chapter 22.

Budgetary control

We have seen how budgeting is an essential part of the planning process of a business, but budgets also form an essential part of the control process. This is known as *budgetary control*. The control of a particular budget is normally the responsibility of the manager in charge of the department concerned who is also responsible for the achievement of that part of the organisation's plan. Although this tends to be the responsibility of such individual managers, members of the accounting department must also be involved. The latter tend to prepare the reports for budgetary control which report on actual performance against the plan, and have the technical expertise to assist managers in understanding and controlling their budgets. Indeed formal procedures, such as budget committees, may exist to formalise such arrangements.

Responsibility accounting is a system of accounting whereby costs and revenues are

analyzed into areas of personal responsibility so that the performance of budget hold-
ers can be evaluated in financial terms. In order to do this it is necessary to divide costs
into controllable and non-controllable items, as follows:

- **Controllable costs** These are items over which the manager has significant influence
  and against which it is possible to evaluate his or her performance.
- **Non-controllable costs** These are items relevant to a particular department or
  budget head but outside the control of the manager responsible. It is therefore not
  possible to judge managerial performance in terms of these costs although it is
  important to remember that they are controllable by someone in the organisation.
  Non-controllable in this context means as far as a particular budget holder is concerned.

Budgetary control therefore provides a means of measuring and evaluating performance for each individual activity within the business as a means of controlling its overall performance. This control is in terms of measuring performance against the initial
plan (i.e. budget) and in terms of assigning responsibility for the achievement of that
plan to individuals within the business. We will see examples of such control in Chapter 21, in terms of variance analysis, and the principle of comparing budgeted costs and
activity against the actual can be extended to all areas of the business. One mechanism
for such control is in terms of flexible budgets (see Chapter 20) by which the initial
budget is altered to provide 'target costs' for the actual level of activity achieved. Thus
control is exercised in terms of budgeted activity levels and budgeted costs and also in
terms of revised budgeted costs (i.e. flexed budgets) for actual activity levels.

Budgetary control forms an essential part of the feedback loop by which an organisation can evaluate performance against the plan (i.e. budget) and alter operations if necessary to ensure future achievement of the objectives of the plan.

The feedback loop in this context can be shown as in Figure 19.2.

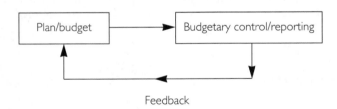

Figure 19.2 The feedback loop

Benefits and problems associated with budgeting

Budgeting can therefore be seen to be an essential part of the planning and control
processes within an organisation. As such it has the following *benefits*:

- it provides a formal way in which the objectives of the organisation and its long-term
  plan can be translated into specific plans and tasks, providing clear guidelines to
  managers regarding current operations

- it facilitates the comparison and evaluation of, and selection between, alternative courses of action
- it provides a means of communicating organisational plans to all members of the organisation
- constraints upon production capability are highlighted (the limiting factor(s))
- preparing budgets provides an opportunity to review operations and revise them if necessary
- performance at all levels of the organisation can be measured and evaluated against an accepted yardstick of the budgeted plan.

Budgeting however also has the following *problems* associated with it:

- as a planning tool budgeting is only as good as the calculations made and limitations on managerial calculation affect this
- the budgeting process can be viewed as a competitive bidding for funds rather than a planning process
- the existence of detailed budgets can cause inflexibility and a resistance to adapting to changed business circumstances (see Chapter 22)
- variations require explanation and this may use managerial time ineffectively if these explanations do not help future performance (see Chapter 8)
- control through budgets can only be exercised by an 'after the event' comparison of actuals with budgets and this may be of little help as a guide to current operations.

Summary

- A budget is a plan for the activity of a business, quantified in financial terms.
- A budget concentrates upon the next period whereas long-term budgeting is incorporated into the corporate plan.
- Budgets are built up from individual activities which are the responsibility of individual managers. Co-ordination is required to ensure that the budget is feasible and achievable.
- The principal budget factor provides an overriding limit to the activities of a business. This factor needs to identified early in the budgeting process to allow the budgets to be built around this limitation.
- Working capital and cash implications from the budget need to be calculated throughout the budget period to allow for any financing requirements.
- Zero based budgeting is a technique which re-evaluates all the activities of the business each time the budget is prepared. It requires the justification of all activities prior to their inclusion in the budget. ZBB can be contrasted with incremental budgeting, which is based upon current levels of activity.
- Budgetary control is an ongoing process of measuring and evaluating performance at individual activity level against the planned budget. Flexed budgets provide a basis for comparing actual costs against expected costs for the actual level of activity. Budgetary control require costs to be divided into controllable and non-controllable ones.
- The budgeting process can lead to undesirable behavioural implication amongst the managers involved in the process.

Bibliography and further reading

Drury C, *Management and Cost Accounting*, 3rd edition, Chapman & Hall 1992, (Chapter 16)

Emmanuel C, Otley D and Merchant K, *Accounting for Management Control*, 2nd edition, Chapman & Hall 1990, (Chapter 7)

Lucey T, *Management Accounting*, 3rd edition, DP Publications 1992, (Chapters 7, 8 and 9)

Sizer J, *An Insight into Management Accounting*, 3rd edition Penguin 1989, (Chapter 9)

Self-review questions

1 What is the essential nature of a budget?
(See page 258.)

2 Distinguish between budgeting and long-term planning.
(See page 259.)

3 Explain how a budget is built up from its components.
(See page 259.)

4 What is the principal budget factor and how does it affect the budgeting process?
(See page 261.)

5 Explain why working capital budgeting is important.
(See page 261.)

6 Explain why the cash budget is important to a business and why the profit and cash budgets differ.
(See page 262.)

7 (a) Distinguish between controllable and non-controllable costs.
(b) Why are these concepts important in the budgeting process?
(See page 266.)

8 What benefits are there to a business in budgeting as far as planning and control are concerned?
(See page 267.)

Additional questions

19.1 The Calculator Company Ltd has collected the following information to be used for the preparation of its budget for the next quarter:

Expected sales	10,000 units
Opening stock of finished goods	2,000 units
Closing stock of finished goods	2,000 units
Direct costs of production:	
Labour	£30,000
Raw materials	£45,000
Overheads	£12,000
Fixed costs	£11,000
Selling price per unit	£15

All sales are for cash payable when the goods are supplied and all expenses are paid when incurred.

Prepare a cash budget for the coming quarter.

19.2 The Carousel Co Ltd is due to commence operations next month. Production costs of its single product are as follows:

Raw materials	£4.00 per unit
Direct labour	£2.00 per unit
Variable overhead	£0.40 per unit
Fixed factory costs	£10,000 per month (including £2,000 depreciation)
Selling and administration expenses	£3,000 per month (including £500 depreciation)

The selling price of the product has been set at £10.00 and it is expected that 75 per cent of sales will be for cash, with the cash being collected at the time of the sale. The remaining sales will be on credit and be paid in the month following the sale.

Stocks of raw materials will be maintained at one month's requirements and all expenses will be paid in the month incurred. There is no opening stock.

Production and sales have been estimated for the first four months of operations as follows:

	Production (units)	**Sales (units)**
Month 1	10,000	6,000
Month 2	10,000	8,000
Month 3	12,000	11,000
Month 4	12,000	12,000

Calculate the working capital requirements of the company in each of its first three months of operations.

19.3 Budgeting is an essential part of the planning and control system of any organisation, and as such has many benefits to the organisation. There are however problems associated with budgeting which need to be recognised by the managers of any organisation. Identify the benefits and drawbacks of budgeting to an organisation.

20 The use of standard costing

Objectives

After studying this chapter you should be able to:

- define standard costing and the types of standards which exist
- explain the objectives of standard costing
- perform costings using standard costs
- discuss the advantages and disadvantages of using standard costing.

Advanced Processors Ltd – manufacturer of electronic components

Advanced Processors Ltd is a company which manufactures electronic components for industrial machinery. It is organised into two cost centres – Department A and Department B. It manufactures two products – the miniprocessor and the transprocessor – and operates a standard costing system.

Joan Walker is the management accountant of the company and has the task of producing a profit and loss statement for each four-week trading period. She has the following information regarding the last period:

The standard variable costs of production for the two products are as follows:

The miniprocessor

Cost centre	Quantity (units)	Price/rate (£ per unit)	Total (£)
1 Direct materials F21	10	6	60.00
2 Direct materials G34	5	16	80.00

	Quantity (hours)	Price/rate (£ per hour)	Total (£)
1 Direct labour grade 1	8	7.80	62.40
1 Direct labour grade 2	7	5.40	37.80
2 Direct labour grade 3	15	4.00	60.00
1 Variable overhead	14	1.25	17.50
2 Variable overhead	16	1.00	16.00
			333.70

The transprocessor

Cost centre	Quantity (units)	Price/rate (£ per unit)	Total (£)
1 Direct materials F21	15	6	90.00
2 Direct materials G35	4	4	16.00

	Quantity (hours)	Price/rate (£ per hour)	Total (£)
1 Direct labour grade 2	15	5.40	81.00
2 Direct labour grade 3	12	4.00	48.00
1 Variable overhead	12	1.25	15.00
2 Variable overhead	14	1.00	14.00
			264.00

Budgeted data for a four-week period of 40 hours per week are:

	Miniprocessor	Transprocessor
Standard selling price per unit	£440	£375
Budgeted output on which standard costs are based	340 units	580 units
Budgeted sales for period	330 units	570 units

Fixed production overhead:
Department A   £27,520
Department B   £18,280

Actual data:

	Miniprocessor	Transprocessor
Actual output	310 units	590 units
Actual sales	300 units	570 units

Actual costs:

	Department A	Department B
Direct materials F21	14,600 @ £5.60	
Direct materials G34		1,120 @ £16.00
Direct materials G35		2,860 @ £4.00
Direct labour grade 1	2,280 hrs @ £8.40	
Direct labour grade 2	12,100 hrs @ £5.20	
Direct labour grade 3		12,720 hrs @ £4.00
Variable overhead	£7,780	£7,460
Fixed overhead	£29,200	£17,600

Joan Walker knows that she needs to use this information to produce a profit and loss statement for the period, comparing actual costs and revenue with those expected from the standard cost information.

Introduction

Standard costing is a technique for control in a business which is based upon the establishment of predetermined expectations of the cost of manufacturing a product. These predetermined expectations of cost are known as *standard costs*. Standard costing therefore is based upon the comparison of these standard costs with actual costs in order to understand the way in which the business is performing. The difference between standard cost and actual cost is known as a *variance* and the use which can be made of these variances in the control of a business is the subject of Chapter 21. Standard costing as a technique is appropriate when repetitive manufacturing takes place, as is the case in Advanced Processors Ltd, so that it is possible to establish cost units. It is therefore a technique which is used primarily in a mass production environment.

A *standard cost* is defined by the Chartered Institute of Management Accountants as:

> A standard expressed in money. It is built up from an assessment of the value of cost elements. Its main uses are providing bases for performance measurement, control by exception reporting, valuing stock and establishing selling prices.

Standard costing therefore can be of considerable benefit to the business manager in controlling the manufacturing operations of the company and in decision making. In order to be useful in measuring and controlling performance it is essential that a standard set for costs of production is realistic, as it is pointless to evaluate performance by comparing actual performance against an unrealistic expectation. Nevertheless, standards can be set in such a way that they provide motivation to the various parts of the production process, and the people employed in production and their managers, to continually strive to improve performance through effectiveness and efficiency improvements. This is one of the objectives of standard costing, and one of the roles of a business manager is to set standards which his or her subordinates consider realistic but at the same time provide a motivation for the improvement of performance. These standards therefore need to be fair but challenging to achieve. The motivational aspects of standard setting are considered further in Chapter 22.

In setting standards there are three types of standard to consider, as follows.

The ideal standard

This is the standard which could be achieved in optimal operating conditions where there are no breakdowns, operating problems or wastage. Such standards are however unattainable in practice and so it is unrealistic to judge performance against them. They should therefore never be used operationally because the failure to attain the standards set in this manner is likely to demotivate the people involved in attempting to meet the unattainable. Nevertheless, ideal standards have a role to play in the manufacturing process as they can be used to represent long-term targets and are a motivator towards continually improving performance.

The attainable standard

This standard is based upon normal but efficient operating conditions and makes allowances for breakdowns, normal losses and problems. Such standards are normally

found in a manufacturing environment and it is against these standards that performance is normally judged. If these standards are set to provide difficult but attainable
targets then they can be used to motivate staff, control costs and measure performance.

The current standard

In the short term it may be necessary to vary the standards used because of changes in
current conditions, such as changed raw material quality. In such a case, the standards
would be changed for a short period to reflect current working conditions, without
affecting the long-term standard, and this is known as the *current standard*. The reason
for setting such standards is to maintain motivation for the people involved who are
thereby able to measure their performance against standards which are attainable under
current working conditions.

The setting of standards therefore is a complex process which requires a thorough
understanding of operating processes and conditions. This process will therefore
involve the accountants and quality/process specialists of the company but it is also
essential that the managers responsible for the various parts of the production process
are involved in the setting of standards. Not only do they possess detailed knowledge
of the processes involved, and any problems which can be encountered, but also they
will have the responsibility for meeting the standards in a production environment.
Their agreement that standards are realistic will enable them to internalise these standards and see them as their own objectives. This will in turn give them ownership of
the standards and hence a greater motivation towards achieving the agreed standards
set.

The revision of standards

The comparison of actual performance with the standards set provides a means of measuring performance within the manufacturing processes of a company. In order to measure performance it is important not just to look at current performance but also to be
able to evaluate changes in performance over time. This implies on the one hand that
standards of performance should not be changed – so that changes over time in levels
of performance can be tracked. On the other hand, it is necessary to recognise that
operating conditions change gradually over time and this has the effect of changing the
expected costs of production and standards of performance. These changes tend to
become more significant in uncertain economic and market conditions, which tend to
make standards unrealistic on a continuing basis. Minor changes in operations on a
continuing basis also mean that standards become less and less realistic the longer they
have been in existence.

In order to motivate current performance it is important that the standards set should
be as realistic as possible. We can see therefore that there is a conflict within a company
between the need that standards once set should be maintained in use and the need that
standards should be continually altered to reflect current operating conditions. To
resolve this conflict most companies compromise between the two sets of needs and it
is normal that all standards are reviewed and altered, as necessary, in one operation at

fixed intervals – often every six or 12 months – rather than being maintained indefinitely or altered on an individual basis as the occasion demands. Changing standards on such a basis is a time consuming activity for the people concerned, and this is one reason for seeking to maintain standards for a length of time.

The objectives of standard costing

The objectives of standard costing can be summarised as follows.

Control of costs

The setting of standards provides targets of reasonable levels of performance and by attempting to meet these targets a manager will concentrate on the various costs of production and seek to keep them under control and within the standards set. In addition, the existence of these standards facilitates a management by exception approach which enables the manager to concentrate upon those costs which are the most problematic and most likely to be outside the standards set.

Performance measurement

The comparison of actual costs and levels of production with the standards provides a way of measuring performance and of assessing the efficiency of manufacturing operations. The setting of standards and their periodic revision requires a review of operating procedures and can provide a way of considering ways of improving performance. A focus on improving upon the standards set in the actual performance and the setting of ideal standards also provide a way of seeking to improve the levels of performance on a continual basis.

Budgeting

The use of standard costs facilitates the setting of budgets because budgeting can be completed on the basis of this formula:

Planned production level x Standard cost = Budget

These standards also enable budgets to be varied according to different production levels without the need for complex recalculation of all the elements of the budget. Only a recalculation based upon the same standards and different volumes is required. The standards can also be used for the estimating and costing of future plans, thereby facilitating planning and decision making, and as a basis for pricing decisions. They also provide a basis for quoting for special orders and variations, and a basis for the valuation of stocks of finished goods and work in progress.

Motivating managers

We have seen that the setting of hard but attainable standards can provide a motivating force for managers and staff in the manufacturing process to seek to improve performance, particularly when they have been involved in the standard setting process. This motivational force can apply to all members of the production departments, from the most senior manager downwards. Setting standards however enables a comparison of standard and actual performance not just at the final level of total product cost but at each level through the stages of manufacture. This makes it possible to assign responsibilities for performance to an individual for any non-standard performance, not just in terms of total cost but also in terms of cost per unit. This accountability at an individual level is part of the motivating force for individual performance and is a way in which standard costing can motivate everyone involved in the production processes.

The motivational effect of standards is considered in detail in Chapter 22.

The relationship between standards and budgets

Although budgets and responsibility accounting are considered in detail in Chapters 19 and 22 respectively, it is important to recognise here that one reason for which budgets are set is in order to forecast the level of activity of a company and the costs and revenues associated with this level of activity. They are also used to allocate responsibilities for the achievement of this planned level of activity to individual managers (see Chapter 19). This responsibility involves not just managing the activity level in the area of the manager's individual responsibility but also managing the costs associated with that level of activity. With this responsibility goes also accountability for the performance level actually achieved.

Budgets therefore are concerned with planning the activity of the business in total while standards are concerned with activity at a unit level. The standards set however can be used in the composition of the budget because the standard cost is a unit cost and will increase in accordance with the level of activity. Thus:

Budget cost = Standard cost x Planned activity level

Standards therefore provide the basis of budget planning and enable budgets to be produced in a relatively simple way which still results in meaningful predictions of cost. Standards also provide a means of budgetary control as in addition to controlling the total budget for any particular activity the manager is able to relate actual costs to individual units and compare not just planned and actual costs in total but also cost per unit, as well as comparing planned and actual levels of activity.

Accounting statements using standard costing

Standard costing is based upon the expectation of managers regarding the unit cost of production and standards are set in advance to project costs and activity levels for the period. It can be expected therefore that the actual costs and actual levels of production will vary from those predicted by the standards.

Thus for Advanced Processors Ltd the standard costs are based upon expected levels of production. A comparison of the planned and actual level of output and sales reveals the following:

	Miniprocessor (units)	Transprocessor (units)
Planned output	340	580
Actual output	310	590
Planned sales	330	620
Actual sales	300	570

The budgeted costs of production for the expected level of output are as follows:

Budgeted cost for expected level of production

Standard costs of producing 340 miniprocessors

	Dept A £	Dept B £	Total £
Direct materials F21 (10 × 6 × 310)	20,400		20,400
Direct materials G34 (5 × 16 × 310)		27,200	27,200
Direct labour grade 1 (8 × 7.8 × 310)	21,216		21,216
Direct labour grade 2 (7 × 5.4 × 310)	12,852		12,852
Direct labour grade 3 (15 × 4.0 × 310)		20,400	20,400
Variable overheads	5,950	5,440	11,390
Total cost	60,418	53,040	113,458

Standard costs of producing 580 transprocessors

	Dept A £	Dept B £	Total £
Direct materials F21 (15 × 6 × 580)	55,200		55,200
Direct materials G35 (4 × 4 × 580)		9,280	9,280
Direct labour grade 2 (15 × 5.4 × 580)	49,980		49,980
Direct labour grade 3 (12 × 4.0 × 580)		27,840	27,840
Variable overheads	8,700	8,120	16,820
Total cost	113,880	45,240	159,120

Total standard costs

	Dept A £	Dept B £	Total £
Miniprocessor	60,418	53,040	113,458
Transprocessor	113,880	45,240	159,120
Fixed overheads	27,520	18,280	45,800
Total departmental cost	201,818	116,560	318,378

Given the actual level of output, it is possible to use the standards to calculate the expected cost of producing this level of output. This calculation is known as a *flexed budget*. The purpose of a flexed budget is to calculate the standard costs of the actual level of production achieved in order to compare this with the actual costs of this level of production.

A calculation of the expected costs of each department based upon standards is:

Flexed budget

Standard costs of producing 310 miniprocessors

	Dept A £	Dept B £	Total £
Direct materials F21 (10 × 6 × 310)	18,600		18,600
Direct materials G34 (5 × 16 × 310)		24,800	24,800
Direct labour grade 1 (8 × 7.8 × 310)	19,344		19,344
Direct labour grade 2 (7 × 5.4 × 310)	11,718		11,718
Direct labour grade 3 (15 × 4.0 × 310)		18,600	18,600
Variable overheads	5,425	4,960	10,385
Total cost	55,087	48,360	103,447

Standard costs of producing 590 transprocessors

	Dept A £	Dept B £	Total £
Direct materials F21 (15 × 6 × 590)	53,100		53,100
Direct materials G35 (4 × 4 × 590)		9,440	9,440
Direct labour grade 2 (15 × 5.4 × 590)	47,790		47,790
Direct labour grade 3 (12 × 4.0 × 590)		28,320	28,320
Variable overheads	8,850	8,260	17,110
Total cost	109,740	46,020	155,760

Total standard costs

	Dept A £	Dept B £	Total £
Miniprocessor	55,087	48,360	103,447
Transprocessor	109,740	46,020	155,760
Fixed overheads	27,520	18,280	45,800
Total departmental cost	192,347	112,660	305,007

A calculation of the actual costs of the two departments is as follows:

Actual costs of production

	Dept A £	Dept B £	Total £
Direct materials F21 (14,600 × 5.6)	81,760		81,760
Direct materials G34 (1,120 × 16.0)		17,920	17,920
Direct materials G35 (2,860 × 4.0)		11,440	11,440
Direct labour grade 1 (2,280 × 8.4)	19,152		19,152
Direct labour grade 2 (12,100 × 5.2)	62,920		62,920
Direct labour grade 3 (12,720 × 4.0)		50,880	50,880
Variable overheads	7,780	7,460	15,240
Fixed overheads	29,200	17,600	46,800
Total cost	200,812	105,300	306,112

A comparison of actual costs and activity with those planned according to standards is one of the main values of standard costing. The difference between the two is known as the *variance* and variance analysis is the subject of the next chapter. At this point it is sufficient to recognise that this variance analysis can point out problems and inefficiencies in production as well as allocating responsibilities.

In the case of Advanced Processors Ltd the differences between the standard cost of production and the actual cost of production are as follows:

Comparison of budgeted and actual costs

	Actual cost £	Flexed budget £	Variance £
Direct materials F21	81,760	71,700	10,000 A
Direct materials G34	17,920	24,800	6,880 F
Direct materials G35	11,440	9,440	2,000 A
Direct labour grade 1	19,152	19,344	192 F
Direct labour grade 2	62,920	59,508	3,412 A
Direct labour grade 3	50,880	46,920	3,960 A
Variable overheads	15,240	27,495	12,255 F
Fixed overheads	46,800	45,800	1,000 A
Total cost	306,112	305,007	1,105 A

Note: the letters A and F stand for:
- adverse (A) – where actual costs exceed the standard
- favourable (F) – where actual costs are less than the standard.

(See Chapter 21 for more explanation.)

It is of course possible that these differences have resulted from problems or inefficiencies in the production process. It is however also possible that these differences have resulted from the standards which were set being unrealistic and impossible to achieve. This therefore illustrates the need for a review and possible revision of standards periodically, as mentioned earlier. This is important in order to ensure that differences between the standard and actual costs of production result from the production itself rather than from unrealistic standards.

Joan Walker is required to produce a profit and loss statement for Advanced Processors Ltd for the period just finished which compares the actual profit with that predicted by the standards. Her statement would be as follows:

Comparison of budgeted profit with actual profit

	Budget £	Actual £
Sales of miniprocessor	145,200	132,000
Sales of transprocessor	232,500	213,750
Total sales	377,700	345,750
Less		
Cost of production	294,863	295,968
Profit	82,837	49,782

This difference in profit is caused partly by changes in the level of sales and production and partly by changes in the costs of production. Variance analysis is used to explain these changes between budget and actual. In practice, this statement would be completed in greater detail by giving an analysis of the variances which have resulted in the different costs and profit. Once you have studied the next chapter you might like to attempt a variance analysis of the activities of Advanced Processors Ltd for this period. A statement of this variance analysis and full profit statement is given as an appendix to Chapter 21.

The advantages of standard costing

We have seen that standard costing is only appropriate in a mass production environment which involves repetitive processing. In such an environment it has a number of advantages which can be summarised as follows.

Guide to pricing

Standard costs represent what it should cost a company to produce its products and operate its processes. They therefore provide a sound basis for valuing inventory and costing a product and hence a sound basis for pricing. They also provide a better basis for considering pricing decisions and quoting for special orders than merely using average or historical cost as a basis for such decision making.

Reappraisal of production methods

Standard costs are revised at periodic intervals and this provides an opportunity for a reappraisal of production methods and a consideration of the ways in which efficiency and effectiveness can be improved. A constant comparison of actual costs against standards also provides an opportunity to review the production methods on a continuing basis. The use of standard costing therefore requires managers involved in production to continually consider the operations involved in the production process and to reconsider the methods used in a constant search for improvements.

Motivation

The setting of standards which are hard but attainable can provide a powerful motivating force not just for managers involved in production but also for all the workforce. These standards have the effect of motivating people not just to maximise output but also to concentrate upon cost per unit. They therefore motivate people to seek efficient operations, cost containment and waste reduction. Standard costing can therefore help a company, not just to achieve cost reduction and high levels of production, but also to achieve its quality objectives and so can have a role to play in TQM (see Chapter 7).

Highlights problem areas

Standard costing breaks down the production process into individual processes and determines cost per unit at individual process level. It therefore enables the cost of a product to be compared with standards at this level and any problems to be pinpointed to the area in which they occur. This enables managers to make more efficient use of their time by not needing to consider the whole production process when problems occur but instead to concentrate their efforts and skills upon the particular problem area.

The disadvantages of standard costing

Standard costing however also has a number of disadvantages, and these can be summarised as follows.

Cost of operating

Standard costing is only of value to a company if the standards in force are realistic and revised sufficiently frequently to keep them so. The setting of standards and their revision at periodic intervals is a time consuming exercise which requires the skills of the managers involved in the production process and those of other specialists. The maintenance of a standard costing system therefore is a costly and time consuming business.

Changing conditions

Standard costing is best suited to an environment which is static as this enables standards to remain meaningful without constant revision. If business conditions are changing rapidly due to product development, technological changes to production methods, inflationary conditions affecting costs, or other economic factors, then this can cause standards to quickly become unrealistic. It is possible to overcome this problem through the use of current standards which override the normal standards but this is costly to implement. In unstable conditions therefore standard costing becomes unreliable and standards tend to lose their control, motivational and performance measurement effectiveness.

Analysis of the past

The comparison of actual performance with standards is by its very nature an analysis of past performance. Such an activity can only be of value to a business manager if it indicates ways in which future performance can be improved. There is a danger therefore with standard costing that too much effort is spent in analysing past performance when this is not relevant to future performance. Without this analysis however it is not possible to isolate those factors which have an important effect upon future performance and therefore need to be addressed.

Relevance to the business environment

The philosophy of standard costing is that standards are set and if production conforms to these standards then all is well as far as the business is concerned. Also, as we have seen, standard costing is appropriate to repetitive processing but modern manufacturing is moving more towards rapid product development, extensive product variations and small processing runs (see Chapter 7). This rapidly changing production environment is becoming the norm for manufacturing businesses and in such an environment standard costing is not appropriate. The value of standard costing as a means of controlling the manufacturing environment and ensuring continual improvement in performance in the production processes and in quality of output is therefore increasingly being questioned by business managers.

Conclusion

We have seen that standard costing is a technique which can be used by the managers of a business to help them in the control of the business. We have also seen however that there are a number of problems associated with the operation of a standard costing system. Nevertheless, standard costing is a method of costing and of production and cost control which is currently widely used in a manufacturing environment and a manager who understands the principles of its operation can therefore make use of the technique to help him or her manage that part of the business for which he or she is responsible.

Summary

- Standard costing is a technique based upon the establishment of predetermined expectations of cost of production.
- Three types of standard exist:
  - the ideal standard
  - the attainable standard
  - the current standard.
- Standards need to reflect current operating conditions but also to remain unchanged for periods of time in order to enable comparisons of performance. In practice, this conflict is resolved by periodic reviews of all standards at fixed intervals.
- The objectives of standard costing are:
  - control of costs
  - measurement of performance
  - budget setting and revision
  - providing motivation for managers.
- Standards are set at unit of production level and provide a basis for building up the budget for the period.
- A flexed budget is produced to compare expected cost for the actual level of production achieved with the actual costs incurred.
- The advantages of standard costing are:
  - it provides a guide to pricing
  - it enables a reappraisal of production methods
  - it provides motivation for managers
  - it highlights problem areas at an individual process level.
- The disadvantages of standard costing are:
  - it is costly to operate
  - it is only suited to static conditions
  - it provides an analysis of past performance not a guide to the future
  - it is of questionable relevance to a modern production environment.

Bibliography and further reading

Arnold J and Hope T, *Accounting for Management Decisions*, Prentice Hall 1983, (Chapter 16)

Biggs C and Benjamin D, *Management Accounting Techniques*, 2nd edition, Butterworth Heinemann 1993, (Chapter 12)

Drury C, *Management and Cost Accounting*, 3rd edition, Chapman & Hall 1992, (Chapters 18 and 19)

Lucey T, *Management Accounting*, 3rd edition, DP Publications 1992, (Chapters 10 and 11)

Self-review questions

1 Define three types of standard and state which is used normally in a manufacturing environment.
(See page 272.)

2 Why do standards need to be revised on a regular basis?
(See page 273.)

3 What is a standard cost?
(See page 272.)

4 Identify three objectives of standard costing and explain how these can help a business manager.
(See page 274.)

5 Explain what is meant by a flexed budget and how it differs from an initial budget.
(See page 277.)

6 Give two reasons for the existence of differences between standard cost and actual cost.
(See page 279.)

7 Explain four different advantages of standard costing.
(See page 280.)

8 Why is standard costing of questionable relevance to a modern production environment?
(See page 281.)

Additional questions

20.1 The management accountant of Jones & Jones Ltd has produced the following performance report for the last month:

	Budget £	Actual £
Factory:		
Direct labour	192,000	179,000
Indirect labour	72,000	63,800

The budget is based upon a production volume of 12,000 units whereas actual production was 10,000 units. Standard direct labour time is 2 hours per unit and actual hours worked were 22,000. Direct labour is a mixed cost and £36,000 is a fixed cost.

You are required to prepare a statement based upon flexed budgeting principles using this information.

20.2 A company manufactures two products, X and Y. The following information is available regarding the production resources required to produce these products:

	Product X	**Product Y**
Direct material A	3 kg	2.5 kg
Direct material B	4 kg	5 kg
Direct labour dept. 1	2 hours	1.5 hours
Direct labour dept. 2	3 hours	2 hours

Costs are as follows:

Direct material A   £900 per 100 kg
Direct material B   £8 per kg
Direct labour costs:
Dept. 1   £157,500 for 21,000 hours productive time
Dept. 2   £126,000 for 18,000 hours productive time
Variable overheads
Dept. 1   £35,700
Dept. 2   £41,400

Overheads are recovered on the basis of direct labour hours.

Calculate the standard cost of production of each product based upon this information.

20.3 The Market Trading Co Ltd manufactures one products which it sells to domestic customers. Budgeted profit, based upon standard costs and expected sales volume of 10,000 units, for the next period was as follows:

	£
Sales revenue	350,000
Less:	
Direct materials	60,000
Direct labour (2 hrs per unit)	160,000
Variable overheads	35,000
(recovered through direct labour hours)	
Fixed overheads	12,000
Net revenue	83,000

In actual fact, the company only produced and sold 9,000 units, although the selling price remained unchanged.

Actual costs were as follows:

	£
Direct materials	52,000
Direct labour	151,000
Variable overheads	32,500
Fixed overheads	11,400

Prepare a flexed budget based upon the actual volume of production and sales, and reconcile the profit expected with the actual level of profit achieved.

21 Analysing variances

Objectives

After studying this chapter you should be able to:

- explain the meaning of variance analysis and the purposes of calculating variances
- calculate appropriate variances in order to measure performance
- describe the steps in variance analysis and the investigations needed
- evaluate whether it is appropriate to investigate any particular variance
- discuss the limitations of variance analysis.

Precision Machining Ltd – manufacturer of machine parts

David Johnson is the management accountant of Precision Machining Ltd, a company which makes machine parts. Gerald Atkinson, the production manager, is concerned that the cost of manufacturing products is different to that budgeted. He believes that this is something to do with the overhead costs and has asked David to investigate.

The company manufactures two products, the X234 and the X365. It operates a full absorption standard costing system.

Gerald has provided the following information for the last period:

	X234	X365
Budgeted production	6,700 units	4,100 units
Standard machine hours per unit	5	6
Actual production	7,100 units	4,000 units
Total machine time used	55,000 hours	
Actual fixed overheads incurred	£120,650	
Actual variable overheads incurred	£86,600	

David Johnson knows that overheads are absorbed as follows:

- The company overheads are applied to production by means of a standard machine hour absorption rate and this is calculated at the start of each period.
- The variable element of the period's absorption rate was £1.50 per standard machine hour and the total overheads for that period were budgeted to be £208,750.
- The budget assumes that one standard machine hour should be produced in one actual hour of machining time.

David knows that this information will enable him to investigate the overhead costs incurred in production and those allocated. He knows that he needs to look at the variances involved in order to provide an answer to Gerald Atkinson.

The purpose of variance analysis

We have seen that an important objective of standard costing is to be able to measure current operational performance by means of comparing this performance with the standards set. This is done by means of variance analysis. A *variance* is the difference between standard cost and actual cost. Variances arise for a variety of reasons:

- differences in rates or prices
- differences in quantities used or proportions combined
- differences in efficiencies
- incorrect standards.

These are the causes of variances and the purpose of variance analysis is to establish the reasons for these causes by means of investigation. The purpose of this analysis is to provide information for the managers of the operations concerning the causes of a performance which is different from standard performance in order to help them improve future performance through:

- increased efficiency
- more effective resource utilisation
- cost reduction.

Any variance from standard can of course be either positive or negative and it is important that the variance is correctly identified. The methods of identification are:

- adverse (A) – where actual costs exceed the standard
- favourable (F) – where actual costs are less than the standard

Any variance therefore consists of a numerical value together with a *signifier*, (A) or (F), in order to be meaningful.

The relationship of variances

The overall objective of variance analysis is to explain the difference between budgeted profit for the period and actual profit. This is known as *operating profit variance* and is explained by subdividing variance into two:

- total cost variance
- total sales margin variance.

Operating profit variance can be explained in terms of these two variances and is given by the following formula:

Operating profit variance = Total cost variance + Total sales margin variance

The *total cost variance* provides an explanation of the difference between the standard cost and the actual cost of the level of production actually achieved while the *total sales margin variance* provides an explanation of differences between actual level of sales and the budgeted level, as well as the difference in selling prices. These two together make up the difference between budgeted profit for the period and actual profit.

Each of these variances is further subdivided into other variances which in their turn are subdivided until a complete picture of the make-up of the operating profit variance is arrived at. Variances can therefore be considered to be hierarchical in nature, as illustrated in Figure 21.1.

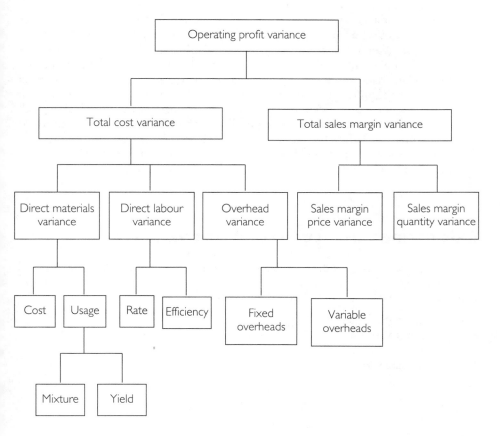

Figure 21.1 Hierarchy of variances

The total variances of each subdivision when added together equal the variance at the next level up in the hierarchy. Thus

Labour rate variance + Labour efficiency variance = Direct labour variance

The analysis of variance

Variance analysis is concerned initially with calculating the variances involved in the production process. It is however essential that these variances are not just calculated but also explanations sought for them in order that the analysis provides some meaningful information to the managers of the processes so that they can act accordingly.

It is important to recognise that the variances calculated are not necessarily independent of each other and that explanations may affect a number of variances. For example, the purchase of a different type of material for a particular job may result in a materials price variance which will be favourable if the new materials are at a lower price but this may be offset by an adverse materials usage variance due to increased wastage and an adverse labour efficiency variance due to the difficulty of working with the new material. It is important therefore that explanations of variances, in order to be helpful to managers, are made not in terms of individual variances but rather in terms of what is happening in the production process as a whole. It is also important to recognise that different stages in the production process (e.g. ordering materials and producing products with those materials) can be the responsibility of a different manager and so the production process needs to be considered as a whole in order to optimise results. Thus the measurement and reporting of performance cannot be treated for each individual manager in isolation, and the consequences of this are considered in detail in Chapter 22.

Calculating variances – total cost variance

The *total cost variance* provides an explanation of the difference between the standard cost of making a product and its actual cost. It is based upon the actual level of output achieved. It can be broken down into the following components:

- direct materials variances
- direct labour variances
- variable overhead variances
- fixed overhead variances.

Each of these will be considered in turn.

Direct materials variances

The difference between the standard cost of direct materials and the actual cost of the materials used for the actual production volume achieved is known as the *direct materials variance*. It can be calculated from the following formula:

> Direct materials variance
> = (Actual production x Standard cost per unit) – Actual materials cost

It can be broken down as follows:

> Direct materials variance
> = Materials price variance + Materials usage variance

Materials price variance can be defined as the difference between the standard price and the actual price of the specific quantity of materials used. It is calculated as follows:

Materials price variance
= (Standard price per unit – Actual price) x Quantity actually used

Materials usage variance can be defined as the difference between the standard quantity required for production and the actual quantity used at the standard price. It is calculated as follows:

Materials usage variance
= (Standard quantity for actual production – Actual quantity used)
  x Standard price per unit

Materials usage variance can be further broken down into the following variances:

- *Mix variance* – which shows the effect on cost of using different proportions of the various materials compared with standard proportions.
- *Yield variance* – which shows the effect on cost of using different total quantities of the mixture used compared with the standard.

These variances can be calculated from the following formulae:

Mix variance = Standard cost of actual quantity of actual mix – Standard cost of
               actual quantity of standard mix

Yield variance = Standard cost of actual quantity of standard mix – Standard cost
                 of standard quantity of standard mix

Typical causes of materials variances are:

- price variances:
  - actual prices different from budgeted price
  - substitute materials used
  - different quantities purchased affecting discounts obtained
  - different qualities of materials used
- usage variances:
  - effect of using substitute materials
  - quality changes affecting wastage
  - different qualities of materials used.

Direct labour variances

The difference between the standard direct labour cost and the actual direct labour cost for the production level actually achieved is known as the *direct labour variance*, which can be calculated by the following formula:

Direct labour variance = (Actual production x Standard labour cost per unit) –
                         Actual labour cost

It can be subdivided into:

- direct labour rate variance
- direct labour efficiency variance;

such that:

Direct labour variance = Direct labour rate variance + Direct labour efficiency variance

Direct labour rate variance can be defined as the difference between the standard and actual cost for the hours actually worked and can be calculated as follows:

Direct labour rate variance = (Standard wage rate per hour – Actual wage rate) x Actual hours worked

Direct labour efficiency variance can be defined as the difference in cost between the standard hours for the actual production level achieved and the actual hours worked to achieve that production level. It can be calculated as follows:

Direct labour efficiency variance = (Standard hours for actual production – Actual hours worked) x Standard rate

Typical causes of labour variances are:

● rate variances:
  – effect of pay awards or bonus payments
  – need for overtime working
  – the use of different grades of labour to the standard
● efficiency variances:
  – problems with materials or the production processes
  – poor organisation of production (e.g. leading to idle time)
  – lack of training or unqualified workers.

Variable overhead variances

The difference between the actual variable overheads incurred and those absorbed (i.e. the over- or under-absorption) is known as the *variable overhead variance*. It can be calculated as follows:

Variable overhead variance = (Actual production x Standard variable overhead rate per unit) – Actual variable overhead costs

This can be subdivided into:

● variable overhead expenditure variance
● variable overhead efficiency variance;

such that:

Variable overhead variance = Variable overhead expenditure variance + Variable overhead efficiency variance

Variable overhead expenditure variance can be defined as the difference between the variable overheads incurred and those absorbed, based on the actual hours worked. It can be calculated as follows:

Variable overhead expenditure variance
= Budgeted variable overheads for actual volume – Actual variable overheads

Variable overhead efficiency variance can be defined as the difference between the variable overheads incurred and those absorbed, and can be calculated as follows:

Variable overhead efficiency variance = (Standard hours for actual production − Actual hours) x Variable overhead rate

Fixed overhead variance

The *fixed overhead variance* is defined as the difference between the fixed overheads absorbed by the actual production and those actually incurred. It can be calculated as follows:

Fixed overhead variance = Budgeted fixed overheads − Actual fixed overheads

Overhead variances − standard absorption costing approach

In a standard absorption costing approach (see Chapter 5) fixed and variable overheads are absorbed into product costs and included in the stock valuation. This means that if the actual production differs from the budget then the amount of fixed overheads absorbed into product costs differs from the actual amount of fixed costs. This gives rise to the calculation of an additional fixed cost variance which is called the *fixed overhead volume variance.*

This can be calculated by the following formula:

Fixed overhead volume variance = (Actual production − Budgeted production) x Fixed overhead absorption rate

This can be subdivided into two further variances:

- volume efficiency variance
- volume capacity variance;

such that:

Fixed overhead volume variance = Volume efficiency variance + Volume capacity variance

Volume efficiency variance can be defined as a measure of the extent to which the labour capacity is used efficiently. It can be calculated by the following formula:

Volume efficiency variance = (Standard hours for actual production − Actual hours) x Fixed overhead absorption rate

Volume capacity variance can be defined as a measure of the failure to use some of the labour capacity available. It can be calculated from the following formula:

Volume capacity variance = (Actual hours worked − Budgeted hours worked) x Fixed overhead absorption rate

Overhead variances arise largely because of the conventions of the overhead absorption process and problems with overhead absorption have been considered in detail in Chapters 4 and 5.

For Precision Machining Ltd fixed and variable overheads are absorbed separately. David Johnson can therefore calculate the following variances for the production achieved:

Variance calculations for Precision Machining Ltd

Workings:

Budgeted machine hours: $(6,700 \times 5) + (4,100 \times 6) = 58,100$

Standard hours for actual production: $(7,100 \times 5) + (4,000 \times 6) = 59,500$

	£
Total budgeted overhead	208,750
Less budgeted variable overheads (58,100 × 1.50)	87,150
Total budgeted fixed overheads	121,600

Budgeted hourly fixed overhead absorption rate (FOAR):
£121,600/58,100 = £2.09

Total overhead absorption rate:
£2.09 + £1.50 = £3.59

Variance calculations:

Fixed overhead volume variance
= (Actual production – Budgeted production) x FOAR
= (59,500 – 58,100) x 2.09
= 2,926 (F)

Volume efficiency variance
= (Standard hours for actual production – Actual hours) x FOAR
= (59,500 – 55,000) x 2.09
= 9,405 (F)

Volume capacity variance
= (Actual hours worked – Budgeted hours worked) x FOAR
= (55,000 – 58,100) x 2.09
= 6,479 (A)

Fixed overhead volume variance
= Volume efficiency variance + Volume capacity variance
= 9,405 (F) + 6,479 (A)
= 2,926 (F)

Fixed overhead variance
= Budgeted fixed overheads – Actual fixed overheads
= 121,600 – 120,650
= 950 (F)

Variable overhead variance
= (Actual production x Standard variable overhead rate per unit)
– Actual variable overhead costs
= (59,500 x 1.50) – 86,800
= 2,450 (F)

Calculating variances – sales margin variances

The sales margin variances provide an explanation of the difference between the budget and actual figures in terms of the revenue from sales and so provide the rest of the explanation of the total operating profit variance. The basic variance is known as the *total sales margin variance* and can be calculated from the following formula:

Total sales margin variance = Total actual contribution – Total budgeted
contribution

The total sales margin variance can be subdivided into:

- sales margin price variance
- sales margin volume variance;

such that:

Total sales margin variance = Sales margin price variance + Sales margin volume
variance

The *sales margin price variance* can be defined as the difference between the standard margin per unit and the actual margin per unit for the number of units actually sold. It can be calculated as follows:

Sales margin price variance = (Actual contribution per unit – Standard
contribution) x Actual sales volume

The *sales margin volume variance* can be defined as the difference between the budgeted and actual number of units sold valued at the standard margin per unit. It can be calculated as follows:

Sales margin volume variance = (Actual sales volume – Budgeted sales volume)
x Standard contribution margin

The term *margin* in these analyses is used to mean contribution margin when a variable standard costing system is in operation (see Chapter 9) and profit margin when an absorption costing system is in operation (see Chapter 5). In all cases the margin can be arrived at from the following formula:

Actual margin = Actual selling price – Standard costs

Explaining variances

The calculation of the appropriate variances is only the first step in variance analysis. The main purpose of the analysis is to provide explanations of the variances which will be of use to the managers involved in the various aspects of the business for the planning of operations in the future. Variance analysis therefore is a control mechanism for the managers of the business by providing a tool by which the performance of the various parts of the production operation can be measured. It is also however a planning tool as it provides a mechanism for understanding the operations, and any problems which are being encountered, and a guide to changing those operations for better future performance.

We have seen, when considering the materials and labour variances, a variety of possible explanations for such variances. We have also seen how a change in one factor in the production process, such as the use of a new material, can have an impact upon several variances being considered. Thus it is possible for a favourable variance to be offset by adverse variances in other areas. The investigation of variances in order to develop explanations which properly account for them can be a time consuming task which requires the specialist knowledge of the managers involved in the process concerned, in order to provide satisfactory explanations. In order to be a valuable use of managerial time therefore it is important that this exercise is not merely an analysis of past performance but also provides benefits in terms of help with future performance. This benefit for the future must of course outweigh the costs of the investigation.

The decision as to whether or not to investigate a variance needs to depend therefore on an expectation of benefits which are likely to arise from the investigation. In this respect it is helpful to categorise variances as follows:

- random variances arising within an operation which is under control and operating satisfactorily
- variances arising from identifiable causes but where the cost of the investigation is likely to exceed the benefits
- variances arising from identifiable causes where the benefits of investigation are likely to exceed the costs of that investigation.

In order to make best use of managerial time it is important that only the third category of variances should be investigated and this should be the aim of variance analysis. One problem of course is that, in reality, until a certain amount of investigatory work has been undertaken it is not always possible to categorise the variances into these three categories. In reality therefore a certain amount of analysis to provide explanations of variances is undertaken by the managers of a business which is not necessarily beneficial to the future performance of that business. This is one reason why variance analysis is often perceived to be merely an investigation into past performance.

It is the case for Precision Machining Ltd that some investigatory work is needed and David Johnson will need to calculate the variances and do some preliminary investigation before he can determine explanations for the difference between budgeted and actual costs of production. His analysis would be as follows:

Explanation of variances for Precision Machining Ltd

Fixed overhead volume variance £2,926 (F)
This can be explained by the fact that actual production is greater than budgeted production.

Volume capacity variance £6,479 (A)
The actual hours worked were less than the budgeted hours, thereby giving some unused capacity.

Volume efficiency variance £9,405 (F)
Machine hours were used more efficiently than anticipated giving rise to this variance.

Fixed overhead variance £950 (F)
The actual fixed overheads were less than budgeted for.

Variable overhead variance £2,450 (F)
Actual variable overheads were less than those expected for the level of production achieved. The reason for this will need to be investigated.

A complete variance analysis of the production of Advanced Processors Ltd for the period reported (see Chapter 20) is included as an appendix to this chapter in order to explain the calculation and all variances using actual figures.

A critique of variance analysis

Variance analysis is a technique which is employed within a standard costing environment and a lot of the advantages and disadvantages of variance analysis are the same as those for standard costing (discussed in detail in Chapter 20). Developing explanations for the variances calculated can however be seen to be useful to managers in understanding more fully the costs of production and hence in controlling the production process. These explanations can also help improve performance in the future and certainly force a review of the operating methods employed. This review of production methods is helpful to any business seeking to improve performance, while the variances themselves can provide valuable feedback to managers about the actual levels of performance achieved.

The problem with this feedback however is that it is evaluated against a plan, in the form of the budget for the period, and the evaluation and feedback are only of value if the original plan was realistic. A further problem with variance analysis is that it is necessarily retrospective and involves analysing past performance which does not necessarily help future performance. Standard costing and variance analysis therefore are of questionable relevance to modern production environments (see Chapter 7).

Variance analysis has the further problem that it is based upon standard costs and actual costs, and for control purposes these may not represent the real costs of scarce factors in the production process. In this situation the economic cost, or opportunity cost, of the resources used may be more relevant. This problem was considered in detail in Chapters 12 and 13.

Despite these limitations however standard costing and variance analysis are used in manufacturing industry to a considerable extent. The techniques can be helpful to business managers working in an environment in which they are used, and who understand them and are therefore able to use them to help plan and control those parts of the business for which they are responsible.

Summary

- Variance analysis is associated with standard costing.
- A variance is the difference between standard and actual cost. It consists of a numerical value and a signifier (adverse or positive).
- The objective of variance analysis is to explain the difference between budgeted profit and actual profit.
- A hierarchy of variances exist building up to:
  - operating profit variance.
    This can be subdivided into:
  - total cost variance
  - total sales variance.
- Variance analysis consists of calculating variances and explaining the reason for the existence of the variance. This explanation is to provide meaningful reasons to managers as a guide to future performance.
- Variances should only be investigated if the likely benefits of investigation are likely to exceed the costs of that investigation.
- Variance analysis is useful to managers in controlling the production process but suffers from the drawback of being based upon historical information. This limitation is discussed in detail in Chapter 20.

Bibliography and further reading

Arnold J and Hope T, *Accounting for Management Decisions*, Prentice Hall 1983, (Chapter 16)

Biggs C and Benjamin D, *Management Accounting Techniques*, 2nd edition, Butterworth Heinemann 1993, (Chapter 12)

Drury C, *Management and Cost Accounting*, 3rd edition, Chapman & Hall 1992, (Chapters 18 and 19)

Lucey T, *Management Accounting*, 3rd edition, DP Publications 1992, (Chapters 10 and 11)

Self-review questions

1 Define (a) three reasons for variances existing and (b) three ways in which analysis of these variances can assist in planning future performance.
(See page 286.)

2 What are the two main variances which explain operating profit variance?
(See page 286.)

3 Describe four different direct materials variance and explain their purpose.
(See page 288.)

4 What are the main causes of direct labour variance?
(See page 290.)

5 Explain the make-up of total sales margin variance and what it represents.
(See page 293.)

6 Give two reasons for investigating variances.
(See page 294.)

7 Explain the meaning of overhead efficiency variance for both variable and fixed costs.
(See page 291.)

8 Explain (a) which variances are worth investigating and why; and (b) which are not worth investigating and why.
(See page 294.)

Additional questions

21.1 Megachemicals Ltd produces a chemical compound, composed of materials A and B, which is sold in 20 kg bags. In the composition of the compound, material A can be substituted for material B but it has been calculated that the most economical mix is as follows:

		£
Material A	4 kg @ £4.00	16.00
Material B	16 kg @ £2.00	32.00
		48.00

Processing of each bag of the compound requires 10 hours of labour, comprising the following:

		£
Labour grade 1	4 hours @ £10.00	40.00
Labour grade 2	6 hours @ £6.00	36.00
		76.00

During the last month a shortage of material B required the substitution of material A to a greater extent than normal, while staffing difficulties have meant that the standard proportions of grade 1 and grade 2 labour has had to be varied. Because of these abnormal conditions there has been abnormally high wastage in production.

Actual costs of completing 100 × 20 kg bags during the month were as follows:

		£
Material A	800 kg @ £4.10	3,280
Material B	1,700 kg @ £2.10	3,570
Labour grade 1	900 hours @ £10.00	9,000
Labour grade 2	300 hours @ £6.00	1,800
		17,650

You are required to calculate the following variances:
(a) materials price variance
(b) materials usage variance
(c) materials mix variance
(d) labour efficiency variance.

21.2 A production department of Ball & Smith Co Ltd has been calculated to have an unfavourable variance on one of the materials used in its production process. Details given by the management accountant are as follows:

	£
Materials variance:	
Actual quantity at actual price	41,800
Standard quantity at standard price	40,000
Unfavourable variance	1,800

As manager of this department you know that materials prices were 10 per cent higher than standard during this period.

How would you revise this analysis?

21.3 Flexible Furniture Ltd makes office furniture. One of its products has the following standard unit cost of production:

Raw materials	100 cc @ £0.20	£20.00
Direct labour	4 hrs @ £7.00	£28.00
Factory overheads		£12.00

Standard capacity is 1,000 units per month, and factory overheads are recovered on the basis of units produced.

Last month the company produced 1,200 units and incurred the following costs:

Raw materials	125,000 cc	£26,250
Direct labour	4,700 hours	£32,430
Factory overheads		£12,850

Using this information prepare a statement of variance analysis.

21.4 Brown's bakery produces a range of cakes which it sells to shops throughout the area. Fred Brown, the owner, has just received the last period's trading figures. A comparison with his original budget is as follows:

	Budget		Actual	
	£	£	£	£
Sales		60,000		64,000
Operating costs:				
Materials	25,000		32,000	
Fuel	5,000		5,500	
Fixed overheads	16,000	46,000	17,500	55,000
Profit		14,000		9,000

After preparing the budget Fred had made some changes which he expected would improve his profit. These were:

● Prices were reduced by 5 per cent in order to increase sales volume.

● Materials were ordered from a new supplier at a 15 per cent reduction in price. Fred realised that these materials were of a lower quality than those from his previous supplier and that this would lead to greater waste.

Fred has asked you to advise him upon the effects of these changes and the reason why his profit was reduced from the budget.

Appendix to Chapter 21: Variance analysis for Advanced Processors Ltd (see Chapter 20)

Materials variances:

Direct materials variance = (Actual production x Standard cost per unit) – Actual materials cost

Material F21: [(310 x 60.00) + (590 x 90.00)] – (14,600 x 5.60) = 10,060 (A)
Material G34: (310 x 80.00) – (1,120 x 16.00) = 6,880 (F)
Material G35: (590 x 16.00) – (2,860 x 4.00) = 2,000 (A)
Total direct materials variance = 10,060 (A) + 6,880 (F) + 2,000 (A)
$$= 5,180 \text{ (A)}$$

Materials price variance = (Standard price per unit – Actual price) x Quantity actually used

Material F21: (6.00 – 5.60) x 14,600 = 5,840 (F)
Material G34: (16.00 – 16.00) x 1,120 = 0
Material G35: (4.00 – 4.00) x 2,860 = 0

Total materials price variance = 5,840 (F)

Materials usage variance = (Standard quantity for actual production –
Actual quantity used) x Standard price per unit

Material F21: [(10 x 310 + 15 x 590) – 14,600] x 6.00 = 15,900 (A)
Material G34: [(5 x 310) – 1,120] x 16.00 = 6,880 (F)
Material G35: [(4 x 590) – 2,860] x 4.00 = 2,000 (A)

Total materials usage variance = 15,900 (A) + 6,880 (F) + 2,000 (A)
= 11,020 (A)

Direct materials variance = Materials price variance + Materials usage
variance

Material F21: 5,840 (F) + 15,900 (A) = 10,060 (A)
Material G34: 0 + 6,880 (F) = 6,880 (F)
Material G34: 0 + 2,000 (A) = 2,000 (A)

Total direct materials variance = 10,060 (A) + 6,880 (F) + 2,000 (A)
= 5,180 (A)

Labour variances:

Direct labour variance = (Actual production x Standard labour cost per
unit) – Actual labour cost

Grade 1: (310 x 62.40) – (2,280 x 8.40) = 192 (F)
Grade 2: [(310 x 37.80) + (590 x 81.00)] – (12,100 x 5.20) = 3,412 (A)
Grade 3: [(310 x 60.00) + (590 x 48.00)] – (12,720 x 4.00) = 3,960 (A)

Total direct labour variance = 192 (F) + 3,412 (A) + 3,960 (A) = 7,180 (A)

Direct labour rate variance = (Standard wage rate per hour – Actual wage
rate) x Actual hours worked

Grade 1: (7.80 – 8.40) x 2,280 = 1,368 (A)
Grade 2: (5.40 – 5.20) x 12,100 = 2,420 (F)
Grade 3: (4.00 – 4.00) x 12,720 = 0

Total labour rate variance = 1,368 (A) + 2,420 (F) + 0 = 1,052 (F)

Direct labour efficiency variance = (Standard hours for actual production –
Actual hours worked) x Standard rate

Grade 1: [(8 x 310) – 2,280] x 7.80 = 1,560 (F)
Grade 2: [(7 x 310 + 15 x 590) – 12,100] x 5.40 = 5,832 (A)
Grade 3: [(15 x 310 + 12 x 590) – 12,720] x 4.00 = 3,960 (A)

Total labour efficiency variance = 1,560 (F) + 5,832 (A) + 3,960 (A)
= 8,232 (A)

Direct labour variance = Direct labour rate variance + Direct labour
efficiency variance

Grade 1: 1,368 (A) + 1,560 (F) = 192 (F)
Grade 2: 2,420 (F) + 5,832 (A) = 3,412 (A)
Grade 3: 0 + 3,960 (A) = 3,960 (A)

Total direct labour variance = 192 (F) + 3,412 (A) + 3,960 (A) = 7,180 (A)

Overhead variances:

Fixed overhead volume variance = (Actual production − Budgeted production) x Fixed overhead absorption rate

$[(310 - 340) \times 15] \times 1.99 + [(590 - 580) \times 15] \times 1.99$
$+ [(310 - 340) \times 14] \times 1.57 + [(590 - 580) \times 12] \times 1.57 = 1,115$ (A)

FOAR department A: $27,520/(340 \times 15 + 580 \times 15) = 1.99$
FOAR department B: $18,280/(340 \times 14 + 580 \times 12) = 1.57$
(based on direct labour hours for absorption)

Budgeted hours $= 340 \times 30 + 580 \times 27 = 25,860$
Standard hours for actual production $= 310 \times 30 + 590 \times 27 = 25,230$
Actual hours $= 2,280 + 12,100 + 12,720 = 27,100$

Volume efficiency variance = (Standard hours for actual production − Actual hours) x Fixed overhead absorption rate

$= [(310 \times 15) + (590 \times 15) - (2,280 + 12,100)] \times 1.99$
$\quad + [(310 \times 15) + (590 \times 12) - 12,720] \times 1.57$
$= 3,305$ (A)

Volume capacity variance = (Actual hours worked − Budgeted hours worked) x Fixed overhead absorption rate

$= [(2,280 + 12,100) - (340 \times 15 + 580 \times 15)] \times 1.99$
$\quad + [12,720 - (340 \times 15 + 580 \times 12)] \times 1.57$
$= 2,190$ (F)

Fixed overhead volume variance = Volume efficiency variance + Volume capacity variance

$= 3,305$ (A) $+ 2,190$ (F)
$= 1,115$ (A)

Fixed overhead variance = Budgeted fixed overheads − Actual fixed over heads

$= (27,520 + 18,280) - (29,200 + 17,600)$
$= 1,000$ (A)

Variable overhead variance = (Actual production x Standard variable overhead rate per unit) − Actual variable overhead costs

$= [(310 \times 33.50) + (590 \times 29.00)] - (7,780 + 7,460)$
$= 12,255$ (F)

Sales variances:

Total sales variance = Sales price variance + Sales volume variance
$= 0 + 31,950$ (A)
$= 31,950$ (A)

Sales price variance = (Actual price per unit − Standard price) x Actual sales volume

$= 0$ (Selling price unchanged)

Sales volume variance = (Actual sales volume − Budgeted sales volume) x
Standard price
= [(300 − 330) x 440.00] + [(570 − 620) x 375.00]
= 31,950 (A)

Reconciliation statement of profit for Advanced Processors Ltd

	£
Budgeted profit	82,837
Sales variance	31,950 (A)
	50,887
Materials variance	5,180 (A)
Labour variance	7,180 (A)
Fixed overhead variance	1,000 (A)
Variable overhead variance	12,255 (F)
Actual profit	49,782

22   Evaluating managerial and divisional performance

Objectives

After studying this chapter you should be able to:

- explain the benefits of divisionalisation
- discuss the objectives of a performance evaluation system
- calculate divisional performance using appropriate measures
- identify possible company objectives
- explain the requirement of target setting for divisions.

Home Improvements plc – DIY stores

Home Improvements plc is a company operating DIY stores throughout the country, as part of its plan to extend its national coverage. It has recently acquired Briggs Ltd which is a regional DIY company operating three stores within a 40 mile radius of each other. Home Improvements plc operated through regional companies, each of which has its own board of directors responsible to the main board. One of these regional companies will take over the three outlets of Briggs Ltd, each of which will have its own manager. New managers have just been appointed to these three stores.

Each store manager is responsible for the store's sales policy, pricing, store layout, purchasing of goods for resale and general running of the outlet. The manager controls staffing and recruitment to meet local needs but the main company is considering controlling this through the introduction of a headcount budget. There is a policy that each store manager can sanction items of capital expenditure up to £1,000 in cost while the regional company can sanction items up to £250,000 per project. Each manager is provided with a car and each store has a delivery vehicle for local delivery to customers.

Sales are made by both cash and credit; debtor and cash control is the responsibility of the regional company. Cash is collected and banked locally but credit sales invoices are raised locally and a copy sent to the regional company for control and collection. Sales can be identified from the till information and credited to the department from which they originated. Goods for resale are obtained either from the manufacturing subsidiaries of Home Improvements plc or directly from authorised suppliers. Invoices are authorised by the store manager before being paid by the regional company. A complete physical stock check is undertaken once each year.

The board of Home Improvements plc is concerned that its system of accounting and reporting does not give sufficient information for it to be able to evaluate the performance of each regional office and each store, taking into account the delegated responsibility available to each manager. The board has therefore employed a consultant, Ashish Patel, and asked him to produce a report outlining the available options and to recommend suitable performance indicators.

Ashish Patel has been supplied with the accounts of the company and of each individual store. The following are the summarised accounts of one of the outlets recently acquired from Briggs Ltd:

Profit and loss account

	£000s	£000s
Sales		4,400
Cost of sales:		
Materials	2,560	
Labour	870	
Store overheads	530	
Depreciation	70	
Regional company overheads	44	4,074
Profit		326

Balance sheet

	£000s	£000s
Fixed assets		700
Current assets:		
Stock	635	
Debtors	400	
Cash	150	
	1,185	
Creditors	300	885
Net capital		1,585

The purpose of divisionalisation

When businesses become very large or diverse in the kinds of product or service which they provide then they become difficult to control as one business. This is one reason that they are organised into divisions. Divisions within a company tend to operate on a day to day basis as independent businesses, although subject to the overall control of the head office management of the company. Holding companies, such as Hanson

Trust, provide an extreme example of a divisionalised company in that all the companies within the group continue to use their original names and operate as independent companies. Other companies are organised in divisions because the separate divisions make completely different products or provide completely different services, and so are able to operate independently of each other. Still other companies are divisionalised because they operate in different markets. This is the case with Home Improvements plc where each store operates in a different geographical area but provides a more or less identical level of service to its customers. Each store within the company can be considered to be a division operating independently but subject to the overall guidance of the head office.

The head office management of a divisionalised company will set guidelines under which each of its divisions must operate, but the level of control exercised will vary from one company to another. In the case of Home Improvements plc the head office imposes detailed control in terms of where the goods for resale can be acquired from, what capital expenditure can be incurred without central authorization, and is even considering imposing control of the staffing of the stores through the introduction of a headcount budget. Other divisionalised companies however will exercise less detailed control from head office and will restrict themselves to controlling capital expenditure centrally, or even to just requiring the division to meet a target level of returns to the company. This target level of returns can be measured in one of several ways, and we will explore the possibilities in detail in this chapter.

A divisionalised company therefore is decentralised in its operations. The object of operating through a divisionalised structure is to enhance the efficiency of the whole company and help ensure that the overall objectives are met.

Divisionalisation has the following advantages.

Local decision making

Local managers of a division are in closer touch with the operations of the division and are able to make speedier and more informed decisions. Local managers are also more aware of local market conditions, trends and tastes. They are therefore in a position to respond more accurately to the conditions under which they are operating than would be the head office.

Flexibility

Communication problems are reduced through divisionalisation and the divisional managers are more able to respond quickly to changes in market or operational conditions. This ability to respond quickly and flexibly depends upon the responsibilities and areas of discretion of the local managers being sufficiently determined.

Strategic decision making

The central management at head office has delegated operational control and is therefore able to concentrate on strategic decision making for the benefit of the organisation as a whole. The purposes of strategic decision making were considered in detail in Chapter 2.

Increased motivation

The greater freedom of divisional managers, together with appropriate performance measurement and reward systems, provides the motivation for these managers to perform well, and this leads to better overall performance within the company. This is probably the most important benefit of divisionalisation, and is an attempt to encourage an entrepreneurial attitude amongst divisional managers.

The disadvantage of divisionalisation

One major problem exists however with divisionalisation, and this is especially the case when divisions are highly interdependent. This problem is that the decisions made by the managers of one division for the beneficial performance of that division might impact upon the performance of another division, causing increased costs or reduced performance for that division and the company as a whole. If the overall performance of the company is reduced by this decision then this will lead to sub-optimality of performance by the company, which defeats the main objective of divisionalisation. Adequate control systems are needed to ensure that this does not happen, and these were considered in detail in Chapter 16, while the implications for managerial behaviour were considered in detail in Chapter 18.

Performance measurement and evaluation

In a divisionalised structure it is important that the central management at head office is able to measure the performance of each division and also to provide motivation for divisional managers to seek to maximise the performance of their division within the overall company performance. The performance evaluation system for such an organisation is therefore an important control mechanism for the company. It is normal in such an organisation for divisional managerial performance to be judged on the basis of the performance of the division for which they are responsible, and for managerial rewards to be related to this divisional performance. It is essential therefore that the performance evaluation system should provide motivation to managers and at the same time encourage them to meet the overall organisational objectives. This evaluation system should therefore have the following objectives.

To provide motivation for divisional managers

Local managers should have autonomy of action, within guidelines, and should feel that their decisions and actions taken can lead to better divisional performance as well as overall company performance, and that this will be recognised in their personal evaluation and rewards.

To promote goal congruence

The autonomy of divisional management should however be directed towards achieving better overall company performance rather than divisional performance, if this is at the expense of other divisions or the company as a whole. The reward systems for managers therefore need to promote goal congruence and motivate managers towards optimising company performance while at the same time recognising their contributions to divisional performance.

To encourage long-term planning

The system should encourage maximising long-term performance for the company rather than the immediate and short-term results of the division (and hence managerial rewards in the short term) if this is not compatible with long-term success. It is for this reason that capital investment decisions are often controlled centrally (see Chapter 14).

Reporting

The system needs to provide regular feedback on performance both to the divisional management and to the head office central management. This feedback needs to be both regular and timely (i.e. the response time needs to be as short as possible) in order to ensure that the reporting is relevant and can enable corrective action to be taken if necessary.

The problems of performance measurement

The performance measurement system therefore needs to be chosen with care to ensure that these objectives are met and the overall objectives of the company are achieved. The basis for evaluating performance needs to be measurable in order to be meaningful. It is for this reason that financial measures of performance are used.

The measure used to evaluate performance needs however to reflect the fact that not all decisions and costs are within the control of the divisional management and performance measurement needs to be related to those which can be affected by the actions of divisional managers. One measure used to evaluate performance therefore is that of *controllable profit.* The profit earned by a division however can be expected to have some relation to the capital employed by that division to generate its profit. A measure used which takes this into account is *residual income.* Different divisions within the company may well employ widely different amounts of capital and make widely different amounts of profit. Comparison between divisions when this is the case is difficult to make unless a comparative measure of performance is employed. A comparative measure used to achieve this is *return on capital employed (ROCE).* These three measures are widely used for the evaluation of divisional performance and will be considered in detail.

A further problem which needs to be considered in the measurement of performance is the extent to which functions overlap or are separated. If functions overlap or are duplicated then the measurement of performance for each individual division is harder to achieve. This is a problem which is of particular concern as far as Home Improvements plc is concerned and one which needs to be considered by Ashish Patel in the production of his report.

It is difficult to see for Home Improvements plc what role the regional companies have in creating benefit for the company. The regional companies perform various functions for the individual stores and make a charge, in the form of overheads, to each individual store. This charge is not within the control of the individual store and this needs to be taken into account when measuring the performance of these stores. Also it is difficult to provide performance measures for the regional companies when their function is to handle some of the responsibilities of the stores and to pass the costs of doing so on to the individual stores in the form of an overhead charge.

The regional companies therefore operate as a service function for the stores and are essentially cost centres rather than divisions. The measures used to evaluate divisional performance are not appropriate to cost centres. Their existence needs to be justified on the basis that performing these functions on a regional basis is better for the company overall, in terms of cost or efficiency, than is delegating these functions to individual stores. The regional companies therefore are concerned with cost containment rather than profit generation and the performance measures appropriate to this are through budgetary control (see Chapter 18 and 19).

Equally, the proposal to introduce a headcount budget by central management is likely to reduce the autonomy of the divisional managers and so reduce their motivation. Hence this action by central management would be likely to negate some of the benefit from divisionalisation and some of the objectives of the performance measurement system. These considerations would need to be mentioned by Ashish Patel in his report together with an evaluation of the three measures of performance which we now consider.

Controllable profit

Controllable profit as a measure is concerned only with those costs and revenues which are controllable at the divisional level by the managers concerned. These costs and revenues are the responsibility of local managers who can affect the levels of costs and revenues through their actions. Some costs are totally uncontrollable by the company. Other costs are outside the control of local management and allocated to them from central management. Such costs would include:

- **central overheads:** these comprise a share of the cost of facilities used jointly by all, or several, divisions
- **fixed asset costs (including depreciation):** capital investment is normally controlled centrally and so investment decisions, and the resultant depreciation charges, are not controllable by the division.

Such costs are classified as uncontrollable costs (see Chapter 12) at a divisional level, although they are controllable within the company overall. Such cost would therefore not included in the controllable profit calculation.

Controllable profit can thus be calculated as follows:

> Controllable profit = Divisional revenue − Divisional controllable costs

While this can be related to divisional profits as follows:

> Controllable profit − Uncontrollable costs = Divisional profit

The overall company profit is the total of all the divisional profits less any central costs not allocated to divisions, and is calculated as follows:

Company profit = Sum of divisional profits − Central costs not allocated

Company profit can therefore be maximised by ensuring that the profits of all the individual divisions are maximised. The performance of divisional managers can therefore be judged on the basis of controllable profit; providing motivation towards maximising this will lead to maximising company performance. Divisional controllable profit can therefore be regarded as a contribution towards central costs and profit, as follows:

Sum of divisional controllable profits − Central costs = Company profit

Company profit can therefore be seen to be maximised by maximising the controllable profit of the divisions and minimising central costs (i.e. the costs of the cost centres).

For the store accounts of the one store of Home Improvements plc which we will consider we can see that the uncontrollable costs are those of depreciation and regional company overheads. The calculation of controllable profit will therefore be as follows:

Calculation of controllable profit

	£000s	£000s
Sales		4,400
Cost of sales:		
Materials	2,560	
Labour	870	
Store overheads	530	3,960
Controllable profit		440

Note: uncontrollable costs are depreciation (£70,000) and regional company overheads (£44,000).

Reconciliation with store profit:

Controllable profit − Uncontrollable costs = Divisional profit

i.e.

£440,000 − £114,000 = £326,000

Residual income

The concept of residual income takes into account the fact that there is an opportunity cost associated with the use of capital by a division and that this needs to be recognised when measuring the performance of that division. The larger the amount of capital employed by the division the greater is the opportunity cost of using that capital to generate the profit of the division. Residual income therefore takes into account the cost of capital employed. It is calculated as follows:

Residual income = Controllable profit − Cost of capital employed

Cost of capital is estimated for the company as a whole in terms of the current opportunity cost of funds. This figure is commonly known as the *weighted average cost of capital (WACC)* and represents the cost to the company as a whole of its capital investment opportunities and financing. It needs therefore to be calculated centrally and advised to individual divisions. This figure is then applied to the net assets employed by the division to calculate the cost of capital for that division, and hence its residual income.

For the store of Home Improvements plc the residual income can therefore be calculated as follows:

Calculation of residual income

Cost of capital (assume to be 15%)
Capital employed = £1,585,000
Cost of capital = £238,000

Residual income = Controllable profit − Cost of capital employed
= £440,000 − £238,000
= £202,000

Return on capital employed

Return on capital employed (ROCE) is a relative measure of performance in that it enables the performance of one division to be compared with that of other divisions. This is because it expresses the performance of the division in terms of a percentage rather than an absolute figure. ROCE can be calculated in the following way:

$$\text{ROCE} = \frac{\text{Profit}}{\text{Capital employed}} \times 100\%$$

It can also be calculated as follows:

$$\text{ROCE} = \frac{\text{Sales}}{\text{Capital employed}} \times \frac{\text{Profit}}{\text{Sales}} \times 100\%$$

This measure is also known as *return on investment (ROI)* and in such cases will be calculated on the basis of investment incurred rather than capital employed. This is particularly the case when used for the evaluation of possible new investment decisions (see Chapter 14) or when then division forms a partly-owned subsidiary of the company rather than a true division.

The fact that ROCE is expressed as a percentage enables the profit made to be related to the capital employed to make that profit and also enables a comparison to the target for the division and a comparison of performance between different divisions.

For the store of Home Improvements plc the ROCE would be calculated as follows:

Calculation of return on capital employed

$$\text{ROCE} = \frac{\text{Profit}}{\text{Capital employed}} \times 100\%$$

$$= \frac{£440,000}{£1,585,000} \times 100\%$$

$$= 27.8\%$$

Evaluating performance using financial measures

The three measures – controllable profit, residual income, and ROCE – are commonly used by companies organised into a divisionalised structure as the basis for measuring and evaluating the performance of the individual divisions of the company and the management of those divisions. In measuring and evaluating performance it is essential to set standards to measure against and so a target level of performance would be set centrally by the head office for the divisions to achieve. This would be in terms of just one of these measures and so the target set would be one of the following:

- a level of controllable profit to be made
- a target level of residual income to be achieved
- a target return on capital employed to be achieved.

Performance could therefore be evaluated against the target set. In order to be realistic the target would need to take into account the industry and market conditions prevailing for each individual division, and it does not therefore follow that the target would be the same for each division within the company or even for one division from one year to the next. Factors which would need to be taken into account would include the following:

- the overall strategy of the company
- the cost of capital for the company
- the level of returns expected by other companies in the same industry as the division concerned
- the level of risk involved in the industry
- the degree of competition and the relative position of the division within that industry
- the extent of over- or under-capacity in the industry generally
- the general economic climate
- the market conditions and level of demand for the product or service provided.

In deciding upon a system for measuring and evaluating the performance of a division the company will opt to use just one of these measures considered. In deciding which one to select the central management of the company will need to recognise the objectives of the company and the way in which these measures can help to motivate the divisional managers to meet them. Possible company objectives other than profit maximisation might include the following:

- growth in terms of asset size or turnover
- sales maximisation
- market share
- productivity or quality improvement.

Any measure of profitability alone is insufficient to measure success against the achievement of any of these objectives and the company will therefore need to look for other measures to supplement the financial measures discussed above in order to help measure performance against these objectives.

In deciding which financial measure to adopt the company will need to consider the relative merits and problems of each measure and the effect which these might have upon divisional and organisational performance. These can be summarised under the following headings.

Pros and cons of controllable profit

Controllable profit is a measure of profit as controlled by the division and will encourage the divisional management to undertake any action which will increase profit. This may however be at the expense of long-term performance and may involve reducing costs as well as increasing sales. This could therefore impact adversely upon a quality objective of the company. As this measure takes no account of the cost of capital the divisional managers may well seek to undertake any investment which increases profit regardless of the opportunity cost of such investment.

Pros and cons of residual income

Taking into account the cost of capital ensures that this opportunity cost is considered and the divisional management will be encouraged to undertake any investment which increases residual income and thereby shows a return on that investment. As capital investment is normally controlled centrally however there may be a demotivating effect if funds for capital investment are denied to a division when the divisional management considers that this would improve its performance.

Pros and cons of return on capital employed

This measure facilitates the ranking of divisions and thus enables the central management to determine where resources could be best employed for the benefit of the organisation as a whole. It has the disadvantage however that the divisional managers will be reluctant to make decisions which would reduce their ROCE even if it would increase profitability and may be in the overall best interest of the company.

The performance of managers in divisionalised companies, and so ultimately the performance of the company itself, can be seen to be dependent upon the measures used for appraising that performance. These measures can affect the decision made by managers and therefore affect the performance of the division and the company itself. Performance measurement therefore needs to recognise these possibilities and systems need to be designed to both motivate managers and lead to performance which benefits the organisation as a whole, as well as leading to behaviour which eliminates conflict between divisions and helps meet the overall company objectives. An understanding of the alternative measures available and their possible effect in use is essential for business managers in designing appraisal systems. Such systems need to ensure that the divisionalisation of the organisation leads to better performance than managing the company centrally as a whole, in order to gain the benefits of divisionalisation.

Summary

- A business is divided into divisions when it is large enough to benefit from treating parts of it independently. The benefits of divisionalisation are:
  - local decision making
  - flexibility
  - increased motivation for divisional managers
  - improved strategic decision making.
- A problem exists when divisions are interdependent in that the performance of one division can be dependent upon the performance of another one.
- The performance evaluation system for a divisionalised company should have the following objectives:
  - to provide motivation for divisional managers
  - to promote goal congruence
  - to encourage long-term planning
  - to provide regular feedback on performance.
- The measures used to evaluate divisional performance are:
  - controllable profit
  - residual income
  - return on capital employed.
- Measures used to evaluate divisional performance are only relevant to trading divisions. Cost centres need to be evaluated using different criteria, through the budgeting process. The performance measures used need to be based upon individual divisional performance which can be affected by the divisional management in order to be effective.
- Targets set for divisions need to take into account the following:
  - cost of capital
  - expected returns and level of competition within the industry
  - market conditions and demand for the product
  - the general economic climate
- Possible company objectives include:
  - profit maximisation
  - growth in asset size or turnover
  - sales maximisation
  - market share
  - productivity or quality improvement.

- The financial performance measure chosen needs to reflect the company objectives. It will need to be supplemented by other measures.

Bibliography and further reading

Drury C, *Management and Cost Accounting*, 3rd edition, Chapman & Hall 1992, (Chapter 17)

Emmanuel C, Otley D and Merchant K, *Accounting for Management Control*, 2nd edition, Chapman and Hall 1990, (Chapters 9 and 12)

Lucey T, *Management Accounting*, 3rd edition, DP Publications 1992, (Chapter 19)

Sizer J, *An Insight into Management Accounting*, 3rd edition, Penguin 1989, (Chapter 10)

Self-review questions

1 What are the main objectives of divisionalisation?
   (See page 304.)

2 How does divisionalisation promote better performance within a division?
   (See page 305.)

3 Explain how controllable profit is calculated.
   (See page 308.)

4 What is the difference between controllable profit and residual income?
   (See page 310.)

5 Define WACC and explain its use.
   (See page 310.)

6 (a) Explain how ROCE differs from the other measures of divisional performance.
   (b) Why is this difference significant?
   (See page 311.)

7 What factors need to be taken into account in setting performance targets for divisions?
   (See page 311.)

8 Outline the main problems in using each of the three performance measures discussed.
   (See page 312.)

Additional questions

22.1 The Sigma Bracket Co Ltd operates two divisions. The reported results of the two divisions are as follows:

	Division A **£000s**	**Division B** **£000s**
Sales	101	52
Cost of goods sold	46	27
Gross profit	55	25
Selling expenses	12	8
Administration expenses	13	13
Net profit	30	4

Notes:

1. Fixed costs are allocated to the divisions as follows:
   production costs:
   division A – £14,000; division B – £10,000
   selling costs:
   division A – £3,000; division B – £4,000.
2. Administrative costs are allocated equally to the two divisions.
3. Assets employed are:
   division A – £250,000; division B – £100,000
4. The cost of capital to the company is 12 per cent.
   Evaluate the performance of each division using:
   (a) controllable profit
   (b) return on capital employed
   (c) residual income.

22.2 (a) Evaluate controllable profit, residual income and return on capital employed as means of evaluating divisional performance.

(b) What other factors need to be taken into account in evaluating performance for divisionalised companies?

22.3 Division B, part of a large company, makes one product. The following data applies to this product:

selling price per unit	£100
variable cost per unit	£60
total fixed costs	£700,000
planned sales	40,000 units
capital employed	£4,500,000
cost of capital	15%

Calculate the residual income and return on capital employed for this division.

The finished product contains one component which the division manufactures at a cost of £10 per component. An outside supplier has offered to supply the component at this price. If the components are purchased from outside then the fixed costs will reduce by £50,000. Should the division make or buy the component if the objective of the division is to maximise residual income?

Answers to additional questions

Chapter 1

1.1   Main inputs:
- materials
- labour
- capital (ie plant & machinery etc
- finance.

Main outputs:
- products or services
- profit.

1.2   Data – a set of facts.
Information – the basis of decision making.
Key elements of information:
- meaningfulness
- relevance
- timeliness
- accuracy
- format.

Chapter 2

2.1   Important factors:
- strategy is affected by day to day decision and so emergent strategy becomes manifest
- changes in the external environment affect the way in strategy is manifest in its implementation
- budgeting and control affect the strategic process through feedback control.

2.2   Features of modern businesses include flatter structures with fewer levels of management and consequent greater responsibility for individual managers.
At the same time this means that fewer accountants are employed within a business to assist managers in using accounting information for decision making.
IT usage means that more information is available to managers to facilitate decision making.
Greater awareness of management accounting is therefore a requirement for a business manager in order to improve business decision making.

Chapter 3

3.1   Prime cost = Direct material + Direct labour

	£
Direct materials:	
Steel	4,000
Plastic	1,800
Other	750
	6,550
Direct labour	8,000
Prime cost	14,550

Total cost = Prime cost + Overheads (i.e. indirect costs)

Overheads:	
Factory rent	2,500
Administration	800
Insurance	350
Cleaning materials	75
	3,725

Total cost = £14,550 + £3,725
= £1,825 × £18295

3.2   Direct costs:
steel used in product manufacture
wages of machine operators
patent royalties on product manufactured
overtime payments for machine operators.
Indirect costs:
floppy discs for the office computer
wages of factory security guard
tools for maintenance mechanics
painting of the factory gates
tyre replacement for the delivery van
telephone rental.

Chapter 4

4.1   Direct labour hour rate:
£25,800/2,600 = £ 9.92 per direct labour hour
Direct materials rate:
£25,800/£12,800 = 202% of direct materials cost
Direct wages rate:
£25,800/£7,200 = 358% of direct wages cost
Unit rate:
£25,800/1075 = £24.00 per unit

4.2

	Cutting	Finishing	Maintenance	Canteen
	£	£	£	£
Actual overheads	71,500	47,300	25,100	24,300
Allocate canteen costs	14,580	7,290	2,430	(24,300)
	86,080	54,590	27,530	–
Allocate maintenance costs	20,647	5,506	(27,530)	1,377
	106,727	60,096	–	1,377
Reallocate canteen costs	918	459	–	–
	107,645	60,555	–	–

Note: final reallocation on the basis of 60:30 to the service departments in order to prevent further iterations.

Chapter 5

5.1   Calculation of fixed manufacturing cost overhead absorption rate is as follows:

	Production departments		Service department	General factory overheads
	1	2		
	£	£	£	£
Allocated	360,000	455,000	220,000	230,000
General factory	103,500	80,500	46,000	(230,000)
	463,500	535,500	266,000	–
Service dept.	51,722	128,728	(133,000)*	
	73,379	59,621	(133,000)**	
	588,601	723,846	–	

* Based on labour hours
** Based on machine hours

Dividing by 150,000 to get the cost per unit gives:
                3.92   4.83

Total cost per unit	£
Direct materials	6.00
Direct labour	6.50
Manufacturing overheads	3.00
Manufacturing overheads:	
Dept. 1	3.92
Dept. 2	4.83
	24.25

Profit statement

	£
Sales (146,000 × 40)	5,840,000
Less cost of sales (24.25 × 146,000)	3,540,500

	£
Gross profit	2,299,500
Less non-manufacturing costs	920,000
	1,379,500
Less under-absorbed overheads	
Dept. 1 (25,000 + 3.92 × 4,000)	15,680
Dept. 2 (4.83 × 40,000	19,320
Net profit	1,344,500

5.2 Factors to be considered:
- depreciation – capital or labour intensive
- capacity – investment for future growth, spare capacity or full capacity
- denominator used – normal capacity or maximum practical capacity
- production based on expected sales or on capacity (ie stock building)
- classification of costs:
  - direct or indirect
  - charged on labour or machine time

Chapter 6

6.1 Factors to consider:
- methods of apportioning joint costs – physical units or sales value
- treatment of by-products as cost reduction
- problems of absorbing overheads generally.

6.2

Costs of producing batch 36	**£**
Raw materials (2.40 × 400)	960
Direct labour (400/20 × 6.80)	136
Machine overheads (400/20 × 2.50)	50
Machine set up	32
Rectification work:	
Labour (10 × 6.80)	68
Machine overheads (10 × 2.50)	25
Machine set-up	36
	1,307
Less scrap (20 × 0.80)	16
	1,291

Units produced: 400 – 20 = 380
Cost per unit 1291/380 = £3.40

Cost of defective work	**£**
Raw materials (2.40 × 400)	960
Direct labour (400/20 × 6.80)	136
Machine overheads (400/20 × 2.50)	50
Machine set-up	32
	1,178

Cost of defective work $= (1,291 - 1,178) + (20/400 \times 1,178)$
$$= £172$$

Chapter 7

7.1 Modern production methods are based upon product innovation, the production of high-quality goods at low cost, shortened product life cycles and short product runs. Advanced manufacturing techniques have been developed to cope with these changed needs. They are, by their nature, capital intensive. This means that a greater proportion of costs are fixed and treated as overheads rather than direct costs. Management accounting has responded as follows:

- new techniques, for example:
  - activity based costing
  - throughput accounting
  - backflush accounting
  - target costing
- changed emphasis in reporting, for example:
  - greater emphasis on non-financial measures
  - introduction of quality management systems.

Chapter 8

8.1

Absorption costing based on machine hours:

Production overheads	**£**
Machine department	8,430
Stores department	5,350
Materials handling	2,100
	15,880

Machine hours used:	
Product A 3 × 100	300
Product B 4 × 120	480
product C 2 × 80	160
	940

Overhead absorption rate:
15,880/940 = £16.89 per machine hour

Product costs:

	Product A	**Product B**	**Product C**
	£	**£**	**£**
Direct materials	40.00	50.00	40.00
Direct labour	21.00	27.00	18.00
Overheads	50.67	67.56	33.78
	111.67	144.56	91.78

Activity based costing:

Machine dept. costs   £8,430
Cost driver – set up per batch
No. of batches 5 (A) + 6 (B) + 4 (C) = 15
Cost per batch = 8,430/15 = £562
Cost per unit = 562/20 = £28.10

Store dept costs   £5,350
Cost driver   Orders
No. of orders = 5 × 2 (A) + 6 × 3 (B) + 4 × 3 (C) = 40
Cost per order = 5350/40 = £133.75
Cost per unit:
A = 133.75 × 2/20 = £13.37
B = 133.75 × 3/20 = £20.06
C = 133.75 × 3/20 = £20.06

Materials handling costs £2,100
Cost driver Batch produced
No. of batches = 15
Cost per batch = 2100/15 = £140
Cost per unit = 140/20 = £7.00

Overhead costs per product:

	A £	B £	C £
Machine dept.	28.10	28.10	28.10
Stores dept.	13.37	20.06	20.06
Materials handling	7.00	7.00	7.00
	48.47	55.16	55.16

Product costs:

	Product A £	Product B £	Product C £
Direct materials	40.00	50.00	40.00
Direct labour	21.00	27.00	18.00
Overheads	48.47	55.16	55.16
	109.17	132.16	113.16

8.2 Factors to consider:
- AMT means that more overhead costs are incurred in producing a product, rather than direct costs of labour. This makes cost allocation less reliable.
- ABC is based on the philosophy that costs are only incurred when activity takes place. Costs are thus related to activity rather than volume.
- ABC enables more costs to be classed as variable and allocated directly to products.
- ABC means that costs can no longer be classified as fixed and variable. Instead the following classification is suggested:
  - short-term variable costs

      – long-term variable costs
    fixed costs.
- ABC provides more realistic costing and facilitates performance measurement. Cost allocations remain somewhat arbitrary however, although less so than under absorption costing.
- ABC is costly to operate and is still based upon historical cost information.

Chapter 9

9.1

Absorption costing method:

	Year 1		Year 2	
	£	£	£	£
Sales		448,000		496,000
Less cost of goods sold:				
Opening stock	16,000		48,000	
Production	256,000		216,000	
Cost of goods available	272,000		264,000	
Less closing stock	48,000	224,000	16,000	248,000
Gross profit		224,000		248,000
Less period costs				
(Over)/under absorption	(6,000)		9,000	
Administration costs	2,100		2,100	
Selling costs	3,600	(300)	3,800	14,900
Net profit		224,300		233,100
Over/under absorption of overheads:				
Overheads absorbed		96,000		81,000
Overheads incurred		90,000		90,000
(Over)/under absorption		6,000)		9,000

Marginal costing method:

	Year 1		Year 2	
	£	£	£	£
Sales		448,000		496,000
Less cost of goods sold:				
Opening stock	10,000		30,000	
Production	160,000		135,000	
Cost of goods available	170,000		165,000	
Less closing stock	30,000	140,000	10,000	155,000
Gross profit		308,000		341,000
Less period costs:				
Fixed factory overheads	90,000		90,000	
Administration costs	2,100		2,100	
Selling costs	3,600	95,700	3,800	95,900
Net profit		212,300		245,100

Summary of differences:

	Year 1 £	Year 2 £
Marginal costing	212,300	245,100
Absorption costing	224,300	233,100
Net profit difference	(12,000)	12,000

Difference in reported profit in each year between the two methods is explained by the stock valuation, which includes fixed costs under the absorption costing method.

9.2

Fixed manufacturing overhead absorption rate:

	Production depts.		Maintenance dept.	Stores dept.	Total
	1 (£000s)	2 (£000s)	(£000s)	(£000s)	£000s
Allocated	360	470	240	170	1,240
Reallocated:					
Stores dept.	59.5	85	25.5	(170)	265.5
Service dept.	45.51	60.69	(106.2)	(40%) labour	
	81.92	77.38	(159.3)	(60%) manufact. cost	
	546.93	693.07			

Dividing by 150,000 to get the cost per unit gives:

	3.65	4.62

Total cost per unit:	£
Direct materials	6.00
Direct labour	7.50
Variable manf oheads	2.40
Fixed manufacturing overheads:	
Dept. 1	3.65
Dept. 2	4.62
	24.17

Profit statement: absorption costing

		£
Sales	144,000 × 35	5,040,000
Cost of sales	144,000 × 24.17	3,480,480
Gross profit		1,559,520
Non-manufacturing costs		765,000
Net profit		794,520
Less		
Under-absorbed overheads		
Dept. 1	20,000 + 4,000 × 3.65	34,600
Dept. 2	4,000 × 4.62	18,480
Net profit		741,440

Profit statement: marginal costing

		£
Sales 144,000 × 35		5,040,000
Variable cost of sales 144000 × 15.90		2,289,600
Contribution		2,750,400
Fixed costs:	manufacturing 1,240 + 20	1,260,000
:	non-manufact	765,000
Profit		725,400

Note: the difference is in stock valuation.

Chapter 10

10.1

(a) Contribution

	£000s
Sales	5,000
Variable cost	3,500
Contribution	1,500

Contribution per unit: 1,500/100 = £15

Break even level of production = Fixed costs/Contribution
= 900,000/15
= 60,000 units

(b)(i)

	£000s	£000s
Sales (100,000 units)		5,000
Direct materials	1,000	
Direct labour	1,000	
Variable production overheads	700	
Variable selling and distribution overheads	450	
Fixed production overheads	900	
Fixed selling and distribution overheads	200	4,250
Net profit		750

(ii)   Current price = £50
New price = 50.00 – (150,000/100,000) = £48.50

(c)

	£
Increased sales revenue	300
Increased fixed costs	250
Increased profit	50

New profit level = £650,000

(d) New selling price   £55
     New sales volume   95,000
     New sales revenue   £5,225,000
     New profit level   £825,000

10.2 Contribution per unit = Price – Variable cost
                              = 10 – 8 = £2

No. of units sold = Sales revenue/Price per unit
                   = 350,000/10
                   = 35,000

Fixed costs = Break-even point (units) × Contribution per unit
            = 350,00 × 2
            = £70,000

New break-even point:

$BEP = f/(p - v)$
    = 50,000/2
    = 25,000 units

Margin of safety $= \dfrac{\text{Actual sales} - \text{Break-even sales}}{\text{Break-even sales}} \times 100\%$

$= \dfrac{35,000 - 25,000}{25,000} \times 100\% = 40\%$

Chapter 11

11.1

Selling price per unit £	Contribution per unit £	Demand in units	Total contribution £
10	2	3,000*	6,000
15	7	3,000	21,000
20	12	2,400	28,800
25	17	2,100	35,700
30	22	1,600	35,200
35	27	900	24,300

* Demand is restricted by capacity.

On the basis of this information a launch price of £25 would appear to maximise the net benefit to the company from this product.

If a competitor launches a rival product at a price of £22 then this will affect the demand for the product at any price in excess of £22. Given the demand–price relationship the best course of action would be to price at slightly less than the price of the competitor, for example £21.

11.2 Factors to consider:

• *Price–demand relationship*

There is no point in pricing at a level where demand exceeds supply (as for the last model introduced) as this is likely to cause adverse customer reaction.

• *Cost based pricing*

Although the costing systems are excellent in this case any cost based pricing policy has the disadvantage of ignoring demand.

• *Demand based pricing*

Premium pricing – this is a quality product with superior after sales service and could be priced accordingly

Penetration pricing – this is not an option given the supply problems in relation to likely demand

Price skimming – as the last product started with a demand level such that second-hand prices exceeded the new price there is opportunity to maximise profits initially in this way. This would also have the effect of reducing demand.

In general, the pricing policy should not be cost related but should recognise the advantages of the vehicle and the likely demand for it, and price accordingly.

Chapter 12

12.1

	Component 32	Component 34	Product V23	Product V46
	£	£	£	£
Direct material	16	24	14	30
Direct labour	18	5	14	27
Variable overheads	6	3	8	11
Relevant cost	40	32	36	68
Unit selling price (£)			45	90
Buying-in price	50	30		
Contribution to fixed costs			9	22

Component 34 should be bought from the outside supplier but all other products should be made by the company.

There would be a need for the company to consider how fixed costs might change in the long term and what alterations could bemade to the total product mix, and the effect upon costs, before this decision should be made.

12.2 Further refining of this fuel oil utilises the spare capacity of the refinery deparment.

Production from refining: Petrol (75%)   22,500 litres; Fuel oil (10%)   3,000 litres

Revenue if refined:

	£
Petrol @ £2	45,000
Fuel oil @ £1	3,000
	48,000
Additional cost of refining	5,000
Net revenue	43,000

Revenue if sold without refining:

Fuel oil @ £1	30,000
Incremental revenue from refining	13,000

The company would gain from further refining this fuel oil.

Chapter 13

13.1

Revised costing statement:

	£	£
Sales revenue	450,000	
Cost of goods sold		
Raw materials	100,000	
Direct labour	230,000	
Factory overhead	25,600	355,600
Gross margin		94,400
Selling expenses	26,000	
Admin. expenses	40,000	66,000
Profit		28,400
Relevant factory overhead costs:		
Indirect labour (fixed)		14,000
Depreciation		8,400
Other fixed cost		3,200
		25,600

Using a relevant costing approach this product is shown to be profitable and should be continued. A longer-term analysis would be needed to ascertain what effect discontinuance would have upon fixed costs.

13.2

Cash flow implications of purchasing new machine:

	£
Reduced production costs (3 years)*	7,500
Sale proceeds of existing machine**	1,700
Purchase cost of new machine	(17,000)
Net cash flow	(7,800)

* The existing machine has a life of only three years and so this is the relevant time scale for the decision.

** Sale proceeds is the difference between current value and value at the end of three years.

Using this analysis it would not be beneficial for the company to purchase the new machine.

Chapter 14

14.1

(a)   Cash flow:

Year	Sales	Cost of sales	Selling	Rent	Net
	£	£	£	£	£
1	750,000	575,000	25,000	20,000	130,000
2	750,000	575,000	25,000	20,000	130,000
3	750,000	575,000	25,000	20,000	130,000
4	750,000	575,000	25,000	20,000	130,000
5	750,000	575,000	25,000	20,000	130,000

Payback period = $\dfrac{\text{Total capital cost}}{\text{Average net cash flow}}$

= £300,000/£130,000

= 2yrs 4 months

(b) Capital outstanding at start of each year

Year	Capital outstanding at start of year	Depreciation	Capital outstanding at end of year
	£	£	£
1	300,000	60,000	240,000
2	240,000	60,000	180,000
3	180,000	60,000	120,000
4	120,000	60,000	60,000
5	60,000	60,000	–

ARR = $\dfrac{\text{Average net cash flow}}{\text{Average net investment}}$

= £130,000/£180,000

= 72%

(c) Internal rate of return:

Discounting factor = $\dfrac{\text{Investment cost}}{\text{Annual cash flow}}$

= £300,000/£130,000

= 2.3077

From tables given in Appendix A:
IRR = 32%

14.2

Payback period = $\dfrac{\text{Total capital cost}}{\text{Average net cash flow}}$

= £350,000/£50,000

= 7 years

ROI:

Year	Capital outstanding at start of year	Net cash flow £	ROI %
1	350,000	50,000	14.3
2	315,000	50,000	15.8
3	280,000	50,000	17.8
4	245,000	50,000	20.4
5	210,000	50,000	23.8
6	175,000	50,000	28.6
7	140,000	50,000	35.7
8	105,000	50,000	47.6
9	70,000	50,000	71.4
10	35,000	50,000	142.9

ARR = $\dfrac{\text{Average net cash flow}}{\text{Average net investment}}$

= £50,000/£192,500

= 26%

Although the project makes an average rate of return in excess of 20% it fails to make this return in the early years. The project also fails to meet the payback criterion.

The proposal should therefore be rejected.

Chapter 15

15.1

Selling price: £5.00

Sales volume (units)	Probability	Expected value (units)	Income £
20,000			
30,000	0.1	3,000	15,000
40,000	0.4	16,000	80,000
50,000	0.3	15,000	75,000
60,000	0.2	12,000	60,000
			230,000

Selling price: £6.00

Sales volume (units)	Probability	Expected value (units)	Income £
20,000	0.2	4,000	24,000
30,000	0.3	9,000	54,000
40,000	0.25	10,000	60,000
50,000	0.2	10,000	60,000
60,000	0.05	3,000	18,000
			216,000

Selling price: £7.00

Sales volume (units)	Probability	Expected value (units)	Income £
20,000	0.6	12,000	84,000
30,000	0.3	9,000	63,000
40,000	0.1	4,000	28,000
50,000			
60,000			
			175,000

Selling price: £8.00

Sales volume (units)	Probability	Expected value (units)	Income £
20,000	0.8	16,000	128,000
30,000	0.2	6,000	48,000
40,000			
50,000			
60,000			
			176,000

Profit will be maximised at a price of £5.00.

15.2

(a)   Calculation of expected value:

Demand	Probability	Expected value (£)
60	0.3	18
70	0.5	35
80	0.2	16
		69

If 60 tyres are ordered:
The company will sell out and income will be 60 × 12 = £720.

If 70 tyres are ordered:
Probability of unsold tyres = 0.3
Storage cost of unsold tyres = 0.3 × 10 × 4 = £12
Income from sales = (0.3 × 60 × 12) = (0.7 × 70 × 12) = £804
Net income = 804 – 12 = £792

If 80 tyres are ordered:

Demand	Probability	Income £	Storage cost £	Net income £
60	0.3	216	80	136
70	0.5	420	40	380
80	0.2	192		192
				708

The company could maximise gross margin by ordering 70 tyres each month.

(b)   Expected value of perfect information:

Value of perfect information = Outcome from perfect information
                                           − Expected value calculated

Outcome from perfect information:

Demand	Probability	Income (£)
60	0.3	216
70	0.5	420
80	0.2	192
		828

Expected value of perfect information = 828 − 792 = £36

Chapter 16

16.1 Production capacity of Division A:
Component Y: 4,000 units @ 3/4 production hour per unit = 3,000 hours
Component X: 7,000 hours available − 1 hour per unit = 7,000 units

Cost of production of component X:
Direct materials − £20
Direct labour − £20
Overheads (170,000/10,000 per labour hour) − £17
Total cost − £97
Selling price = Cost + £50% = £145.50

Variable cost of production for Division A:
Direct costs − £80
Variable overheads £6.80
Total variable cost £86.80

Price range for Division A: £86.80 − £145.50

Division B:
Selling price £200
Processing costs £35
Maximum price for component £165

The price range should allow some profit for each division and should therefore be
between the normal selling price of Division A and its variable cost in order to provide some motivation for each division.

16.2 Objectives of a transfer pricing system:
to encourage goal congruence
to ensure divisional autonomy
to facilitate divisional performance evaluation
to promote internal competition.
Methods of cost based transfer pricing:
full cost; full cost plus; variable cost; variable cost plus; dual pricing.

The relative merits of these various methods are summarised in the following table:

Advantages and disadvantages of the various cost plus transfer pricing methods

Method	Advantages	Disadvantages
Full cost	Basis of pricing decision	No incentive to reduce costs
Full cost plus	Profit motivation for division	No incentive to reduce costs
Variable cost	Leads to decisions which are in company's interest	No motivation for division
Variable cost plus	Motivation for division	Limited performance evaluation possibilities
Dual pricing	Motivation for both divisions involved	Separate performance evaluation difficult

Alternative methods of pricing:
- market based pricing
- negotiated pricing.

Chapter 17

17.1

Using FIFO basis:

	£		£
1st Jan purchases (1,000 × 1.00)	1,000	5th Jan sales (100 × 1.00)	100
12th Jan purchases (1,000 × 1.20)	1,200	13th Jan sales (600 × 1.00)	600
25th Jan purchases (1,000 × 1.30)	1,300	23rd Jan sales (300 × 1.00)	300
		sales (200 × 1.20)	240
		27th Jan sales (800 × 1.20)	960
		sales (100 × 1.30)	130
		31st Jan closing stock	1,170
	3,500		3,500

Using LIFO basis:

	£		£
1st Jan purchases (1,000 × 1.00)	1,000	5th Jan sales (100 × 1.00)	100
12th Jan purchases (1,000 × 1.20)	1,200	13th Jan sales (600 × 1.20)	720
25th Jan purchases (1,000 × 1.30)	1,300	23rd Jan sales (400 × 1.20)	480
		sales (100 × 1.00)	100
		27th Jan sales (800 × 1.30)	1,040
		31st Jan closing stock	1,060
	3,500		3,500

Using average cost basis:

	£		£
1st Jan purchases (1,000 × 1.00)	1,000	5th Jan sales (100 × 1.00)	100
12th Jan purchases (1,000 × 1.20)	1,200		
average cost (900 × 1 + 1,000 × 1.2 = 1.11)		13th Jan sales (600 × 1.11)	666
		23rd Jan sales (500 × 1.11)	555
25th Jan purchases (1,000 × 1.30)	1,300		
average cost (800 × 1.11 + 1,000 × 1.30 = 1.22)		27th Jan sales (1,000 × 1.22)	1,220
		31st Jan closing stock	959
	3,500		3,500

17.2

$$EOQ = \sqrt{\frac{2DS}{I}}$$

Where
D = demand per period
S = cost of placing an order
I = cost of holding one unit of stock for one period

Therefore:

D = 200 units
S = £30
I = £0.10

$$EOQ = \sqrt{\frac{2 \times 200}{0.10} \times 30}$$

$= 346$ units

Reorder point:

Expected usage during lead time (200 × 2) =	400
Safety stock	50
Reorder point	450

Chapter 18

18.1 Problems:
- lack of motivation due to non-involvement
- targets set may be unrealistic
- budget includes costs which are not controllable
- bonus not directly linked to controllable performance.

Essential features of a budgeting system:
- setting of agreed targets
- mechanisms for feedback
- ownership of budget
- goal congruence
- recognising achievements.

18.2 Main points to consider:
- targets set need to be regarded as achievable by managers; targets set are imposed centrally without regard as to whether or not managers regard them as achievable
- ownership of targets is best achieved through participation in target setting; targets are set centrally without the involvement of managers
- individuals set more difficult target for themselves than those allocated to them, and this could lead to an improvement in company performance as the managers would be motivated to achieve these targets; the managers have no motivation to achieve targets imposed upon them and this is one reason for their failure to achieve the targets set
- allocation of resources is optimised through using the expertise of those involved in operations; this is not the case in this company
- managers should only be held responsible for performance which they can influence, i.e. they should only be accountable for their performance with respect to controllable costs
- central management appears to assume Theory X behaviour by the imposition of targets; perhaps the assumption of Theory Y would lead to improved performance
- feedback needs to be timely to enable corrective action to be taken; there is no indication of what feedback is given and under what time scale
- performance measurement needs to promote goal congruence and the feedback and rewards systems need to be allied to this objective; the motivation of managers is dependent on this and this is one reason why targets fail to be met.

Chapter 19

19.1

	£	£
Sales		150,000
Production expenses		
Labour	30,000	
Raw materials	45,000	
Overheads	12,000	87,000
Fixed costs		11,000
Net cash inflow		52,000

19.2

	Month 1 £	Month 2 £	Month 3 £
Income			
Cash sales (75%)	45,000	60,000	82,500
Credit sales (25%)		15,000	20,000
Total cash inflow	45,000	75,000	102,500

	Month 1 £	Month 2 £	Month 3 £
Expenditure			
Raw materials*	80,000	48,000	48,000
Labour	20,000	20,000	36,000
Overheads	4,000	4,000	4,800
Fixed factory costs**	8,000	8,000	8,000
Selling and admin expenses**	2,500	2,500	2,500
Total cash outflow	114,500	82,500	99,300
Net cash flow	(69,500)	(7,500)	3,200
Cumulative cash flow	(69,500)	(77,000)	(73,800)

Cumulative cash flow = Working capital requirement

* Raw materials cost = Requirements for following month but for month 1 equates to requirements for first two months
** Cash costs exclude depreciation

Chapter 20
20.1

	Budget £	Flexed budget £	Actual £	Variance £
Direct labour	192,000	160,000	179,000	19,000 (A)
Indirect labour:				
Variable	36,000	30,000	27,800	2,200 (F)
Fixed	36,000	36,000	36,000	—

20.2

Costs:

Direct material A: 900/100 = £9 per kg
Direct material B: £8 per kg
Direct labour dept. 1: 157,500/21,000 = £7.50 per direct labour hour
Direct labour dept. 2: 126,000/18,000 = £7 per direct labour hour
Variable overheads dept. 1: 35,700/21,000 = £1.70 per direct labour hour
Variable overheads dept. 2: 41,400/18,000 = £2.30 per direct labour hour

Standard costs:

	Product X £	Product Y £
Direct material A	27.00	22.50
Direct material B	32.00	40.00
Direct labour dept. 1	15.00	11.25
Direct labour dept. 2	21.00	14.00
Variable overheads dept. 1	3.40	2.55
Variable overheads dept. 2	6.90	4.60
Standard cost	105.30	94.90

Chapter 21

21.1

(a) Materials price variance = (Standard price − Actual price) × Actual quantity

Material A: (4.00 − 4.10) × 800 = £80.00 (A)
Material B: (2.00 − 2.10) × 1700 = £170.00 (A)
Total materials = £250.00 (A)

(b) Materials usage variance = (Standard quantity − Actual quantity) × Standard price

Material A: (4 × 100 − 800) × 4.00 = £1,600.00 (A)
Material B: (16 × 100 − 1700) × 2.00 = £100.00 (A)
Total materials = £1,700.00 (A)

Materials mix variance = Standard cost of actual quantity of actual mix − Standard cost of actual quantity of standard mix
= (800 × 4.00 + 1700 × 2.00) − (100 × 48.00)
= £1,800 (A)

Labour efficiency variance = (Standard hours − Actual hours) × Standard rate

Grade 1: (4 × 100 − 900) × 10.00 = 5,000.00 (A)
Grade 2: (6 × 100 − 300) × 6.00 = £1,800.00 (F)
Total labour = £3,200.00 (A)

21.2

	£
Standard quantity at standard price	40,000
Standard quantity at actual price	44,000
Actual quantity at actual price	41,800
Materials price variance	4,000 (A)
Materials usage variance	2,200 (F)
Materials variance	1,800 (A)

Chapter 22

22.1

	Division A £	Division B £
Controllable profit:		
Sales	101,000	52,000
Controllable cost of goods sold	34,000	17,000
Gross profit	67,000	35,000
Controllable selling expenses	9,000	4,000
Controllable profit	58,000	31,000

	Division A £	Division B £
Residual income:		
Controllable profit	58,000	31,000
Cost of capital	30,000	12,000
Residual income	28,000	19,000
Return on capital employed:		
Controllable profit	58,000	31,000
Capital employed	250,000	100,000
ROCE = Profit/Capital employed	23.2%	31%

22.2 Evaluation of the three measures:

- **Controllable profit**

  This is a measure of profit as controlled by the division and will encourage the divisional management to undertake any action which will increase profit. This may however be at the expense of long-term performance and may involve reducing costs as well as increasing sales. This could therefore impact adversely upon a quality objective of the company. As this measure takes no account of the cost of capital the divisional managers may well seek to undertake any investment which increases profit regardless of the opportunity cost of such investment.

- **Residual income**

  Taking into account the cost of capital ensures that this opportunity cost is considered and the divisional management will be encouraged to undertake any investment which increases residual income and thereby shows a return on that investment. As capital investment is normally controlled centrally however there may be a demotivating effect if funds for capital investment are denied to a division when the divisional management consider that it would improve its performance.

- **Return on capital employed**

  This measure facilitates the ranking of divisions and thus enables the central management to determine where resources could be best employed for the benefit of the organisation as a whole. It has the disadvantage however that the divisional managers will be reluctant to make decisions which would reduce their ROCE even if it would increase profitability and may be in the overall best interest of the company.

Factors which would need to be taken into account would include the following:
- the overall strategy of the company
- the cost of capital for the company
- the level of returns expected by other companies in the same industry as the division concerned
- the level of risk involved in the industry
- the degree of competition and the relative position of the division within that industry
- the extent of over- or under-capacity in the industry generally
- the general economic climate
- the market conditions and level of demand for the product or service provided.

Present value interest factor: PVIF $_{t,r}$ = 1/(1 + r)t

t/r	1%	2%	3%	4%	5%	6%	7%	8%	9%	10%	11%	12%	15%	20%	25%	30%	35%
1	.990	.980	.971	.962	.952	.943	.935	.926	.917	.909	.901	.893	.870	.833	.800	.769	.741
2	.980	.961	.943	.925	.907	.890	.873	.857	.842	.826	.812	.797	.756	.694	.640	.592	.549
3	.971	.942	.915	.889	.864	.840	.816	.794	.772	.751	.731	.712	.658	.579	.512	.455	.406
4	.961	.924	.888	.855	.823	.792	.763	.735	.708	.683	.659	.636	.572	.482	.410	.350	.301
5	.951	.906	.863	.822	.784	.747	.713	.681	.650	.621	.593	.567	.497	.402	.328	.269	.223
6	.942	.888	.837	.790	.746	.705	.666	.630	.596	.564	.535	.507	.432	.335	.262	.207	.165
7	.933	.871	.813	.760	.711	.665	.623	.583	.547	.513	.482	.452	.376	.279	.210	.159	.122
8	.923	.853	.789	.731	.677	.627	.582	.540	.502	.467	.434	.404	.327	.233	.168	.123	.091
9	.914	.837	.766	.703	.645	.592	.544	.500	.460	.424	.391	.361	.284	.194	.134	.094	.067
10	.905	.820	.744	.676	.614	.558	.508	.463	.422	.386	.352	.322	.247	.162	.107	.073	.050
11	.896	.804	.722	.650	.585	.527	.475	.429	.388	.350	.317	.287	.215	.135	.086	.056	.037
12	.887	.789	.701	.625	.557	.497	.444	.397	.356	.319	.286	.257	.187	.112	.069	.043	.027
13	.879	.773	.681	.601	.530	.469	.415	.368	.326	.290	.258	.229	.163	.093	.055	.033	.020
14	.870	.758	.661	.577	.505	.442	.388	.340	.299	.263	.232	.205	.141	.078	.044	.025	.015
15	.861	.743	.642	.555	.481	.417	.362	.315	.275	.239	.209	.183	.123	.065	.035	.020	.011
16	.853	.728	.623	.534	.458	.394	.339	.292	.252	.218	.188	.163	.107	.054	.028	.015	.008
17	.844	.714	.605	.513	.436	.371	.317	.270	.231	.198	.170	.146	.093	.045	.023	.012	.006
18	.836	.700	.587	.494	.416	.350	.296	.250	.212	.180	.153	.130	.081	.038	.018	.009	.005
19	.828	.686	.570	.475	.396	.331	.277	.232	.194	.164	.138	.116	.070	.031	.014	.007	.003
20	.820	.673	.554	.456	.377	.312	.258	.215	.178	.149	.124	.104	.061	.026	.012	.005	.002
21	.811	.660	.538	.439	.359	.294	.242	.199	.164	.135	.112	.093	.053	.022	.009	.004	.002
22	.803	.647	.522	.422	.342	.278	.226	.184	.150	.123	.101	.083	.046	.018	.007	.003	.001
23	.795	.634	.507	.406	.326	.262	.211	.170	.138	.112	.091	.074	.040	.015	.006	.002	.001
24	.788	.622	.492	.390	.310	.247	.197	.158	.126	.102	.082	.066	.035	.013	.005	.002	.001
25	.780	.610	.478	.375	.295	.233	.184	.146	.116	.092	.074	.059	.030	.010	.004	.001	.001
30	.742	.552	.412	.308	.231	.174	.131	.099	.075	.057	.044	.033	.015	.004	.001		

Present value interest factor of an annuity: $PVIFA_{t,r} = \left[\dfrac{1-(1+r)^{-t}}{r}\right]$

t\r	1%	2%	3%	4%	5%	6%	7%	8%	9%	10%	11%	12%	15%	20%	25%	30%	35%
1	.990	.980	.971	.962	.952	.943	.935	.926	.917	.909	.901	.893	.870	.833	.800	.769	.741
2	1.970	1.942	1.913	1.886	1.859	1.833	1.808	1.783	1.759	1.736	1.713	1.690	1.626	1.528	1.440	1.361	1.289
3	2.941	2.884	2.829	2.775	2.723	2.673	2.624	2.577	2.531	2.487	2.444	2.402	2.283	2.106	1.952	1.816	1.696
4	3.902	3.808	3.717	3.630	3.546	3.465	3.387	3.312	3.240	3.170	3.102	3.037	2.855	2.589	2.362	2.166	1.997
5	4.853	4.713	4.580	4.452	4.329	4.212	4.100	3.993	3.890	3.791	3.696	3.605	3.352	2.991	2.689	2.436	2.220
6	5.795	5.601	5.417	5.242	5.076	4.917	4.767	4.623	4.486	4.355	4.231	4.111	3.784	3.326	2.951	2.643	2.385
7	6.728	6.472	6.230	6.002	5.786	5.582	5.389	5.206	5.033	4.868	4.712	4.564	4.160	3.605	3.161	2.802	2.508
8	7.652	7.326	7.020	6.733	6.463	6.210	5.971	5.747	5.535	5.335	5.146	4.968	4.487	3.837	3.329	2.925	2.598
9	8.566	8.162	7.786	7.435	7.108	6.802	6.515	6.247	5.995	5.759	5.537	5.328	4.772	4.031	3.463	3.019	2.665
10	9.471	8.983	8.530	8.111	7.722	7.360	7.024	6.710	6.418	6.145	5.889	5.650	5.019	4.192	3.570	3.092	2.715
11	10.368	9.787	9.253	8.760	8.306	7.887	7.499	7.139	6.805	6.495	6.207	5.938	5.234	4.327	3.656	3.147	2.752
12	11.255	10.575	9.954	9.385	8.863	8.384	7.943	7.536	7.161	6.814	6.492	6.194	5.421	4.439	3.725	3.190	2.779
13	12.134	11.348	10.635	9.986	9.394	8.853	8.358	7.904	7.487	7.013	6.750	6.424	5.583	4.533	3.780	3.223	2.799
14	13.004	12.106	11.296	10.563	9.899	9.295	8.745	8.244	7.786	7.367	6.982	6.628	5.724	4.611	3.824	3.249	2.814
15	13.865	12.849	11.938	11.118	10.380	9.712	9.108	8.560	8.061	7.606	7.191	6.811	5.847	4.675	3.859	3.268	2.825
16	14.718	13.578	12.561	11.652	10.838	10.106	9.447	8.851	8.313	7.824	7.379	6.974	5.954	4.730	3.887	3.283	2.834
17	15.562	14.292	13.166	12.166	11.274	10.477	9.763	9.122	8.544	8.022	7.549	7.120	6.047	4.775	3.910	3.295	2.840
18	16.398	14.992	13.754	12.659	11.690	10.828	10.059	9.372	8.756	8.201	7.702	7.250	6.128	4.812	3.928	3.304	2.844
19	17.226	15.679	14.324	13.134	12.085	11.158	10.336	9.604	8.950	8.365	7.839	7.366	6.198	4.843	3.942	3.311	2.848
20	18.046	16.352	14.878	13.590	12.462	11.470	10.594	9.818	9.129	8.514	7.963	7.469	6.259	4.870	3.954	3.316	2.850
21	18.857	17.011	15.415	14.029	12.821	11.764	10.836	10.017	9.292	8.649	8.075	7.562	6.312	4.891	3.963	3.320	2.852
22	19.661	17.658	15.937	14.451	13.163	12.042	11.061	10.210	9.442	8.772	8.176	7.645	6.359	4.909	3.970	3.323	2.853
23	20.456	18.292	16.444	14.857	13.489	12.303	11.272	10.371	9.580	8.883	8.266	7.718	6.399	4.925	3.976	3.325	2.854
24	21.244	18.914	16.936	15.247	13.799	12.550	11.469	10.529	9.707	8.985	8.348	7.784	6.434	4.937	3.981	3.327	2.855
25	22.023	19.524	17.413	15.622	14.094	12.783	11.654	10.675	9.823	9.077	8.422	7.843	6.464	4.948	3.985	3.329	2.856
30	25.808	22.396	19.601	17.292	15.373	13.765	12.409	11.258	10.274	9.427	8.694	8.055	6.566	4.979	3.995	3.332	2.857

Index